Hussey Vivian: Wellington's Hussar General

RICHARD HUSSEY VIVIAN

Hussey Vivian: Wellington's Hussar General

The career of Richard Hussey Vivian
during the Campaigns in the
Low Countries, the Peninsular War &
the Waterloo Campaign of 1815

Claud Vivian

*Hussey Vivian: Wellington's
Hussar General
The career of Richard Hussey Vivian
during the Campaigns in the
Low Countries, the Peninsular War &
the Waterloo Campaign of 1815*
by Claud Vivian

First published under the title
*Richard Hussey Vivian
First Baron Vivian
A Memoir*

Leonaur is an imprint
of Oakpast Ltd

Copyright in this form © 2010 Oakpast Ltd

ISBN: 978-0-85706-066-2 (hardcover)
ISBN: 978-0-85706-065-5 (softcover)

http://www.leonaur.com

Publisher's Notes

In the interests of authenticity, the spellings, grammar and place names used have been retained from the original editions.

The opinions of the authors represent a view of events in which he was a participant related from his own perspective,
as such the text is relevant as an historical document.

The views expressed in this book are not necessarily
those of the publisher.

Contents

Early Years—Flanders and the Helder	9
Corunna Campaign, 1808-9	57
Campaign of 1813	117
Quatre-Bras and the Retreat of June 17	215
Waterloo 1815	260

To
The Past and Present Officers
Non-Commissioned Officers and Men
of the
7th, 10th and 18th Hussars
This Memoir of One Who Frequently Acted as
a Leader of Their Regiments During the
Peninsular Wars is Respectfully
Dedicated by His Grandson
Claud Vivian

Chapter 1

Early Years—Flanders and the Helder

Richard Hussey Vivian, who was created first Baron Vivian in the year 1841, but who was better known as "Sir Hussey" throughout his life, was born at Truro on July 28, 1775.

When about eight years old he was sent to the Grammar School at Truro, under Dr. Cardew. Here, however, he did not remain long, as from 1784 to 1787 he was at school at Lostwithiel, from which place he went direct to Harrow.

Three years of his life were passed at Harrow; and in 1790 he entered at the old West Country College, "Exeter," at Oxford.

He appears, however, only to have kept two terms, when he went to France to complete his education.

The first letter I possess of his is one written from—

Montreuil, July 18, 1791.

Dear Mother,—I hope that my late silence has not alarmed you, but I wished not to write till I should be perfectly settled, which I am happy to inform you I am at present; and that in as comfortable a place as I could wish for.

My uncle has also taken lodgings here, and means to study the French language; not but that at present he knows it as well as most people who are not perfect Frenchmen—that is, grammatically, but as to speaking it he can hardly hold a conversation!

A history of our journey would fill a sheet of paper. I shall therefore abridge it a little.

Last Tuesday [July 12] we left Oxford and went to Southampton, where the rascals, by telling us lies, contrived to make us stay some hours without giving us a satisfactory answer till late in the evening, when they told us the packet had sailed that morning.

Thence we proceeded to London; thence to Dover; and then had a bad passage to Boulogne, in which I was sea-sick, but not much.

We stayed there one day, but liked not the place. We then came here, where we have settled ourselves comfortably, and in a good place to learn the language.

Everything is quite quiet, so that you need not fright yourself. My uncle tells me to say that for my next you must get your French dictionary. What he means I know not, unless that it will be so exceedingly unintelligible as not to be understood without trouble.

The uncle referred to in the above letter was the Rev. Richard Vivian, Rector of Bushey, Herts. The next letter is from the same place.

Montreuil, August 8, 1791.

My dear Mother,—After having waited in vain for a letter from you, take another from me.

Since the last we have seen and heard many things. We have been at the 'Grand Mass,' where we saw abundance of fine priests and heard a grand instrument called a 'serpent.'

We have seen volunteers in the cause of liberty assembled for the purpose of marching to the frontier.

We have been at a wedding dinner, the magnificence of which it is almost impossible for me to describe. *Un prevuer service—l'entrée*—and *le dessert—café—noyau—et l'eau de vie.*

The company, our friends, *le Directeur, le Curé, et sa nièce.*

A description of the rest I shall defer till we meet, only observing that the bride is fifty-two, and weighs eighteen stone; the bridegroom about half as much in both age and weight.

I have been often *au convent*, where, besides the nuns, are some very pretty English girls, imprisoned for love. Their situation is truly deplorable, not being allowed out but once in three weeks.

My uncle is not able to creep in through the *tournez*; I am not grown very big, though! How do you like to hear it? I have tied my hair! Enter the hairdresser, in full national uniform and sword by his side; he is just going *à la garde.* The spirit of these men who buy arms and clothing, when they dress [hair] for three-halfpence a day, appears admirable.

An interval of nearly two years takes place between the dates of the two letters I have quoted, and that of the next in my possession.

During this period, the time arrived for Hussey Vivian to choose a profession. Mr. Vivian wished his heir to follow a pursuit in which distinction had been gained both by himself and other members of the family.

Hussey Vivian was accordingly articled to a Mr. Jonathan Elford, a solicitor of Devonport, with a view to his becoming a "counsellor learned in the law." But the attractions presented by the lives and uniforms of the officers of a garrison town were an all-powerful opposing force; and besides, he could urge family precedents for a military career; for his great uncle. Colonel Hussey, had been amongst the heroes who fell with Wolfe on the heights of Abraham. Accordingly an ensign's commission in the 20th Regiment of Infantry was procured for him on July 31, 1793.

It is doubtful if he ever joined this regiment, for on October 20, he obtained a lieutenancy in an Independent Company of Foot, from which, on the 30th of the same month, he exchanged into the 54th Regiment.

At the time when the following letter was written, he had expected that his regiment would make part of an expedition which the British Government had prepared to act against the French colonies in the West Indies. This expedition, the land forces of which were commanded by Sir C. Grey, sailed on November 3, 1793.

William and Mary Transport,
Portsmouth, November 22, 1793.

My dear Mother,—I have received your very kind letter, for which I return you my sincere thanks; nor can I possibly proceed any further without first assuring my father that he has always acted with the greatest liberality towards me.

You propose so many questions that I really do not know where I shall find room to write all I have to say.

I will first begin by informing you in what state things are at present in this place.

I have already informed you by a short letter that we were then immediately ordered on board, and expected to sail immediately; to what place I know not.

Since then it has, I believe, been certainly proved that St. Malo is our destination; a cutter having sailed on Monday for Guernsey to procure pilots against our arrival; and it is, I believe, generally supposed that we shall sail before Sunday. Lord Moira, who commands the expedition, comes tomorrow.

There are at present here, the 3rd, 27th, 28th, 42nd, 19th, 54th, 57th, 58th, and 59th Regiments, a troop of horse, and two companies of artillery. Besides these we expect four regiments from Ireland, and, if report speaks true, 5000 Hessians.

We are all ordered on board our respective transports to be ready to sail at a moment's notice. There are great murmurs here about our being ordered and counter-ordered so, and a petition to Sir C, Grey is, I believe, thought of; for no pay or fortune can possibly support the enormous expense.

In the first place we were ordered to lay in ten weeks' provisions, and prepare our clothing for a West India campaign. Besides the £18—the bare payment for our provisions—we were obliged to find kettles, plates, &c. &c.; in fact all the necessaries for cooking.

All this being laid in, and expecting every day to be sent on a ten weeks' voyage, an order came on Monday to prepare with all possible expedition for a cold climate.

This additional expense besides the loss of all our former stock, which will become useless to us on our leaving the ship, will, I fear, my dear mother, occasion a greater expense than I can afford; and, had I not saved money by omitting to purchase shirts, more than I could possibly have done. At present I have a few guineas left to buy flannel and thick clothes. Whilst this lasts I will never call for another farthing. How long that will be it is impossible for me to know; so very different are our necessaries. We hope nevertheless to receive some sort of redress for our heavy expenses.

I forgot to say that our orders did not say prepare for a cold climate, but for a winter campaign—a pleasant thing! Thank God we are all well, in good spirits, and highly rejoiced at exchanging the West Indies for France.

Now for answering your questions. My father comes first.

The officers are as good a corps as I ever met with; you really have the worst at Truro. The men are a very fine body.

Mr. Stewart is much mistaken about my getting a company soon, unless a strange fatality happens; for there is not at present a captain in the regiment inclined to sell, and there are second lieutenants, every one of whom would purchase. Nevertheless, it is so far from my wish to squander more money than is absolutely necessary that I am very happy in supposing that in four years hence I may probably be near being a captain.

I wrote a week ago to Captain John desiring that Harry might come into the regiment, as I thought it very probable he would soon be a lieutenant. I told him that before six months were at an end I should probably get a company, but a conversation with Col. Strutt has proved to the contrary. I must here only mention one circumstance. Capt. Hall (who by the way is just now reading very loud) has been in the army but two years, and has, by raising his independent company and purchasing an exchange, got his company cheaper than an officer who has just now, for £2200, got his company, after having for nine years been a subaltern in the regiment.

The officers are Lieut-Col. Strutt, Major Paget, Capts. Darby, Layard, Montgomery, Harrison, Garden, Hall, Wright, and Seton; Lieuts. Warren, Gott, Fell, Warren, Gibson, Williams, Baynton, Frederick, Robinson, Vivian, and Frederick; Ensigns Cunningham, Caimes, Spence, and Maister. My great friends are Paget, Harrison, Garden, and Frederick senior. As for quarrels, a duel was never fought in the regiment.

Thus far have I answered your questions and I am really come to a standstill. As soon as we arrive anywhere I will write. It is impossible you can expect a letter as regular as from the post; wind may not permit, perhaps despatches may not be sent. You must not, therefore, fancy I am killed if you do not hear for these three weeks again. As soon as possible I will write

I have opened this to say that an express from Guernsey is arrived, which, they say, brings news of an action having been fought, but that St. Malo is still in the hands of the Republicans. We are therefore ordered to get up our yards and topmasts to sail at a minute's notice.

Presumably the expedition referred to in the above letter was the one commanded by Lord Moira, which sailed with the object of assisting the Royalists, who had for some time been strenuously fighting (and at first with some success) against the Republican forces in Brittany.

The latter were, however, decisively defeated in December (23rd), before the English forces arrived.

Alison alludes to the expedition thus:

In war everything depends upon rapidity of execution, and an accurate attention to time. The moment of success once allowed to escape, never returns. Hardly had the Royalist standards disappeared from the shores of Brittany when the tardy English succours, commanded by Lord Moira, who had exerted himself to the utmost to accelerate the preparations, appeared on the coast of Cherbourg, having on board eight English battalions, 4000 Hanoverians, and 2000 emigrants— in all 10,000 men.

They looked out in vain for the expected signals, and after remaining on the coast for some days, and receiving intelligence of the defeat of the Royalists, returned to Guernsey, where the expedition was broken up.

Had this succour arrived on the coast a fortnight sooner; had even a few English frigates appeared off Granville during the assault, to intimidate the Republicans and encourage the Royalists, the town would have been taken, the junction of the English troops with the Royalists effected, and the united forces marched in triumph to Paris.

The next letter is written two months later than the last, from—

Southampton, January 26, 1794.

My Dear Father,—I sit down to answer as much of your letter as this paper will contain.

First, then, I must inform you that I like the Isle of Wight most amazingly, and look upon it that it must be a most enchanting spot in summer. What places you can fancy prettier than Yarmouth, or Newport, I know not: than Cowes, certainly not. The castle and view from it are charming.

Our return from Guernsey to England, about which you enquire, was not voluntary; a very hard wind compelled us to it, and the ships left behind were too near the rocks to venture getting under weigh.

Mr. ——'s being disliked in the regiment is entirely owing to his being rather a coxcomb. The report you heard is very true; but he is a bad hand at running away. Their being disappointed was entirely owing to his neglect; the lady is since married, and her husband, they say, is the happiest man in the world!

The ball at Lord G.'s was full of officers, and about twenty island ladies, with one of whom (the prettiest girl I ever saw in my life) I had the honour of dancing, and you may depend I was not backward in calling on her the next morning. Between you and me I must confess I was most desperately smitten. She unfortunately had no fortune, so that anyone who takes her will make a bad bargain.

My great friends are Capt. Hall, Major Paget, and Lieut. Robinson, three very good young men! Since Paget has become Major I do not see so much of him as before; he has so much to do. The others I am constantly with. Hall is on board our ship.

We left Cowes on Thursday and arrived here on Friday

Two of our officers are to go recruiting—one to Romsey, and one to Salisbury. I expect to be ordered on the duty

The assemblies are few here; I believe only once a fortnight.

The next letter has no date, but was evidently written when Hussey Vivian was thinking of exchanging into the 28th Regiment. It has the postmark "Lyndhurst."

My dear Father,—I have received your letter of the 21st, and I assure you had taken even precaution that is therein mentioned before I went to any lengths.

The case is just this. Lord Moira has the *absolute* disposal of every commission in his army below the rank of field officers, and of those he has the recommendation.

Indeed, had this not been the case, it differs widely from Col. Buller's business; this resignation is given in conditionally on my being the successor. Col. B. depended on his interest; my money is lodged, and is to be *paid only when I am gazetted as Captain of the 28th, vice Wilson.*

The proposal about Lord Falmouth was made to me only by some of our own old officers, and my own anxiety. Capt. Twysden of the 28th, when I told him of it (for he is my great friend) said, 'Nonsense, you need not think of it.'

I hope to be at Bath about the middle of April, about which time we shall be encamped at Romsey.

The 3rd and 78th sailed yesterday to the relief of Jersey. About four hours after they passed the Needles a violent cannonade was heard. What it was we know not. The convoy was small I understand.

My mother's alarms and the papers infamous falsehoods agree

very well. I have had the fever, and am now, thank God, about again. I mentioned to you the number we have lost, and nearly 3000 have been ill, and our fever is by far the most dangerous. When at Cowes we were the strongest regiment, and we are now nearly the weakest in the expedition

I forgot to mention some reasons which induced me to take the company in the 28th. Stewart says in a letter of the 17th of this month, that exchanges are not to be had under £100, and Lowrie is easily bribed oft' his bargain; as was the case with Capt. Groves of the 28th, for whom he engaged to raise a company. At the end of three months Groves asked for his men. Lowrie had sold them to a higher bidder, and Groves, at the expense of £2300, raised an independent company. Lord Amherst heard of this, and being his friend, and a vacancy happening in the 28th, gave it him.

Another letter, undated, but evidently written about the same time as the last, from "Ironhill" says:

My Dear Mother,—I had determined previous to the receipt of your letter to have written to you by today's post; my reasons for not writing before were two. First, I hoped that you would have heard of my being perfectly recovered, from my father; indeed, from him I understood that you did not know of my being ill.

You will, I am confident, excuse me from having been guilty of any sort of neglect when I inform you, secondly, that on the day I received your letter we were ordered to march from Lyndhurst to this place, about two miles from it; since which we have been in a continued state of confusion, and at this moment I am obliged to borrow paper, &c., to write to you.

The place and situation is wonderfully pleasant, but we have not got our things comfortable, as the house has not been inhabited this sometime past; some part of it never.

The 28th Regiment still remains at Lyndhurst; we are alone.

"My company goes on very well. I wait for nothing but to be gazetted, the commission being already signed '*par le Roi*.' We go into camp May 13; where we know not. Some say Stony cross, and others Romsey Common.

I shall be much obliged to you to have the bed, &c., you had made for me at Truro sent me here by the wagon, as soon as possible; the bed I have is nothing but a cot, which was best on shipboard, and when I bought it we expected to make a four-months' voyage! I now sleep on the ground, and that will not do in camp; there I must have a bedstead....

As soon as I am in the 28th Regiment you will see me. When that will be I know not, but very probably on Saturday next (tomorrow). Should it be so, I shall see Bath on Monday or Tuesday.

Hussey Vivian obtained his company in the 28th Regiment on May 7, 1794, and formed part of the Duke of York's forces which, in the spring of 1794, went to Flanders to fight against the Republicans. In May, 1794, Pichegru, who commanded the Republican forces in West Flanders, laid siege to Ypres; whilst in June another French army under Jourdan crossed the Meuse and besieged Charleroi. The major portion of the allied forces were then moved in that direction; the Duke of York with the English and Hanoverians being alone left on the Scheldt.

This separation of the Allies contributed not a little to augment the misunderstandings which already prevailed between them, and was the forerunner of numberless disasters to both monarchies.

No sooner was the departure of the Emperor of Austria with reinforcements to the army on the Sambre known to Pichegru, than he resolved to take advantage of the weakness of his adversaries by seriously prosecuting the siege of Ypres. On June 17, in consequence of the defeat of Clairfait with the Prussians, Ypres capitulated, and its garrison consisting of 6000 men, were made prisoners of war.

At this time 30,000 Austrians lay inactive at Tournav, and 6000 English were reposing from the fatigues of their sea voyage at Ostend.—*Alison*, vol. 2 p. 387.

On June 26, Hussey Vivian writes:

Ostend, June 26, 1794.

My dear Father,—I have just time to tell you that Ypres and Bruges are both taken, and that the French are advancing with all possible speed to take this place; but I hope it will be the lot of Lord Moira's army to give them a good drubbing. Our army are all in the highest possible spirits, anxious to meet them, and, I may say, feel themselves pretty confident of victory.

We expect the French this night. Bruges was evacuated yesterday morning, and the French took possession last night.

This is all the news I have at present to tell, but should anything extraordinary happen, you may depend on hearing from me immediately.

Tournay was abandoned on June 24; Nieuport capitulated; Fort Ecluse, the key of the Scheldt, was blockaded; and the Island of Cadsand was overrun by the Republicans who crossed the arm of the sea, which separated it from the mainland, by swimming. Clairfait was reinforced by the 6000 men, who marched from Ostend under Lord Moira.

Major Paget, who was in the same regiment as Vivian, gives the following account of part of this march:

> We quitted our position at Oestaker on July 3, at night, and encamped near Dendermont on the 4th.
>
> We considered ourselves lucky in having accomplished our tedious march, when Graham's Brigade, in which you know I am, received orders to take a post at Wiesse, about half-way to Alost. We remained there during the night, and, being joined early in the morning by the rest of the army, we proceeded to Alost, where we joined the army of Clairfait.
>
> During the night of the 5th Clairfait advanced, and early the next morning, the 6th, he took his position about a quarter of a mile from the town. About 12 o'clock the enemy (to the shame of the Hanoverians, *entre nous*) entered Alost, where, after a severe skirmish, they were obliged to fly. The 8th Dragoons lost one officer and some men, several wounded. Lieut.-Col. Vandeleur of the 8th was wounded. Col. Doyle also is wounded. My old friends, the 54th, had one killed and five wounded. The French left behind them not above twenty killed, though it is said that they took with them several wounded.
>
> Understanding; that the enemy were in great force and near the town, we burnt down all the bridges, which were the only communication to our camp, during the night of the 6th and day of the 7th. On the night of the 7th we *retreated* (if I may be allowed the expression) to Thiesselt, where we arrived at 10 a.m. on the 8th. At 12 the same night we marched, passed through Malines, and arrived here this morning at 11 o'clock. Thus having finished our march, I shall now enter into the

merits of it; and since I have used the word *merit*, I must humbly confess that I conceive Lord Moira has as completely saved the Duke of York and his army as—you'll excuse a simile. From what I *know* the Duke of York was in a most critical situation when we arrived at Ostend. It became so great an object of the enemy to impede our progress into Flanders that the whole force opposed to the Duke of York and Clairfait were immediately sent to prevent our advancing; but, all glory to our commander-in-chief, he out-generaled them and joined the Duke of York this morning at Malines; and this, I may say, he performed, advancing in the front of an enemy, without firing a shot.

The fact is this—that our marches have been so unprecedentedly expeditious, and our manoeuvres so grand, that at no one instant could the enemy conceive where we were, and the consequence is that they are left behind to bewail the loss of the destruction of the Duke of York's army, and to lament their want of generalship is not impeding *us*.

I cannot finish this letter without giving the sentiment of our army: that, though greater hardships never have befallen an army in so short a period, there is not an individual who would not offer up his life in support of what he considers the first of men and generals—Lord Moira.

In spite of these reinforcements, however, Clairfait found himself unable to make head against Pichegru.

After in vain attempting, in conjunction with Coburg, to cover Brussels, he was compelled to fall back behind the Dyle; while the Duke of York also retired in the same direction, and encamped between Malines and Louvain

The English forces posted behind the canal of Malines amounted to above 30,000 British and Hanoverians and 15,000 Dutch The English were intent on covering

Antwerp and Holland; the Imperialists on drawing nearer to their resources at Cologne and Coblentz. Neither recollected that by separating their forces they gave the enemy means of crushing either separately at pleasure. . .

On July 15 the canal at Malines was forced, after an inconsiderable resistance by the Dutch troops, and the Duke of York retired to Antwerp, which was soon after evacuated and his whole forces concentrated towards Breda for the defence of Holland.—*Alison*, vol. 2. p. 392 *et seq.*

For about two months the English forces had a rest here, as the Republicans, for some inexplicable reason, left them unmolested. During this respite Hussey Vivian wrote the following letter:

Camp near Breda,
August 20, 1794.

My dear Mother,—Having heard from several correspondents that they have never received one half of the letters I have written them, I take the opportunity of Robinson's going; to England to write you a long letter of our late proceedings.

The last camp I wrote from was behind Antwerp, since which time we have marched through Antwerp, Calemthout, Roosendale, and Breda, and are at present encamped within two miles of the latter place.

At Calemthout we encamped for one day on a most barren, extensive plain, famous only for a battle fought there by Louis XIV. The troops were for two days here in a complete state of starvation; in want of bread, water, and everything else.

From hence to Roosendale, twenty-four miles, through a very heavy road, the poor soldiers were obliged to march without any sort of halt or provisions.

We were encamped at Roosendale a fortnight, and found it a better place (though in itself very bad) than Calemthout.

From hence I went to Bergen-op-Zoom, a very strong town, and capable of withstanding a siege of ten years.

After having remained at Roosendale a fortnight, we marched to the position we are now in, which is wonderfully strong, and famous for having been the position of every retreating army. Bois le Duc on our left; Breda on our right; in front we are throwing up batteries innumerable, and in our rear there is a strong wood.

The situation is a pleasant one; within an hour's ride of Breda, Oosterhout, and Gertrudenberg, and a day's ride off Dortwilliamstadt and Rotterdam.

The country is very flat and in some parts very pretty. The houses the neatest things imaginable; every article, either tin, copper, or plate, would serve for a looking-glass; and the scales in particular are as bright as if made of gold; in fact, it is not possible to conceive anything so neat and clean.

Dort is the only town in the heart of the country I have as yet seen, and, I must confess, it is the cleanest and neatest I ever saw in my life.

We are at present perfectly undisturbed; nor from all accounts is there any idea of an enemy being at hand; indeed from all accounts we are to advance again; but all this we learn from the English papers. What we are to do is never known to us a week, or three days, before.

The weather has been very bad here, and, contrary to the opinion of every one, the soldiers have borne it very well, and are in high health and spirits; our only remedy is to smoke and drink grog—the wines of the country are far too thin for the climate, and all the physicians advise us not to drink them—in fact we are at present curious figures. I am confident you would laugh to see me of an evening with my hair cut quite short, no powder, blue trousers and waistcoat, smoking and drinking grog.

One thing I beg is that you will not think I am growing fond of spirits; indeed, were I so, I should not be quite so candid as to mention drinking them. Nothing but the full conviction of their being the only thing good in this climate makes me drink them; consequently not in quantities....

The French are not about to lay siege to any city but Valenciennes, which I have never seen, consequently can say nothing of the inhabitants. The people here seem more to wish, than dread, their coming.

I succeeded very well in purchasing my horses at Southampton, and on coming away delivered them up to the commissary who issued them out to me again here; but not the same or so good—the ones being English, and the others Flemish.

I forgot to say that an order has just been issued for all officers to give in a return of their losses, and should I receive any recompense for my baggage, which I expect, I will immediately remit to Mr. Grenfell, to reimburse my father.

Col. Moorshead and Capt. McMurdo have been so good as to invite me to dinner twice, and have been wonderfully civil.

It may not perhaps be uninteresting to you to know the state of our army which I give at the end of this long letter.

Adieu. You shall hear soon from your most affectionate son.

Return of H.R.H. the Duke of York's army, August 20, 1794. Effective, fit for duty.

Cavalry.	Officers.	Sergts.	Trumpets.	File.
British	165	231	72	4274
Hanoverians	112	184	44	1395
Hesse Cassel	46	116	23	860
Hesse Darmstadt	10	36	—	280
	333	567	139	6809
Infantry.				
British	583	924	511	19,734
Hanoverians	143	273	213	3284
Hesse Cassel	135	403	160	3029
Hesse Darmstadt	44	93	—	1327
	905	1693	884	27,374
Grand Total	1238	2260	1023	34,183

After an inexplicable delay of two months the Republican armies recommenced those active operations which their immense superiority in numbers speedily rendered decisive.

The army of the North had 70,000 men under its banners; that of the Sambre and Meuse, nominally 145,000 strong, presented an efficient force of 116,000 men; while the Duke of York, to cover the united provinces, had hardly 50,000; and General Clairfait, who had replaced Coburg, could only muster 100,000 to maintain the footing of the Imperialists in the Flemish provinces.

All anxiety about their rear having been removed by the reduction of Condé, Valenciennes, Quesney, and Landreçy, the Republicans, in the end of August, assumed the offensive.

The fort of Ecluse having surrendered to Gen. Moreau, the army of the North, reinforced by his division, commenced the invasion of Holland; while the States General obstinately insisted in maintaining half their forces, amounting to 20,000 men, in garrison in the interior, thirty leagues from the theatre of war; thereby leaving the protection of the frontier to the inconsiderable force of the British commander.

With little more than half the invaders' force the Duke of York was charged with the defence of a frontier twenty leagues in extent. He first took up a defensive position behind the Aa, but, his advanced posts having been defeated by the French, he was compelled to retire to the right bank of the Meuse, leaving the important places of Bergen-op- Zoom, Breda, and Bois le Due, to their own resources.—*Alison*, vol. 2. p. 411.

Maestricht and Bois le Duc were both taken by the Republicans, and the Duke of York was again forced to retire:

"He distributed his forces along the line of the Waal, in hopes of being able to maintain a communication with the fortress of Grave now threatened with a siege; but Pichegru, continuing his career of success, crossed the Meuse and attacked the advanced posts of the allies with so much vigour that they were compelled to fall back with considerable loss across the Waal."

Capt. Vivian, writing from the scene of war, says:

Nimeguen, November 2, 1794.

After having been a month on the Continent, and about fifty times drawn out in line of battle, without firing as many shots, we have at last got in the hot of it.

For these last four days and nights I have never closed my eyes. The enemy have been continually attacking and throwing up works, and five British regiments consisting of scarcely more than 300 men each, are ill able to defend a large town against a victorious army.

The hottest battle for the whole war happened here the other day. Two hundred British and Hanoverians opposed, and even repulsed, 300 of the enemy's riflemen, after an action of thirteen hours. The Buffs were considerably engaged, and the party altogether from being 200 were reduced to 76.

Towards the end of October, Pichegru undertook the siege of Nimeguen, which was defended by a numerous garrison, and covered by the Duke of York, who from his camp at Arnheim was enabled at any time to throw in supplies.

The enemy, after forcing the British outposts in front of the place, immediately attacked Fort St. André, and Lieut.- Gen. Abercromby and General Clarke were slightly wounded in the skirmish, as was also Captain Picton in a sally from the place.

At length the French broke ground under the direction of General

Souham, and began to construct batteries and earthworks; on which Count Walmoden marched out suddenly with a body of British infantry, consisting of the 27th, 28th, 55th, 63rd, and 78th Regiments of Infantry and the 7th and 15th Light Horse, two battalions of Dutch troops, and a few other troops.

On this occasion the infantry advanced under a severe fire and jumping into the trenches without returning a shot, charged with the bayonet, and by this check greatly retarded the enemy's works.

Returning to Captain Vivian's letter, he continues:

I myself have been three times on picket, and as often have had my hands full of it, but for my part have luckily escaped.

As the garrison duty is taken between the whole regiments, you seldom are on duty with your own company alone, excepting when in the lunettes; and I am happy to say our regiment as yet has only had three men wounded, one of whom was the finest fellow in my whole company—his wound from a rifleman, under the shoulder—and I hope he will soon recover.

The last picket I was on, four of the Hanoverians and three of the 59th Regiment were killed and wounded. We had a picket out last night, and Twysden, who was the Captain, I understand, has gained great credit from having charged the French and driven them from a post. He has sent in twice for ammunition, and when the last messenger came, he had lost no men (an Hanoverian officer who was with him excepted, being killed).

At the moment I am now writing my ears are deafened by the heavy cannonade on all sides. Twysden is still engaged, and has been since six last night. I expect that before long I shall either go out with a reinforcement for him, or relieve him, being first for duty.

They are busy taking the cannon off the ramparts, the place not being considered as a tenable post, and consequently not worth hazarding five British regiments for; for should the bridge of boats be cut off, which they say is more than probable, in all probability a trip to Paris would be the consequence.

What is to be done I know not, but the enemy are in such superior force that our little army, discouraged by frequent retreats, is very unequal to withstand them; and the opinion here is that this winter must bring peace. Should it be the case I shall return happy in seeing what every soldier ought to see to know his duty and his profession—a campaign; and that, as fatiguing an one as ever was undergone.

What think you of lying out four nights following, in the latter end of October, on the bare ground, without any other cover than a single blanket, and continually harassed by the enemy, and wet and chilled with the rain and winds? Even the old Americans are astonished, and allow their campaign to be far surpassed.

Alison describes the end of the siege of Nimeguen thus:

Shortly after (*the siege had begun*) the French established some batteries destined to command the bridge which connected the town with the intrenched camp in its rear, and soon sunk some of the pontoons composing it, which so much disconcerted the Allies that they hastily evacuated the place with the bulk of the garrison in the night, leaving its defence to an inadequate garrison of 3000 men.

These troops, discouraged by the flight of their fellow soldiers, overawed by the redoubled fire of the besiegers, and despairing of maintaining the place, immediately attempted to follow their example.

Terror seized their ranks; they precipitated themselves upon the bridge which was burnt before the rear-guard had passed over; one regiment was obliged to capitulate, and part of another, embarked on a flying bridge, was stranded on the left bank, and the next day made prisoners by the French; and this splendid fortress, which rendered them masters of the passage of the Waal, fell into the hands of the French.[1] . . . .

The evacuation of Nimeguen completed the misunderstanding

---

1. When visiting Nymergen in the course of the last tour ever made by him (1842), Lord Vivian wrote: "At Nymergen, on my approach, I recognised many buildings, &c., that reminded me of the events that took place nearly 47 years ago, when as a young captain of the 28th Regiment, I was left with my company and Captain Warren's company of the 27th to bring up the rear of the British Army in their retreat from this town after a short siege, and when I had with my Company to cross the bridge of boats in the depth of winter (January 1795) up to our middles in water, the French having sunk by their fire five of the boats which formed the centre of the bridge. On the ramparts at Nymergen I met an old retired general officer of the Dutch service, now resident in the house at the Bellevue, but whose name I forget. He informed me that after Nymergen was evacuated, it was discovered that a man employed on the bridge had been bribed to bore holes in the centre boats, and that it was to this rather than to the fire of the enemy that the destruction of the bridge was to be attributed."

between the Allied Powers, and by spreading the belief in Holland that their cause was hopeless, and that the English were going to abandon them, contributed to the easy conquest of the United Provinces which so soon followed.

Grave, six weeks after, capitulated; and Breda, one of the last of the Dutch barrier towns, was invested

Early in December the Duke of York, conceiving the campaign finished, set out for England, leaving to General Walmoden the task of protecting, with an inferior and defeated army, a divided country, against a numerous and enterprising enemy.

But a severe frost which soon afterwards set in made the Republicans conceive the design of invading Holland while the frost made the canals and rivers passable for troops and artillery.

The prospect of that danger excited the utmost alarm in the mind of General Walmoden, who was afraid that the same cold that exposed his line to the attacks of the enemy would render the passage of the arms of the sea impracticable in the event of a retreat.

Influenced by these apprehensions he passed his heavy cavalry to the other side of the Waal, evacuated his magazines upon the Dwenter, and ordered the Prince of Hesse Darmstadt, cantoned with the most advanced corps in the Isle of Bommel, to abandon it on the first intelligence of the passage of the Meuse by the enemy.

At the end of December, the Meuse being entirely frozen over, the French army commenced its winter campaign by an attack on two columns of the Dutch advanced posts.

The result was what might have been expected from an irruption into a cordon of posts by concentrated forces. The Dutch troops after a slight resistance fled in confusion, some to Utrecht and others to Gorcum, leaving 60 pieces of cannon and 1600 prisoners in the hands of the invaders.

In the general confusion the Republicans even made themselves masters of some forts on the Waal, and crossed that river; but the stream not being yet passable for heavy artillery, Pichegru withdrew his troops to the left bank.

Walmoden then wanted to concentrate his forces on the Waal, between Nimeguen and St. André, but the Prince of Orange insisted on the allied forces approaching Gorcum in order to cover the direct road to Amsterdam, where a revolutionary spirit had for some time been showing itself.

Thus thwarted in the only rational way of carrying on the campaign, Walmoden resolved to abandon the United Provinces, and, with a view to secure his retreat to Hanover, concentrated the English forces behind the Lingen and covered them on the left by the Austrian contingents.

Thiel was abandoned in a panic, and the troops, with the exception of a small vanguard, were withdrawn behind the Rhine.

On January 8, the French crossed the Waal; whereupon Walmoden "abandoned Holland altogether, and retiring to the line of the Issel, from Arnheim to Zutphen, left the United Provinces to their fate."

The Prince of Orange did the same and embarked for England.

A revolution soon after broke out in Amsterdam in favour of the French; the Dutch fleet was captured by the French crossing with their cavalry on the ice; and the British troops embarked and returned to England.

Captain Vivian wrote the following letter in connection with these movements of the British forces.

Schalwych on the Rhine,
Friday, January 9, 1795.

My dear Father,—I have no doubt but for some time past you have been anxiously waiting to hear how I have been going on; but having written to my grandmother from Thiel, and having often begged you not to be surprised should you miss hearing from me for a week or a fortnight, and with the addition of having nothing to say, I deferred writing until about ten days ago.

What has prevented me since that a journal of the time will best tell you.

General D. Dundas, who commanded at Thiel, where our regiment was, having received advice that about 4000 of the enemy had crossed the Waal at Bommel (which the cowardly Dutch had so infamously given up) on the ice, ordered out our regiment, supported by the 80th, 19th, 27th, Hessians, &c., to drive them back.

We marched on Monday night at eight o'clock and arrived at the place of action, twenty-two miles distant, at daylight on Tuesday; but the French could not stand the charge, and the light companies drove all their sharpshooters from the woods, with very little loss. Our company did not lose a man.

As soon as the frost had lasted long enough to make the passage of troops over the ice practicable, Pichegru sent two brigades across to the isle of Bommel; a detachment was at the same time sent against Fort St. André, and the two places were captured almost without bloodshed, which at any other time would have been attended with great slaughter.

The Duke of York having returned to England, the command devolved upon General Walmoden who achieved everything that was possible to be performed by an army destined to contend against an enemy superior in numbers, inured to hardships, and accustomed to success.

But although Major-Gen. Dundas had succeeded in an expedition, in the course of which he carried Thiel, and drove a body of the enemy across the ice with the loss of a number of men and four pieces of cannon, yet it was deemed necessary in the course of a few days to fall back during the night, first upon Buern, and soon after they took refuge behind the Leck.

They, however, at times attacked the enemy, and proved successful in an affair of posts at Geldermalsen, on which occasion Major-Gen. Lord Cathcart, with three English regiments (the 14th, 27th, and 28th) and the British Hulans, distinguished himself greatly, and this too during a period when the troops, notwithstanding the inclemency of the season, were frequently obliged to pass the night in the open air.

Captain Vivian was at Thiel, as he states in his letter, and he gives an account of the affair at Geldermalsen:

We remained all this night and day on the bare snow (rather a cold bath at the end of December).

The next morning our regiments were ordered into the Château of Haften, from which we had just driven the Carmagnoles.

I cannot pass this over without thanking kind fate for not having sent a war into England. Here is I suppose as elegant an house as you ever saw, furnished in the highest possible style, pillaged to such a degree that out of forty-three pier glasses in the different chambers but one remains sound. Every bed, chair, and table, &c., were all broken. In fact words cannot express the horrid situation in which it was left.

We remained here this day and Thursday until eight at night, when we retired to the village of Beest, about six miles distant, on the river Lingen, between the Waal and the Rhine.

We slept out all the remainder of this night and the next day, and at length obtained billets for our poor soldiers, harassed with fatigue and cold. We remained here Saturday, Sunday, and Monday.

At eleven o'clock on Monday night we marched to Buern, covering the retreat of the army over the Rhine. We slept all Tuesday and the night once more on the bare ground, still covered with snow.

On Wednesday we marched to the village where I write this.

Here, my dear sir, you will fancy an end of our troubles must be drawing near; but the wise generals at headquarters, determined to try the strength of our unfortunate soldiers, sent an order for us once more to pass the Rhine and march to Buern, January 10, they having determined to take possession of the Waal, if possible—not unlike a falling man grasping at a straw.

Before we had got half way to Buern we heard a very smart firing, which was occasioned by the French making an attack on our outposts.

The 27th and 14th Regiments were ordered immiediately to their support, and we were directed to follow as quickly as possible in case the enemy's force should be too great for them.

"The two regiments no sooner saw the enemy than they charged bayonets and drove them to the village of Geldermalsen, with trifling loss; and so elated were they at their success that they (as was the case at Toulon) rushed impetuously through the village, and were checked only by a body of 4000 of the enemy.

It was now they that were obliged to retreat, and I am sorry to say with considerable loss, both of officers and men.

Lord Cathcart, who commanded, immediately sent off an express to us, saying if we did not run for it the two regiments were lost; and luckily for them we arrived just in the nick of time, so that we formed on one side of the Rhine and Lingen, under an immensely heavy fire from the enemy, whilst the two regiments retired over the ice from the village.

It was just here that I was unfortunate enough to see poor Colonel Buller and two more of the officers knocked down by a discharge of grape; the other two officers died immediately and I am sorry to add Buller died this morning, having had his thigh broken by the ball.

During the whole of this time our regiment was sustaining their fire, ourselves not firing a shot; and I am sorry to add, with great loss. From my own company, in less than ten minutes, I lost nine men wounded severely, besides numbers hit with spent balls; amongst the former was a wonderfully fine lad, my servant, who, although shot in two places through the arm, would never quit me. He is, I am happy to say, out of danger; and you may depend I'll spare no pains to get him well as soon as possible.

During this business, which did not last a quarter of an hour, our regiment lost two sergeants and sixty-five privates wounded; and what is more astonishing, out of twenty-one officers not one was touched; in fact our regiment was always lucky in this respect. I am sorry to add out of our wounded men many are dead, and the surgeon says that two-thirds will either die or be unfit to serve again. Out of my nine I shall lose but two. I forgot to mention that this loss was only from nine companies, the grenadier company not being engaged.

The chief part of the loss was sustained by Captain Twysden, Captain Potter, and my own; the wings being divided and one company on the flanks. Captain Twysden lost one sergeant, one corporal, and twelve rank and file. Potter, one sergeant, one corporal, and ten rank and file; and mine, nine rank and file.

Continued on January 20.

Once more have I been obliged to break off, and as you will perceive, for no inconsiderable time.

Just as I was writing, an order came out for our regiment to march from our quarters to the Dyke across the Rhine, not above 400 yards distant, to cover the retreat of the 27th, 14th, 33rd, 80th, and 19th Regiments, then stationed in Cuylenberg, which place the enemy were expected to attack every minute. Although so near our quarters the necessity was such that our regiment was again obliged, day and night, until the 16th, to lie under the Dyke.

This night, one of the most wretched ever was, we marched to Amersfoort, seven leagues.

17th.—Remain here this day.

18th.—Six o'clock, morning. Marched to Gardner, six leagues;

a bleak village in the centre of Gelderland.

19th.—Set off, six o'clock, and marched six leagues more to Elburg, from whence I write this.

It is impossible for me to express the wretched state our unfortunate army is reduced to. I will satisfy myself by telling you what alone has been our loss since we left Thiel; and other regiments much more. We marched from Thiel 403 privates, besides non-commissioned officers; and our utmost strength on this morning's parade was 157. In fact, the British army, from being 34,000 men before Breda, are now reduced to less than 7000.

You who have been in Holland must know what marching over the dreary heaths of Gelderland by night, in a severe snow, must be. Suffice it to say that some regiments have 200 missing, others 150, and others 100. The 27th and we were more lucky. They have lost about sixty and we thirty-nine. Shocking to say most of these men are supposed to be dead with the frost.

The general report is that the French army from Maestricht are advancing to cut off our retreat, and it is supposed not one of our sick can escape. We may, perhaps, escape with our skeletons of regiments.

From all accounts nothing can exceed the confusion at headquarters; no one seems to know what they are about. How Mr. Pitt will be able to stand this I must confess I know not; but certain I am if England knew the half her soldiers are suffering the war would soon be at an end. The Coldstream Regiment of Guards alone lost the night before last, in a march of six leagues, twenty-five men from frost; in fact, as I have said already, words cannot express the wretched situation we are in.

Holland, you will see from the last date of this letter, is relinquished to her fate.

The last accounts we have is that Pichegru is at Utrecht with the advanced guard; he entered the town amidst the acclamations of the inhabitants, who were provided with the national cockade; and I have no doubt but that before you receive this, Amsterdam will be in their possession. This, I should suppose, will make a great crash among the merchants of London, and if I do not mistake, will have, I fear, an effect on Mr. Grenfell and his brother.

At present the communication is stopped between this and

England. I shall therefore keep this open lest anything new turns up. For the present I must conclude, and I fear now having tired you with a long and tedious letter.

I forgot to mention that during the whole of this business I have been as well as ever I was in my life,

I must also beg to be excused any irregularity in the writing, &c. This is no place to stand on ceremonies. You will see by the difference of the ink that I have caught every opportunity to write.

Lieut. Gough of our regiment, who has just come in, tells me that Lord Cathcart, our General, is just going to send off to England; so that I must finish.—January 21, '95.

A further letter, not without interest, was written by Captain Vivian about a month later to a female relative, from

> Bellingwolda, near Seer sur l'Ems,
> February 26, 1795.

You certainly deserve well of your country, my dear Betsy, for even affording the slightest amusement to any one billeted under the dykes of Holland; and I really believe were I near enough I should be inclined to give you the fraternal embrace—for your patriotism

In your letter there is a requisition for red-coats; they are not plenty enough here to spare any; the exportation from hence to the next world is too great to be able to spare any at present.

If a man perchance should happen to escape from fire and smoke, and visit Truro once more, is there any chance of a fresh brood of chickens? for by that time, as the present call for those articles is so great, none of the old ones will be left.

I must, nevertheless, confess that as the call for red-coats is also great, should I ever happen to return, I shall esteem myself at no small price; perhaps even higher than the highest bidder— although a campaign in a Dutch winter is at least a five years' addition to a man's age, and although the inconveniences arising from it are, by me, not yet found out, about ten years hence you may expect to see a poor rheumatic old wretch, bound up in flannels, leaning on a wife as on a walking-stick; for this is, in my opinion, the only proper time when a soldier should marry.

The general report here is that we are all soon to come home.

Should this be the case, I will, if possible, see Truro; but I doubt it.

Perhaps we may even have something more to do than we expect before that time; for at this moment the French are cannonading our advanced posts, about six miles on, whom, should they happen to drive in, our regiment is to support.

In June 1795, Captain Vivian's regiment, together with the rest of the British troops, returned to England. From passages in subsequent letters it would appear that the troops remained for some months on board ship.

At this time there was every prospect of the 28th forming part of the expedition which the British Government were then fitting out for the West Indies.

Captain Vivian writes:

Gosport, June 13, 1795.

My dear Father,—You have, I doubt not, seen by the papers that orders are sent to the ten regiments in this neighbourhood to hold themselves in readiness for immediate foreign service.

A letter has just now been received from Lord Paget saying that the fifteen regiments embark in ten days on a secret expedition—generally supposed to be the coast of Brittany—in which parts, if we may believe reports, the Royalists are in great force.

A letter has also been received by the Master of the Ordnance at Portsmouth, ordering him to issue arms immediately to the ten regiments without the regular writ. Who is to command the expedition I know not; but, if to the coast of France, Lord Moira most probably; and I have no doubt but that it will end the same way as his last—tossed up and down Channel for four or five months, and eat our Christmas dinner in old England.

There is also a report that the Grenadiers and Light Infantry companies are to be completed to one hundred strong. If this is the case, and they are detached, or form part of a separate corps. Otter, as paymaster, must give the former up, and I succeed to them.

If this expedition all ends in a bubble, as I very much suspect, you may expect me either before a month is out, or not before September. The latter is most probable; not but that I shall be induced to catch the first opportunity, for fear of getting none at all.

Both Captain and Lieut. Hall are at home with a month's leave; but this unexpected call will make them join sooner than they would wish, I expect. In fact, I am at present the only captain with the regiment, Major Potter commands, every opportunity being given to officers who wish fourteen days'"leave to see their friends. A month's leave must be obtained by application to the General, whereas the commanding officer is empowered to give a fortnight's, from the 7th to the 14th of each month, and from the 14th to the 21st.

We expect half a dozen of our lads in tonight; and tomorrow half a dozen more go to London—which is just the same as being here present—twelve hours brings them down.

The grand fleet under Lord Bridport sailed yesterday, as is generally supposed, to look into Brest.

Camp, Southampton,
August 21, 1795.

My dear Father,—I have just now received your letter of the 10th, which in all probability would have lain in the Gosport post-office a twelvemonth, had not Captain Paget happened to go there and see it.

You will have received my letter stating that we were going to the West Indies. Since that I have been offered various purchases and exchanges, two of which I will mention. One a majority in the 117th Regiment, for £1800; the other a troop in the Carbineers—a Dragoon regiment, now on the Continent, for the regulation of £3000.

In case I get the majority of the 117th, my company falls to Government; and of course the sum is too large; and if I could lower the price, the purchase would be so much the better, as Colonel St. John engages to carry it through for me.

As we certainly are going to the West Indies, the question is, is it worthwhile to avoid the climate? If so, you certainly do so effectually by getting into the Dragoons, which many of our army are about to do. I should get £1800 for my company in the latter case.

P.S.—An account is just arrived to say that Charette, with 20,000 men, has forced his way to the coast. If so, we are off directly.

Charette was the leader of the Royalist adherents in La Vendée. After varying success he was captured and executed by the Republicans in March 1796.

He was constantly promised support by the English Government, and was at times even sent it, but as a rule, the expeditions arrived too late to be of service.

Captain Vivian's regiment did not apparently start as soon as he anticipated, for in September he writes from

Handley, September 6, 1795.

My Dear Father,—Since the 1st I have been spending my time with my uncle at this place. I came, as you may suppose, with an intent to shoot; but birds really never were so wild or scarce; altogether we have killed about thirty brace in five days.

You will, of course, have seen by the papers that our destination is positively the West Indies, under Sir Ralph Abercromby, and many other Scotch generals. The Guards, very much to their astonishment, are to be a party concerned.

We expect to sail somewhere about the beginning of October. The army is immensely large, and St. Domingo is certainly the destination of one part. I hope that by the time we arrive the yellow fever will be nearly done away.

As during this long voyage, and also to encounter the climate, there are many luxuries necessary, to which a captain's pay is altogether unequal; and as, in all probability, I shall not suddenly in the West Indies have an opportunity of troubling you for money, I shall be much obliged to you to allow me something to lay in stock, &c., for the passage, and also for my arrival there, as there are a great many things which I am recommended to carry out; and also to purchase light dress, as a total change of clothing of course takes place on your arrival there. This is an indulgence which all our officers receive, and which I hope you will not think unreasonable.

Two months later Captain Vivian, having then rejoined his regiment, writes from

Gosport, November 30, 1795.

My Dear Mother,—Your joint letter of the 24th, which I received yesterday, gave me the greatest pleasure; and amidst the hurry of changing ships, I take the first opportunity of answering the questions you propose.

In the first instance I must answer ray father by assuring him that it is with the greatest satisfaction that I can say we have not a sick man on board, nor have had any since embarkation. Fourteen months [? *weeks*] on board ship has been a pretty good lesson to us how to keep our men healthy. From eight in the morning until sunset of a fine day, our men are all on deck, except at meal times; their bedding, &c., is also always on deck during fine weather; and the decks are cleaned every day and fumigated twice a week.

With regard to provisions, Government allows us fresh beef, if we can get it; but the bustle of fitting out so large an armament renders it frequently impossible, although you have an order to the purpose.

We are not empowered to allow our men to go on shore for fear of desertion, which, among the drafts, is not an uncommon thing.

Thus far I think I have answered all the questions proposed, and I will now explain the riddle (as I have no doubt you think it) contained in the beginning of this letter, under the words 'changing ships.'

You must know the good ship *Lyde*, being built in the year 1737, did not much relish the knocking about she got in the last place, and proved it by weeping most bitterly on our arrival at Spithead; so much so as to render it necessary to pump about twice every twenty-four hours—to avoid which we applied for a new ship, and got the *Lord Hood*—a very fine ship, but not quite so roomy for the men.

In answering the questions I forgot to say that we are allowed daily a quart of porter, or half a pint of rum, alternately.

The part of your letter concerning the health of the men is already answered, and I am happy to say that the whole regiments are equally well and safe; and Gough, who is on board the same ship as myself, begs me, with his compliments, to say that his love affair is, like all others ought to be, laid aside to serve his country in the West Indies.

The storm frightened me very little, and, if being seasick proves it, believe me I was plentifully so, although so old a sailor. The 63rd lost a transport and 180 men, with the captain, Bancroft, Mr. Ashe (nephew to Captain Ashe), and the surgeon's mate; and Captain Godley tells me that there were 14 officers and

235 bodies of soldiers lying on the beach of Portland at the same time. Had the wind not lulled when it did, his ship, the *Lady Jane*, had certainly perished. As it is, she will never move out of the Weymouth harbour again.

The troops were brought round in the *Alemene* frigate, on board of which is Warren, a Truro man, and to whom I really am very much obliged for the greatest possible attention.

We expect to go out of harbour tomorrow, and the fleet are positively to sail the first fine wind. We have been using every possible exertion to get ready to go with them. I have therefore no chance of the pleasure of having another letter from you before we sail. Depend on it the moment anything happens, you shall hear, and the first packet that leaves Barbadoes after our arrival brings a letter from me.

As will be seen from the next letter. Captain Vivian's regiment was not destined to go to the West Indies.

Portsmouth, February 4, 1796.

My dear Mother,—I always told you that the 28th was the luckiest in the army; and you will acknowledge it when I tell you we are *not to go to the West Indies*.

The expedition is given over, and the regiments to go are the 8th, 44th, 55th, 62nd, and two battalions Scotch Brigade. There was at one time an idea that the two battalions of the Grenadiers were to go, but that is given over.

The whole of this alteration seems to have taken place on account of the news from Spain, which is none of the best. Government is afraid for Gibraltar, and the Guards are to go there, and I think in all possibility we shall go there too.

The quartermaster-general is just gone to the Isle of Wight to get quarters for our brigade, and we are to land there, and be ready for any call. If we remain in England till next April, I will come down among you, but I think in all probability Mr. Pitt will cut out some other employment for us by that time.

The force in the West Indies will, with the six regiments ordered, be fully sufficient to defend our islands; particularly as it is supposed that the part of the regiments already there will be drafted in those going out, so that our four companies will be lost to us.

To see the different countenances of the officers here is really curious; those who have escaped going, and those ordered to go. You cannot conceive how anxious everyone was until the orders came out. We should certainly have gone had we not been so long on board ship.

An interval of four months occurs between the date of the last letter and that of the following one:

Lyndhurst, June 13, 1796.

My dear Father,—I arrived here last night, and found everything just as when I left it, except the regiment having moved; otherwise there is nothing new, nor is there any idea of our going abroad.

Paget has applied for Lymington as our quarters for the summer, and there is every probability we shall go; not but that the inhabitants have petitioned against us, as having the small-pox in the regiment.

We have received many letters from our friends in the West Indies—all going to St. Lucia—more chance of promotion.

Godley has gained a good deal of credit for frightening off a sloop-of-war of fourteen guns, after he had parted convoy in his little bark. He fell in with a national sloop-of-war, on which he heated all the pokers, loaded his six guns, and manned the tops with soldiers.

The sloop did the same, and they came within hail; but seeing him determined, thought proper to sheer off, and Godley, of course, having gained his purpose, did not think proper to stir up their anger by firing on them.

Gosport, July 10, 1796.

My dear Father,—I have the pleasure to inform you that, owing to an application from Paget, we are destined for Gibraltar, for which place we expect to sail the latter end of next week.

In general the idea is that the West Indies will be our destination in September next; but Paget, who has every- thing his own way, says it will not. How far he has a right to say so you may judge when I tell you that within this last week he has made no fewer than the following applications.

In the first place he applied for Fort Monkton, about half a mile from this, as our barracks; and a Militia regiment was to have given them up to us.

Secondly, to go to Gibraltar.

Thirdly, for a Lieut.-Colonelcy for Hall, and a Majority for Twysden.

Fourthly, for 280 of the best men in the country. He succeeded in all, although very strong opposition was made to everything except our going to Gibraltar; and what is more extraordinary, his father, who was here when we heard of Colonel Scott's death, absolutely refused to assist him, and said that he had asked too much already; but Paget trusted to his brother Arthur, who is a most intimate friend of the Duke of York, and who no sooner made the applications than they were granted.

With regard to the Majority of the 64th, I care very little about it, and perfectly coincide with you in thinking that, even if you had money to throw away on it, it is useless; but when it is almost one's all, it is ridiculous. No one knows what may happen. Something perhaps may turn up in the 28th, and how foolish both you and I should look supposing I should sell out, and Otter (even at the distance of live or six years) should get the Majority for nothing.

Portsmouth, July 31, 1796.

My dear Father,—The signal is just now made for the fleet to get under weigh and drop down to St. Helen's, so that there is little probability of my having the pleasure of seeing you on your return into Cornwall.

Two of our wounded officers are returned from the West Indies. Grady died two hours after he received his wounds, having both his thighs broken.

The companies are drafted into the 14th Regiment, and the officers are on their return.

I have no news to tell you, and must, therefore, conclude by wishing you a pleasant journey and myself a quiet passage.

The next letter from Captain Vivian is of two months' later date, some of which time had been taken up by the passage out to Gibraltar.

Gibraltar, October 22, 1796.

My Dear Father,—I wrote a long letter about two days since, with an intention to send it by a lugger at that time lying here; but just as I had finished it I had the mortification to see her get under weigh, and my labour was in vain.

Every person here is in a great bustle on account of the Spanish war. The troops are all encamped in the South, in consequence of a threat from the Dons to set the town on tire, and storm in the confusion.

You may perhaps have read an account of the last siege. If so, you will remember that when the fire on the town first commenced, the shells entered the houses and opened all the cellars. The consequence was that the soldiers were in a continual state of drunkenness and mutiny for four days; and, certainly, had an attempt to storm been then made, it would probably have been successful. It is therefore to avoid anything of that sort again, and, should the enemy attempt to put their threat into execution, to have it in his power to meet them with cool troops, that O'Hara has encamped us, immediately on the beginning of the rainy season.

With regard to the policy of the thing, it is very much doubted by many; for when we consider that the enemy have not above 7000 troops in the neighbourhood, and that the batteries are not at all in a state to begin firing, the chance of their attempting to storm is not equal to the certainty of a sickness prevailing amongst the men owing to their being encamped on the side of the brook during the heavy rains, and the probable attack of gunboats on the encampment.

You will have heard long before this of the narrow escape Admiral Mann had from the Spanish fleet. They passed by this a fortnight since. At that time war was not declared, and they pretended to say was not about to be; but in a few days they met Admiral Mann and immediately gave chase to him, but, fortunately, he happened to be rather nearer to the Rock than they were, and owing to their prime sailers being afraid to engage without the whole fleet, he got off. There were some of their fleet close up; one in particular—an 80-gun ship, and by all accounts an uncommon sailer—was ahead of her fleet and coming fast up with a transport, when Admiral Mann made the signal for the *Hector* to put about and take her in tow. Although the *Hector* was then a league astern of the fleet, as soon as this 80-gun ship saw her put about, she did the same, and ran immediately into the Spanish fleet.

In fact everybody says that had they not been the most arrant cowards they might certainly have brought the fleet to action; and probably, owing to the superiority of fifteen sail to seven, might have taken some ships; the only thing they took, as it happens, was an hospital ship belonging to the 100th Regiment. A very pretty beginning of a war!

To make up for it, we have taken the *Mahonesa* frigate by the *Terpsichore*—Captain V. Bowen.

She came in the day before yesterday. The action lasted about an hour, but after the first two broadsides the Spaniards ran from their guns, and got into the chains on the opposite side from which they were engaged. In fact, so infamously did they behave, that their captain put one of them to death and wounded four more.

She is a fine frigate of 32 guns, and an immense number of four-pound swivels; her guns are thirteen-pounders. She had upwards of 300 men, out of which one officer and 28 men were killed, and one officer and 30 men wounded.

The *Terpsichore*, owing to a bad fever which raged on board her, had only 150 men on board, out of whom one only was wounded in the thigh, and, being unable to move, was afterwards jammed by a gun and was obliged to have his thigh amputated. In fact, never was British naval superiority more evident. A frigate of 650 tons and 32 twelve-pounders, with 150 men, has taken one of 1150 tons and 32 thirteen-pounders, besides 12 four-pound brass swivels, with 300 men; and whilst the Spaniards were running from their guns, 25 British sick on board the *Terpsichore* were crawling on deck, if possible, to assist in fighting ours.

After this, all alarms on account of Sir John Jervis must vanish; for although he has but fifteen sail, and the Spaniards twenty-two, there can be little doubt but that he will thrash them, and very likely bring their admiral once more to visit Gibraltar.

We have various reports here. One party says that the French (20,000) and 30,000 Spaniards are coming determined to take this place. If so, they will, I can tell them, get a warm reception; for, in addition to the present garrison, which is upwards of 5000 men, 3000 more are coming from Corsica. Indeed, so strong shall we be, that I fear lest they should send some of us to the West Indies.

But talking of the reports, others there are who say there certainly will be a general peace very shortly.

I forgot to say that young Devonshire is first lieutenant of the

Terpsichore, and consequently, will get a ship—a very fortunate thing for him and his family, I think.

Gibraltar, November 26, 1796.

My dear Father,—I had determined to have written you a long letter this night, and taken the opportunity of sending it by Lieut. Hamline, of the navy; but he has just now sent to say that Admiral Thompson, who commands here at present, considers his dispatches so urgent that he had ordered him instantly to proceed. What the nature of the dispatches is, you will know before us; but Hamline says that so secret are they that Sir J. Jervis would not allow him to stop and take a letter from any person belonging to the fleet except Admiral Waldegrave.

Everything goes on very well. General O'Hara has at length found out that the Spanish were humbugging him, and that his troops were getting sickly.

A glorious campaign he has made of it! A full set of camp equipage spoilt, and an epidemical disorder, owing to the inclemency of the weather, amongst the troops! Our regiment alone had on leaving camp 104 sick out of 560, and all the rest, I believe, worse.

I have only time to add that we are all getting better, -and our regiment has lost only about eight or ten men as yet; not one of whom, I have the satisfaction to add, was out of my company, who, not to flatter myself or them too much, are about some of the finest fellows you ever saw.

I myself am just as well as ever. Excuse all mistakes; I have written this in about two minutes, and have not had time to read it over; perhaps there are a great many."

Gibraltar, January 15, 1797.

My dear Mother,—At this instant I certainly am in great wrath; whether I shall cool or not by proceeding remains to be proved; but you will, I am sure, allow that I have some reason to be annoyed when I tell you that five mails are arrived and not one letter for me; nearly six months, and not one syllable from any correspondent in England.

But, as I have always professed the principle of returning good for evil, I shall continue to maintain it by writing you every opportunity that occurs; and at the same time I beg and beseech you, at least, for the future, once in three months to write and tell me you are alive; if not, I shall be asking leave to return some of these odd days with the expectation of finding you all dead—for what else can possibly hinder you writing? Letters for every officer but myself! Try what directing them to the care of Messrs. Ross and Ogilvie, agents, will do. Perhaps they will find some method of forwarding them.

But to proceed. With regard to news no place is more destitute than Gibraltar; and how can it be otherwise, seeing that we have no communication with any ports but African, from whence we get all our supplies?

Captain Bowen,[2] in the *Terpsichore*, has taken another frigate, the *Vestale*—French—after a desperate action of an hour and a half; but, owing to the badness of the weather, he could put but nine men on board, and in the night the crew rose and recaptured her.

Immense fortunes are made here by the privateers; many men, from a share of only one-eighth, costing £150, have made £35,000. Colonel Hall, Otter, and our quartermaster, have all a share in one that sails on Monday for the first time, and they have great expectations from her. Indeed, nothing is more common than for one of these row-boats (for they are nothing more) to go out into the Gutt in the morning, and return with a South Sea man with £30,000 in the evening.

Devonshire is acting-captain in the *Mahonesa*, the ship the *Terpsichore* took, and is fitting her out very fast in hopes to be able to get to sea before her captain (Giffard) comes from the Elbe, where he is at present. I sincerely hope he will succeed—if so, he in all probability, will make his fortune, and be able to make some provision for his mother, &c.

Lord Garlics, in the *Lively* frigate, is cruising off Cadiz with a squadron; they have taken prizes to the amount of £200,000.

I have never told you whom I send this by; it is Colonel Paget, who has got leave to return to England, and I sincerely hope that before long I shall write to you from Portugal. If any British troops go there he will certainly apply for us to go, and we all know what Lord Uxbridge's interest is when put in force.

---

2. Captain Bowen was killed in the unsuccessful attempt made by Nelson to take the Isle of Teneriffe, on July 15, 1797, when Nelson was himself wounded in the arm.

Gibraltar, February 12, 1797.

My Dear Father,—In conformance to my promise to write to you by every opportunity, I again sit down to tell you how we go on here, and what has happened since I wrote to you by Gough.

I think I concluded that letter by telling you that the Spanish fleet was hourly expected. I shall now commence by telling you it has passed by, consisting of twenty-seven sail of the line, seven frigates, and a vast number of gunboats, ten of which latter, with three sail of the line, remained at Algesiras; the others, it is supposed, are gone to Cadiz.

As Sir J. Jervis is cruising somewhere off that port, we all sincerely hope he may fall in with them, as, from all accounts of their condition, if he was so fortunate, there is every prospect of his giving a good account of them; although to me (being but little of a sailor) they appeared to pass by in good style. At all events, I will venture to pronounce that they looked very well, and that the sight was a very fine one; the number of vessels being immense, as their whole Mediterranean fleet have accompanied them.

That their order is not very good, or that they are not very alert, is very evident by what happened last night. Two of our very heavy sailing 44-gun ships, a frigate, and a brig, passed through from the eastward, and within a league of the squadron now lying in the bay, without their taking the slightest notice of them; although it was clear to everybody had they cut their cables and chased, the 44s, at least, must have fallen; in fact our frigates, &c., are constantly running in and out, unmolested. This certainly argues a fault somewhere.[3]

The governor is, as usual, in a most terrible fright on account of the gunboats. He declares that he expects them to fire upon us, and has ordered everything ready for another campaign to the South. In fact, any man half so anxious you cannot conceive, and, if there is a shot fired, he will, I am convinced, be the first man killed.

It is allowed by all hands that he certainly has, in some meas-

---

3. On February 13, Sir J. Jervis received intelligence that the Spanish fleet was at sea, and immediately set sail in quest of it. At dawn of the succeeding day the enemy were descried off Cape St. Vincent, and Sir J. Jervis gained the memorable victory, for which he was created Earl of St. Vincent.

ure, more reason for this alarm than the first; since their having gunboats intimates an idea of acting against the place; and if anything is to be apprehended, it is from them, their size being so small that it is not once out of a thousand times that we hit them, and almost every shot or shell they fire takes effect.

About 1500 men arrived in the squadron to do duty in the lines. This, by all accounts, but makes them equal in number to us, and that will not be for very long, from the quantity of deserters constantly coming in; scarce ever a night passing without some. Three only are known to have deserted from the garrison to the enemy, although many more are absent, but supposed to be on board ship.

We are all in anxious expectation of hearing from England, in hopes of being ordered to Portugal (being heartily tired of this place). If we do not leave this, and should not the Spaniards commence an attack, with the governor's permission, you may expect to see me before the year is at an end.

I mean next week, if possible, to get leave to make a fortnights' excursion with a party into Africa, and see what sort of fellows those Moors are. If I succeed you may expect to see in my next an account of them.

Devonshire (who is made master and commander) expects to go to sea in the *Mahonesa* every day, as he only wants a few men. I sincerely hope he may be successful, as from a conversation I had with him, I am convinced, should he be, he would do something for his mother.

I have no letters from Captain Vivian for a space of fifteen months, when he still wrote from

Gibraltar, June 3, 1798.

My dear Father,—After a month's anxious expectation we have again been blessed with the sight of a vessel from England, bringing with her also the mails from Lisbon. I unfortunately am of the few to whom it has brought no letters; I confess it rather hurts me, when I consider that all my friends and correspondents live within ten miles of the Packet office, and have it in their power to know to a day when she sails.

The accounts in the papers, which we have up to May 17, are very good.

The troops in Ireland have fine times of it in free quarters.

Thank God, the spirit of the English has shown itself in a different manner, and I really think it will puzzle the Great Nation even to make a landing good; any further, I am convinced they cannot go. Their defeat at St. Marcon will show them how difficult an attack is, and how seldom it succeeds.

Nevertheless I wish our regiment were with the expedition from Margate. It would seem as though they were about to pay a visit to our old friends, the Dutch.

During the spring of this year an expedition was fitted out against maritime Flanders, for the express purpose of blowing up the Bruges canal.

An armament sailed from Margate roads on May 18, under Captain Popham, with a body of troops under Major-Gen. Coote.

Ostend was set on fire, and on the 19th a landing was effected without opposition, and as soon as the soldiers had formed, they proceeded to burn several boats, demolish the sluice gates, and attempted to blow up the canal.

Having, it was supposed, rendered the canal unserviceable, the commander-in-chief attempted, about noon, to return on board the shipping, but he soon discovered that the wind was so high, and the surf so great, that the attempt was impracticable.

He thereupon occupied a position upon the sandhills at a little distance from the beach, and, by way of gaining time, the governor of Ostend was summoned to surrender; but this fate was unhappily reserved for the invaders themselves, as the governor found means in the course of the night to assemble a great force with which he hemmed in the English early in the morning, and all resistance being in vain, they surrendered after a gallant defence, in the course of which Major-Gen. Coote was wounded.

By the way, talking of our regiment, I give you in great confidence an extract from a letter from Lord Paget to his brother, which he has just shown me: 'I can tell you that H.R.H. means to move your regiment, and regrets very much that it is not the 28th, instead of the 100th, on its return to England; and as nothing is better worth taking care of than this little island, I do not think it at all improbable but that I shall see the "Slashers" here before the end of '98.'

Of course, this prospect has made me very happy, and I am fully convinced that if we do not return to England we shall not remain here very long; nor do I think we shall be sent to the West Indies, from another part of Lord Paget's letter: 'I know of no expedition abroad worth your attending to, nor do I think anything can prevent your return but our friend Tippoo, in the East.'

A few days since, we were under the melancholy necessity of shooting a soldier of ours for desertion to the enemy. I hope the example will have a good effect; but to tell you the truth, the troops in this garrison are in a very relaxed state of discipline, nor can the most active officers prevent it, owing to one-half of our men being constantly at work.

Admiral Nelson, with twelve sail of the line—picked ships—is gone up the Mediterranean; and Sir Roger Curtis has joined the Earl St. Vincent with ten sail from Ireland, which proves that the Government has no apprehension in that quarter.

Amongst all the Volunteer Corps and various other descriptions of loyal defenders, who every day spring up, I do not see any mention of a Cornish Association. I hope you are taking means to drive the 'Carmagnoles,' from off your coast if they should dare attempt to invade them; for although my countrymen are rather riotous now and then, I believe them loyal. I recollect particularly well, when at the bottom of 'Wheel Unity,' a miner telling me that if the French were to come, they (meaning the tinners) would 'scat their brains out.'

Owing to the preparations that were being made by the French for the invasion of England, and also to the number of troops that had been sent to Ireland, a spirit of military ardour seemed at once to seize and pervade the whole kingdom at this time.

All ranks and orders of men eagerly formed themselves into Volunteer Corps, commanded by officers of their own choice acting under temporary commissions, till England presented to her foe the glorious picture of an armed people inspired with the magnanimous resolution of sacrificing; their lives in defence of their country.

Gibraltar, July 17, 1798.

My dear Father,—Paget brings this, and will, I think, most probably deliver it himself. He declares that he will use his utmost exertions to get us out of this horrid prison, rendered worse than ever by the uncommon heat of the weather, the thermometer in the shade at noon having two or three days stood at 86° and 87°.

You may, perhaps, have heard that had the supplementary Militia enlisted (as it was supposed they would) the 28th, 37th, and 42nd Regiments were to have been relieved by three other regiments completed from them, and to have returned to England.

We still live in hopes that Paget will be able to get us away, particularly as this rebellion in Ireland has taken place; to which place I have no doubt but that he will immediately propose our being sent.

I feel myself exceedingly obliged to you for the pains you have been at to procure me an exchange with the Dragoons; and I am really of opinion that were it possible to get a troop out of the break it would be a very desirable purchase, provided also it could be obtained at a reasonable price; but really in these critical times, when the whole world seems upside down, to give a large price for any commission seems to me an imprudent thing.

I cannot agree with Twysden in thinking it probable that I shall get a majority in our regiment soon. Godley will certainly purchase, and I believe Groves will also; Hall wants a larger price than any of us will give.

Godley is on his return home. I fear the same good luck does not await me soon. Two captains must join before I can get leave, and I know of no two likely to do so.

By advices from Admiral Nelson, by the French frigate *Sensible* (captured by the *Seahorse* after a short action), we learn that the French have taken Malta with the loss of only five men; and that Buonaparte has proceeded on his way, supposed to Alexandria, with Nelson within twenty leagues of him. Now, as he is encumbered with transports, it is more than probable that he will be overtaken; so that we may daily expect good news from aloft.

A dreadful mutiny has lately been discovered on board the *Princess of Wales* off Cadiz. Two hours after it was found out they were to have murdered all their officers, and, in concert with the *Hector*, to have attacked the *Ville de Paris*—there also to have committed like enormities; and after having reduced the whole fleet they meant to have gone into Cadiz. Happily it was discovered to Admiral Orde, who secured sixty of the ringleaders—five of whom have been executed. God only knows where the next mutiny will break out. Thank God, in this garrison we have more English and Scotch than Irish.

Gibraltar, July 19, 1798.

Colonel Paget is, I understand, to sail today. I must therefore close this.

Nothing new. As soon as the wind changes we expect a mail from the West. God send good news from Ireland. Gough is in a great fright for his friends and acres.

On August 1, the Battle of the Nile was fought by Nelson who gained a signal victory over the French.

The Great Irish Rebellion broke out in the spring of this year.

More than a year's interval takes place between the date of the last letter from Captain Vivian and the date of the one that follows. During this time Captain Vivian had exchanged (in August, 1798) from his old regiment, the 28th, into the 7th Light Dragoons (7th Hussars); and with them took part in the expedition to the Helder.

In the summer of 1799 the British Government prepared an expedition against Holland, and, by a treaty concluded in June, England was to furnish 13,000 men, and Russia 17,000.

On August 13, the First Division of the English army sailed from Deal, under Sir Ralph Abercromby. On the 27th they landed at the Helder which was taken possession of by the English after an action; and the Dutch fleet was also, very soon afterwards, captured without a shot being fired, owing to the mutiny of their crews. Between September 12 and 15 the Russian contingent arrived, as well as the remainder of the English troops; and the Duke of York took command.

> The English general, finding himself now at the head of 35,000 men, and being aware that extensive reinforcements were advancing to the support of the Republicans, resolved to move forward and attack the enemy. As the nature of the ground precluded the employment of large masses the force was divided into four columns.
>
> The first, composed of 8000 Russians and a brigade of English, was destined to advance by the Sand dyke against the left of Brune, resting on the sea; the second, consisting of 7000 men, of whom 5000 were English, was charged with an attack on the French centre; the third, under Sir J. Pulteney, was intended rather to make a diversion than a serious attack, and was not to push far forward unless in the event of an unlocked for success;

while the fourth, under Sir R. Abercromby, was destined to turn the enemy's right.

The action commenced at daybreak on September 19 with a furious attack by the Russians under Hermann, who speedily drove in the advance guard of the Republicans, and pressing forward along the Sand dyke, made themselves masters of Schorldam and Bergen, and drove back Vandamme, who commanded in that quarter, to within half a league of Alkmaer.

But the assailants fell into disorder in consequence of the rapidity of their advance, and, reinforcements having been moved from the centre to the support of the left, Vandamme was enabled to resume the offensive, and the Russians were attacked at once in front and both flanks in the village of Bergen, from whence, after a murderous conflict, they were driven at the point of the bayonet.

Their retreat, which at first was conducted with some degree of order, was soon turned into a total rout by the sudden appearance of two French regiments on the flank of their column...

While the Russians were undergoing these disasters on the right, the Duke of York was successful in the centre and left....

Indeed, everything promised decisive success in the centre and left of the Allies, when intelligence was brought to the Duke of York of the disaster on the right, and the rapid advance of the Republicans in pursuit of the flying Russians.

He instantly halted his victorious troops in the centre, and marched upon Schorl with two brigades of English and three Russian regiments, which was speedily carried, and if the Russians could have been rallied, decisive success might yet have been attained.

But all the efforts of their commander could not restore order, or rescue the soldiers from the state of discouragement into which they had fallen; and the consequence was that, as they continued to retreat to the entrenchments of Zyp, the Republicans were enabled to accumulate their forces against the Duke of York, who, thus pressed, had no alternative but to evacuate Schorl, and draw back his troops to their fortified lines.

In this battle the Republicans lost 3000 men in killed, wounded, and prisoners; but the British lost 500 killed and wounded, and as many prisoners; while the Russians were weakened by 3500 killed and wounded, twenty-six pieces of cannon, and seven standards.—*Alison*, vol. 4. p. 151 *et seq.*

Major Vivian, who was present at the battle thus writes of it:

Callante Ooge, September 20, 1799.

My dear Father,—You will be anxious, I have no doubt, to hear an account of the action of the 19th—yesterday. I am myself so excessively fatigued that I cannot possibly enter into particulars.

I can only say that the Russians, after advancing like a brave mob, retreated like a cowardly one.

The slaughter was dreadful, and they made it worse by their savage acts of cruelty to the wounded French.

Our left succeeded completely, and but for 'Russeman' the day would have been a brilliant one.

The country was such that we could not act; narrow lanes bounded by immense sandhills; and woods, intersected by ditches. We had some cannon shot at us, but without effect, and a few horses wounded by rifle balls.

I am just off picket and am going to bed. We were on horseback from 11 o'clock on the night of the 18th, till 10 on that of the 19th.

The action commenced at three in the morning, and ended at night.

Our loss is dreadful; that of the enemy 3200 prisoners, but I should guess, from what I saw, not near so many killed as we had. I should think our loss nearly 5000, if not more. The British have lost a quarter of their officers.

Adieu. I will write again soon. I expect another attack on Monday.

The Duke of York was not discouraged by the issue of the attack on September 19. Although heavy rains prevented him doing so for some time, he resumed the offensive on October 2.

> The recollection of the success which had everywhere crowned their efforts in the preceding action, animated the English troops, while the Russians were burning with anxiety to wash out the stain which their disasters on that occasion had affixed to the Imperial eagles...
>
> At six in the morning, the attack was commenced at all points. The Russian division of Essen, anxious to efface its former disgrace, supported by the English division of Dundas, advanced to the attack in the centre with such impetuosity that the villages of Schorl and Schorldam were quickly carried, and the

Republicans driven in confusion to the downs above Bergen. An attack was there projected by the Duke of York; but Essen, who recollected the consequence of the former rashness of the Russians on the same ground, refused to move till the advance of Abercromby on the right was ascertained; a circumstance which paralysed the operations.

Abercromby advanced gallantly along the Sand dyke, and, notwithstanding a hot fire of musketry and grape, by which he had two horses shot under him, succeeded in forcing the French left and expelling them from the sandhills and downs on which they rested.—*Alison*, vol. 4 p. 155.

The shades of night now began to prevail, when the enemy, determined to make one more effort to retrieve the fortune of the day, advanced with his *chasseurs* in the face of the British column, and charged the horse artillery with such impetuosity as to cut down several of the troops and to carry off two guns in triumph.

But this success was of short duration; for several squadrons of the 7th and 11th Dragoons, with Lord Paget at their head, suddenly issuing from a recess between two sandhills, fell upon the cavalry of the enemy, who, incapable of sustaining the shock, rushed into the sea to avoid the British sabres.

The rout now became complete, but a small portion of the enemy, favoured by the approaching darkness, effected their escape, leaving their prize cannon behind.

The British cavalry remained all night on the beach, forming a line with the infantry on the sandhills. Neither horses nor men could get any water. When day broke it was expected the column would move forward. The troops, however, were so worn out with fatigue and the want of food, that it was determined not to advance till they had been refreshed. But the road was so bad that neither the bread, nor the wagons for the wounded, could arrive before four o'clock in the afternoon.

An order had just been issued for the regiments to send for their rations, when a report was received that the French were retiring from Egmont-op-Zee. Not a moment was to be lost. The troops were ordered to arms. They instantly marched forwards without expressing a murmur, leaving their provisions on the beach.

The French, however, had retired two hours, and not one Frenchman was overtaken in a pursuit of three miles.

The cavalry lay again on the beach all night, and were again without water. Altogether the horses were fifty hours without hay or drink—some, indeed, were sixty. The whole army suffered as much as human nature could support.

The English entered Alkmaer on October 3. During the whole of the 4th and 5th, the two armies rested on their arms. But on the 6th, in the morning, a general order was given by the Duke of York to make an attack upon the entire front of the enemy's line.

The action commenced at seven in the morning, and was obstinately contested during the whole day.

In the centre the Allies were successful in the first instance; Essen bore down all opposition, and the Republicans were on the point of succumbing when Brune strengthened them with the greater part of a fresh division, and a vigorous charge threw back the Allies in confusion towards their own position.

In their turn, however, the victorious Republicans were charged, when disordered by success, by an English regiment of cavalry, thrown into confusion, and driven back with great loss to Kastricum, where they were with difficulty rallied by Vandamme who succeeded in checking the advance of the pursuers.—*Alison*, vol. 4 p. 156.

On the whole the battle was indecisive. Haarlem was the object of the English general, without the possession of which he could not maintain himself in the country during the inclement weather which was approaching; and Haarlem was still in the enemy's hands. The Republican forces were daily increasing; and the total absence of all the necessary supplies in the corner of land within which our army was confined, rendered it impossible to remain there for any length of time.

In these circumstances the Duke of York, with the unanimous concurrence of a council of war, resolved to fall back to the entrenchments at Zyp, there to await reinforcements, or commands from the British Cabinet.—*Ibid.* p. 158.

On the day after the battle, therefore, the Allies retired to the position they had occupied before the battle of Bergen.

Brune lost no time in following up the retreating English. . . . The situation of the Duke of York was now daily becoming more desperate; his forces were reduced by sickness and the sword to 20,000 men; the number of those in hospital were daily increasing; there remained but eleven days, provisions for the troops; and no supplies or assistance could be looked for from the inhabitants. . . . In these circumstances, he rightly judged that it was necessary to lose no time in embarking the sick, wounded, and stores.—*Ibid.*

Accordingly, he proposed a suspension of arms to General Brune, preparatory to the evacuation of Holland by the allied troops. This was eventually agreed to, and before December 1 the British troops had regained the shores of England, and the Russians were quartered in Jersey and Guernsey.

Such was the disastrous issue of the greatest expedition which had yet sailed from the British harbours during the war, and the only one at all commensurate to the power or character of England.—*Alison*, vol. 4. p. 159.

In a letter written when the English were retreating in 1799, Major Vivian says:

Callante Ooge, October 13, 1799.
What we are to do they keep secret, but it is generally believed that we are to return. Advance we cannot; and if the frost sets in our retreat is cut off. The only alternative appears to be either to retire immediately, or become prisoners.
Of this I am convinced—that if 20,000 men more are sent, we shall never be able to reach Amsterdam.

In December, Vivian returned with his regiment to England and on March 9 he was promoted to a majority.

The only letter from Major Vivian, that I possess, written in the interval between the expedition to the Helder and the Corunna campaign, is one dated August 1803—nearly four years after the Helder. During this time, Malta had been taken, and the battles of Copenhagen and Aboukir fought.

In March 1802, a peace was signed at Amiens between France and England. Previous to this, however. Napoleon had been making great preparations for the invasion of England, which had called forth the national spirit in a remarkable degree. The whole kingdom was filled with volunteers, who were not daunted by the renown lately gained by the French in the victories of Marengo and Hohenlinden. It is to these efforts on the part of the nation that Major Vivian alludes in the following letter.

Woodbridge, August 14, 1803.
My Dear Father,—What with business and pleasure, my time

has for ten days been so much employed that I find myself in your debt for two letters.

Since I last wrote to you I have been making myself acquainted with the coast toward Yarmouth on the one side,, and the Essex coast on the other. Add to this balls, fetes, and dinners, given by Thelluson and other gents of the neighbourhood, and I really have had scarcely time to write a line.

You may imagine how thick engagements are here, when I tell you that I have now been here seven weeks and have dined at home but five times. I make a point of sleeping in my quarters, unless absent on duty, which was the case last week.

They tell me this is the best defended district of any; if so, I can only say others are very bad, for we have not, in the whole of it, 20,000 men, and there is no one spot where we could bring above 5000 men to act under twelve hours at least. The volunteers are few, and those not armed. So much for the exertions of Government!

The army of reserve are here perfectly satisfied, with immense bounties; but still I find at Bury they have deserted dreadfully; forty guineas for a substitute has been very common.

I agree with you in thinking Government are in a hobble about the Defence Bill; but I think Sheridan's motion, and the consequent resolutions, will produce more volunteers than anything; else. The fellows like the idea of the thanks of the House, and the handing down to posterity the services of their forefathers. Our establishment is eight troops of eighty-five men, and seventy-five horses; but we want 104 men more to complete, and recruiting is at an end.

I certainly think you and Gwatkin most proper and able men to have a corps; pray let it be a good, rattling battalion.

We expect the Duke of York here on Saturday to inspect the district and review the troops. In our whole brigade of Light Cavalry we have not at present effective above 700 men—we have so many recruits, and recruiting.

Since I have been here I have seen a great deal of a very great man—Sir Sidney Smith. I have been several times on board the *Antelope*, and, in fact, generally see him every day. He is one of the pleasantest possible men to live with, full of anecdote, but, if anything, rather too fond of talking about Acre. He is extremely volatile and very intelligent, and nothing I really believe could put him in a passion.

Lord Paget, Sir Robert and Lady Harland, the Thellusons, and myself, last week were very nearly drowned in going off with him to the *Antelope*. The wind was hard and we struck on the bar of the Aide River, and if all the sailors and Lord P. and myself had not jumped out up to our middles in water to lighten the barge, she must have gone to pieces; for the sea was making a fair breach over her, and the ladies were just as wet as if they had been drawn through a pond. When we got into deep water the boat was full half-way up the leg. So much for water parties!

It seems I was fated to get duckings last week, for the very next evening I had another, in a much more agreeable way. I happened to be walking on the quay at this place and saw an unfortunate fellow, who could not swim, out of his depth and in the act of drowning. Fifty people were present, and no one attempted to assist! Knowing I could swim very well I felt it my duty to do my best, and without hesitation, in full regimentals, in I jumped, and had the good fortune to fetch the poor fellow, almost lifeless, to the shore.

I have gained a good deal more credit for this than I deserve; for it strikes me now, as it did then, that it was only my duty to do an act of humanity to a fellow creature when I could do it with very little risk to myself. The man I must tell you offered liberally to reward me with a crown bowl of punch!

During the time that he spent at home, between his return from the Helder and his going on active service again in the Corunna campaign, Hussey Vivian turned his thoughts from war to love, and became engaged to Eliza, daughter of Philip Champion De Crespigny, of Aldborough.

As this match, however, did not meet with the approval of the relatives of either party, the young couple settled the question for themselves by running away to Gretna Green. The bride was descended from an old French family, refugees from the Edict of Nantes; and the fruit of the marriage was two sons and three daughters.

On September 20, 1804, Vivian became Lieut.-Col. of the 25th Light Dragoons, but three months later, December 1, he exchanged back into the 7th Hussars.

CHAPTER 2

Corunna Campaign, 1808-9

In the interval of five years that elapsed between the date of the letter written by Major Vivian in August 1803, and the commencement of the Corunna campaign in September 1808 great and interesting events were taking place both on the Continent and in England, and I much regret that I have no correspondence of my grandfather on such exciting and important matters.

In March 1802, peace had been signed between France and England at Amiens; but it was not destined to be of long duration, for in May 1803, Napoleon, complaining of the countenance given by England to French emigrants, and of the delay in surrendering Malta to the Knights of St. John, publicly insulted the British ambassador (Lord Whitworth), and war was again declared.

A huge camp was formed at Boulogne for the invasion of England, but 30,000 volunteers immediately enrolled themselves to protect these shores.

The British fleet swept the Channel and recaptured the French and Dutch colonies, which had been surrendered by the English Government at the peace of Amiens.

In May 1804, Napoleon had assumed the title of Emperor of the French; and with the exception of Prussia, most of the European powers were combined against him.

The invasion of England was organised, and Napoleon only awaited the junction of his fleets from Toulon, Cadiz, and Brest, to make the attack. Nelson, however, signally defeated the French admiral, Villeneuve, at the battle of Trafalgar, on October 21, 1805, and completely shattered all Napoleon's hopes of successfully invading this country; and the latter thereupon marched his "Grand Army" from the shores of the Channel to the banks of the Danube, against the Austrians, over whom he gained the celebrated battle of Austerlitz on December 2, 1805.

The news of this victory is said to have been Pitt's deathblow; and that statesman's death was shortly after followed by that of his great rival, Fox.

On land the English had, at first, but little success against their foes; for, though the brilliant victory of Sir John Stuart over the French at Maida (July 1806) raised the prestige of the British arms, the expedition of Sir John Duckworth to Constantinople, and that of General Frazer to Egypt, were unsuccessful.

Meanwhile Napoleon was in the full tide of success. He had declared war with, and had virtually conquered, Prussia, by the battle of Jena, in October 1806; and the victories of Eylau and Friedland had resulted in a close alliance between him and the Emperor Alexander of Russia, at Tilsit, in July 1807.

In order to prevent the fleet of the Northern Powers falling into Napoleon's hands, the surrender of the Danish navy was demanded by the English, and enforced by the bombardment of Copenhagen in September 1807, and the seizure of that nation's fleet.

In the autumn of 1807 Napoleon began his schemes of conquest in Spain. An army under Junot overran Portugal and entered Lisbon on November 30, the royal family fleeing to the Brazils.

Napoleon then decoyed Charles IV. of Spain, and his son, Ferdinand, to Bayonne; and obtaining from them a renunciation of the throne of Spain, conferred the sovereignty on his brother, Joseph Buonaparte, who entered Madrid on July 20, 1808. The inhabitants of Spain, however, soon rose in revolt against the French yoke, and proclaimed Ferdinand VII. as their king.

The British Government determined to support the Spaniards in their insurrection against the usurper; and the greatest valour was shown by the Spaniards in their efforts to rid themselves of the French, more especially in the defence of Saragossa, where women and children flew to the ramparts with the men, and the most heroic resistance was made to the French besiegers. Even when the latter had obtained an entrance into the town, the Spaniards fought so desperately from house to house, that between August 4 and 14 the besiegers were only able to make themselves masters of four houses; and eventually the French retreated, after having besieged the place for two months, abandoning their cannon and heavy stores. The inhabitants of Valencia behaved in the same gallant manner and also repulsed the French.

In the meantime, however, the Spaniards elsewhere were not so successful. Generals Cuesta and Blake, with 25,000 infantry, 400 cavalry, and 80 cannon, were forced to retreat at Rio Seco, on July 14, by Bessière's force of considerably less number.

Cordova was taken and sacked by Dupont; but the latter eventually retired towards Baylen, after having wasted a considerable time at Cordova, which gave the Spanish general, Castaños, an opportunity of instilling a certain degree of order into his tumultuous array of peasants.

A battle took place at Baylen on July 19, in which both the French and Spanish armies became intermixed in a most extraordinary manner, with, however, the result that the French army eventually laid down their arms to the Spanish forces, to the immense astonishment and joy of Europe. This capitulation caused Joseph Buonaparte to retire hastily from Madrid.

In 1808 the British Government sent an expedition to Portugal, under Sir Arthur Wellesley, consisting of 10,000 men. Two smaller divisions were soon after prepared, and sailed from Margate and Ramsgate; and orders were sent to Sir John Moore, who with 12,000 men had been sent to Gottenberg to aid the Swedes, to return and form a further reinforcement of the armies in the Peninsula.

The expedition under Sir A. Wellesley sailed on July 12, and landed in Mondego Bay on August 1, where it was joined by a further division, under General Spencer, making the force 13,000 strong. On August 9 this force commenced their march inland, and on the 15th a skirmish occurred at Obidos, which is memorable as being the first conflict in which any British soldiers fell in the Peninsular War.

A battle took place at Rolica in which the French were defeated, and would, on the following morning, have been pursued but for news having arrived that Generals Anstruther and Acland, with their respective brigades, were off the coast, and that Junot was marching with all his forces from Lisbon to bring matters to an issue.

On the 19th and 20th of August, Anstruther's and Acland's troops were landed, bringing the number of the English army up to 16,000 men. Sir Harry Burrard now arrived, and, as superior to Sir A. Wellesley, took command.

The troops were concentrated at Vimiera, where Junot, who attacked them on the 21st, was completely routed. Had he been at once pursued, as Sir A. Wellesley advised, it is probable that he would have been annihilated. Sir Harry Burrard, however, gave orders for the troops to halt at all points and to remain in position at Vimiera till Sir J. Moore arrived with reinforcements.

Sir Harry Burrard's tenure of office was short; for on the morning of August 22nd Sir Hew Dalrymple arrived and assumed command; so that within thirty hours a pitched battle had been fought, a decisive operation rejected, and three successive generals had been in command!

Sir Hew resolved to advance on the 23rd, but as he was about to do so a flag of truce arrived from Junot, agreeing to evacuate Portugal on conditions that the French army were not to be considered prisoners, but were to be sent back to France by sea, with their artillery and arms. The Russian fleet, which was in Lisbon, was to be conducted to England, and remain there till peace was declared, the officers and crews being transported to Russia without restrictions as to future service. This arrangement, known as the Convention of Cintra, was agreed to by the English generals, but caused such great dissatisfaction in England that a Court of Inquiry was held upon them.

On the 15th of September the first of the French troops sailed from the Tagus, in accordance with the Convention. By the 30th the whole were embarked, and before the middle of October not a French soldier remained on the soil of Portugal.

Sir Hew Dalrymple, Sir Harry Burrard, and Sir A. Wellesley were obliged to return to England, to undergo the Court of Inquiry before alluded to; and the command of the army thereupon devolved upon Sir J. Moore, whose division had landed at Lisbon; whilst another corps, 15,100 strong, under Sir David Baird, was destined about this time to land at Corunna, and descend through Gallicia, to co-operate with the troops of Sir J. Moore, which were advancing from Portugal, in the plains of Leon.

Sir J. Moore's forces set out on their march from Lisbon in the middle of October; but for the sake of procuring better roads for the artillery and wagon train, broke into two columns; and whilst the main body, under Sir J. Moore, followed the direct road by Abrantes, Almeida, and Ciudad Rodrigo, a lesser division, but with all the reserve and most of the guns, under General Hope, took a more circuitous route by Elvas, Badajos, Talavera, and Madrid.

On the 11th Sir J, Moore crossed the Spanish frontier, and on the 18th had collected the bulk of his forces at Salamanca; but Sir D. Baird, who had landed at Corunna on the 13th of October, had (and then only by great exertions) not got further than Astorga, four days' march from Salamanca, on the 20th of November.

Thus the British army, in all not more than 30,000 strong, was split into three divisions, severally stationed at the Escurial (near Madrid), Salamanca, and Astorga—distant eighty or ninety miles from each other! Napoleon, on the other hand, lay with 180,000 veteran troops concentrated near Vittoria.

Major Vivian had by this time become Colonel of the 7th Hussars, which regiment was ordered to form part of the forces that landed at Corunna, and was consequently, at first, under the command of Sir D. Baird.

A diary was kept by Colonel Vivian during this campaign, which is now in the possession of the present Lord Vivian, as head of the family. From that diary (whilst it was in my mother's possession) I made the following copy.

Journal of March from Corunna and Sir John Moore's Campaign, 1808.

September 23, 1808. Guildford.—On Friday, September 23, received orders for eight troops of the regiment to be held in readiness for immediate embarkation.

September 25.—On Sunday inspected the regiment in watering order, and selected the men and horses to form the troops.

September 28.—On Wednesday assembled the regiment again in complete marching order, and formed the troops.

September 29.—On Thursday received an order, by orderly dragoon, for the regiment to march in three divisions—three troops in each of the two first, and two troops in the third—to Portsmouth, to embark.

September 30.—On Friday, the 30th, the First Division, under the command of Lieut.-Col. Kerrison, marched.

October 1.—The Second Division, under the command of Captain Denshire, marched.

October 2.—The Third Division, with the band, under Major Cavendish, marched.

On the same day the First Division embarked, having halted the first day at Liphook, the second at Petersfield.

I saw the Third Division off, and then proceeded to Portsmouth to see the first embark, and so on the others, which embarked the two following days; and, much to the credit of the regiment, not a man appeared on any parade during the march the least in liquor.

The following is a list of the officers, number of men, &c., that embarked:—

	Horses	
Lieut.-Col. Vivian	5	
Lieut.-Col. Kerrison	5	
Major Paget	4	
Major Cavendish	4	(Dead. Drowned coming from Corunna)
Captains Denshire	3	
Cholmley	3	
Hodge	3	(Dead. Killed at Waterloo)
Treveake	3	(A clergyman)
Thornhill	3	
Dukenfield	3	(Dead. Drowned coming from Corunna)
Lovelace	3	
Pipon	3	
Verner	3	
Lieuts. Long	2	
Crawford	2	
Waldegrave	2	(Dead. Drowned coming from Corunna)
Stow	2	
Robeck	2	
Lowther	2	
Wildman	2	
Cornets Champion	2	(Dead)
Goodwin	2	
Meyer	0	(Killed at Waterloo. I mounted him. He was very poor, and had a wife and child. As gallant a soldier as ever drew sword)
1 Paymaster	2	
1 Surgeon	2	
1 Asst.-Surgeon	1	
1 Vet. Surgeon	1	(N.B.— Mr. Parker was arrested at Portsmouth)
6 Quartermasters	4	
36 Sergeants	—	
8 Trumpeters	—	
672 Rank and File	—	

751

The ships went out to Spithead as soon as we embarked; and on Thursday, the 6th, the whole convoy, under the *Egeria*, got under weigh and sailed to St. Helens.

October 7.—Lying at St. Helens. The wind north-west.

* * * * *

The troops were some time before they were able to make a start. In *St. James Chronicle* of October 13, 1808, I find this:

On the 13th the *Egeria*, of eighteen guns, lying at St. Helens, with the 7th Regiment of Dragoons for Falmouth, was recalled, it is supposed in consequence of Sir D. Baird, whom they were to join, having sailed.

The *Egeria* attempted to sail on the 18th, but owing to foul winds, did not actually depart till the 31st.

* * * * *

On October 24, Major Paget and myself embarked on board *La Sibylle* frigate, and on November 8, in the morning, we arrived, after a favourable passage, in Corunna Harbour.

The kindness and civility of Captain Upton was beyond anything, and such that I can never forget.

On the 9th the regiment began disembarking from the eleven transports. Five of the transports had not arrived. The others were not able to haul in close enough.

On this and the three following days, the whole regiment disembarked, having lost only seven horses on the passage, and one drowned disembarking.

The 10th Hussars also disembarked. On the second and third days, disembarkation of the 10th and part of the 15th. On the last day part of the 10th, and so on till all were landed.

Two of the transports of the 15th parted company and were driven into Muros Bay—one, after being taken and liberated, having lost their arms and on parole not to serve again."

The captain of the French ship which took the above transport proposed to kill all the horses; but the men declared that they would suffer anything rather than submit to this cruel massacre of animals they regarded as companions.

The Frenchman, touched by this display of feeling, consented to spare them, and put the men on parole not to serve again.—
St. James' Chronicle, November 22, 1808.

The first day's disembarkation of the 7th was truly deplorable; it rained in torrents; and from the transports not being able to haul up to the quays, the horses were slung into the water and most of them obliged to swim on shore. The poor men, most miserably soaked, having no place to go to but an open shed—many of them having lost their appointments and necessaries, and no man having a dry article to put on. Add to all this the easy rate at which the men obtained wine, and consequent drunkenness, and the misery and confusion of the scene may be imagined!

Fortunately the following days were very fine, and the regiment had an opportunity of getting into some sort of order; but still, from the distance to which it was necessary for them to go for procuring forage, &:c., nothing could possibly be more harassing than the duty of the soldier, who had scarcely an instant to himself from morning till night.

With great exertions, however, on the part of all, officers and men, the regiment was in a state to move on on the 15th of November, on which day the First Division, consisting of the right squadron under the command of Lieut.-Col. Kerrison, and one troop of R.H.A, under that of Colonel Downes, commenced their march.

It is now time to say something of Corunna itself. the town is situated in a very fine harbour, at the foot of a mountainous country, and is excessively well supplied with provisions of all sorts.

The streets are in some parts very wide, and the foot-pavement most excellent; the shops very good; and, what appeared to us rather extraordinary, the very strict blockade to which it had been liable did not prevent their being well furnished.

The officers were quartered on the different families, and experienced, most generally, the kindest attention.

The playhouse is far from bad; indeed, very superior to what you will see in any provincial town in England; the dresses magnificent, and the *bolero* dances with the castanets most admirable.

The British officers were invited to a ball given by a lady of distinction, which, although not in the style of magnificence which is shown at parties of this sort in England, was very far from disagreeable, and the dancing was most excellent.

The costumes and manners of the inhabitants were to us something truly different to what we had been accustomed, and in many points they are certainly very much behind the rest of the world; but still Corunna is, even at the present time, a fine city, and capable of vast improvement. It is true it is dirty, but this might very easily be earned off on account of a great part of it being situated on the side of a hill; and the *tout ensemble*, both for comfort and convenience, was very superior to anything we had been led to expect.

We heard, shortly after our arrival here, of the army under Blake having been obliged to evacuate Bilbao, after a considerable loss; but this appeared to have very little effect upon the inhabitants, who seemed fully determined to continue the conflict. The women, we understand, in particular, are most zealous in the cause.

I cannot here omit relating an anecdote I heard from my landlord, of a Spanish lady of distinction of this city, who, having lost three sons in the last action, lamented only that she had not as many more to supply their places.

A spirit even beyond this, if possible, actuated the women of Saragossa, where the women worked the guns and in the trenches even after the men had deserted them. It is said that the women of Corunna requested to be permitted to form a battalion. While such a spirit reigns, however successful the battalions of Buonaparte may be at first, it is impossible that they can be so eventually. At least this is my opinion. I know I differ from those who ought to be better judges.

★ ★ ★ ★ ★

Colonel Vivian mentions above the report the army had received as to Blake having been defeated. This was the fact.

The Spanish troops had been divided into three armies—the right, under Palafox, were near Saragossa; the centre, under Castaños, were near Tarazona, opposite the French; and the left, under Blake, were at Reynosa.

On September 18, Blake advanced from Reynosa to Santander. The French thereupon concentrated their forces near Vittoria. Blake attacked and took Bilbao, but his men were ill equipped, worse drilled; he had scant stores, and still less ammunition to rely on. He however was reinforced by Romana's troops, and attempted to interpose between Lefevre and Ney and their communications with the French frontier.

Blake's forces were, however, so scattered that, though he had 36,000 men under his orders, only 17,000, without any artillery, were ever actually in front of the enemy.

Lefevre, under cover of a thick fog, suddenly attacked the Spanish army, on October 31, and drove them into Bilbao, whence they retreated towards the Asturias; and the French took possession of Bilbao.

About this time Napoleon arrived at the seat of war; and, on November 10, Marshal Victor, with 25,000 men, attacked the Spanish near Espinosa, whilst Lefevre, with 15,000 more, marched upon the Spanish line of retreat.

Though the Spanish for some time fought gallantly they were eventually completely routed, and Blake fell back, with 7000 disorganised troops, on Reynosa. He was, however, again attacked by Soult and Lefevre, on November 13, and completely defeated, and driven, with a few hundred followers, into the heart of the Asturian mountains. Bilbao, Santander, and the remainder of the intermediate coast, together with great stores that had been landed at Santander by the British, fell into the hands of the French.

The Spanish centre was also defeated by the French near Burgos, on November 10, at which place Napoleon then established his headquarters, and proceeded to organise movements for the destruction of the remaining Spanish army, under Castaños and Palafox, who retreated towards Tudela.

At this time, as has already been pointed out, Sir J. Moore was, with part of his forces, near Salamanca; the remainder of his force, under General Hope, was near Madrid; and Sir D. Baird was on his way from Corunna towards Astorga, with the object of uniting his forces with those of Sir J. Moore.

Colonel Vivian's diary continues:

★ ★ ★ ★ ★

Sir D. Baird's army had commenced their march previous to our arrival, and we found Sir David himself just ready to depart.

November 14.—On the 14th he (Sir D. Baird) actually set out, accompanied by the whole '*Etat Majeur*'; and the command devolved upon Lieut-Gen. Lord Paget, who was chief of the cavalry.

During our stay here a curious and ludicrous circumstance occurred, which afforded us much amusement.

In order to conciliate the inhabitants, orders had been given to show all possible respect to their religious customs, and especially when the Host was passing, the guards were directed to turn out and present arms.

A large crowd of people, accompanied by priests, was seen one day approaching the main guard, and the sentry (supposing it could be nothing but the Host) turned out the guard, which in all due form presented arms, when, lo and behold! to the great amusement of all present it turned out to be an unfortunate fellow, chained hands and feet on a mule, doing penance.

On the 15th, the 7th Light Dragoons commenced their march to join the British army assembling at Astorga.

The First Division consisted of two troops, commanded by Lieut.-Colonel Kerrison, and accompanied by one troop of R.H.A.

The Second Division, three troops, commanded by Major Cavendish.

The Third Division, three troops, accompanied by Lord Paget and Major Paget.[1]

November 16.—The 10th Hussars, in three divisions, accompanied by a troop of R.H.A., and the 15th, in two divisions marched.

On the 17th, the Division of the 7th which I commanded, commenced their march under most favourable circumstances. A finer day

---

1. The Major Paget referred to above, was Berkeley, a younger brother of Lord Paget. Writing to his father (Lord Uxbridge) on November 16, 1808, Major Paget says: "Bladen Capel returns to England in a few days, and as I march tomorrow morning with the last division of the 7th I shall give this letter into his custody.

"Our present route is only as far as Astorga. What is to become of us when we get there I have not yet heard. We are to reach it on the 30th of this month. The 10th and 15th follow us, in three divisions each; the former first, so that the Hussars will not be assembled till December 6.

"We have always plenty of reports here, but none to be depended on We look for news from England. I, however, believe that Blake has been licked. Two or three Spanish generals have been discovered as rogues having been bought by Buonaparte. They are in custody. I daresay he will buy them all at last. I'm confident, at least, that he will try. I hope that we shall be able to show a good example, and if we meet the French upon equal terms I do not think they will have to boast of much. They outnumber us in cavalry considerably. We are told they have 8000. If we can muster 3000 it will be as much as we can do. The odds are high. I think, nevertheless, that we shall tackle them, as they probably will not be all together.

"The inhabitants, on whom we are quartered here, are particularly attentive and kind. I dine today with Paget's host, who insisted on his asking twenty of his friends. I dined the other day with my landlady, and a sorry meal I made of it. The Spanish cookery does not suit me. A touch of garlic I have no objection to, but my breath was taken away when one dish was put on the table, which was a sausage as large as a line-of-battle ship's mainyard, cram full of garlic, a dish of macaroni poisoned with saffron, and a salad mixed with lamp-oil. I was obliged to eat out of compliment, and lie through thick and thin by saying that I thought it delightful. The market nevertheless is plentifully supplied with red-legged partridges, which I was happy to see, as I mean to try my luck at them with my gun. (Cont. next page.)

never was seen, and the country through which we passed was romantic, and in many parts most beautiful so far as scenery goes.

Of its cultivation I cannot boast much, although in many parts it was far from bad, and the number of vineyards, when in leaf, must have added much to its appearance in this respect and to its general beauty. Turnips are cultivated in very great abundance, and although not brought to that perfection that they are to be found in England, they are still much superior to what I had been led to suspect from the accounts I had read of the country.

During our first day's march to Betanzos, we remarked several houses, evidently the property of persons of consequence, round which the cultivation was better than in other parts, and about which we observed plantations of fine ash trees. Furze appears to be cultivated in great abundance; it grows, to a large size, and is the common firewood of the country; indeed, woods of all sorts are scarce, although here and there we observed some coppice beautifully situated on the borders of mountain rivers; and, excepting that the scenery is on a much grander scale, in many parts it reminded me of Devonshire.

Having marched at about half-past nine o'clock, we arrived at Betanzos, a small, dirty town, situated at the head of a small arm of the sea, into which a little river empties itself. Here we were billeted on the inhabitants; and it is but justice to say they did, in most instances, their utmost to make the men comfortable. The place itself is very dirty, and abominably stinking. Its market appears remarkably well supplied.

Lieut.-General Lord Paget was quartered upon the house of a colonel serving with the Gallician army. His wife—a pretty woman—was remarkably civil to us, and gave us an excellent dinner, and afterwards

On our march we may find plenty.

"Paget marches with my division, and we mean to take our guns. He has plenty to do; indeed, I do not think he has time to write to England. We have 160 or 170 miles to Astorga, which will occupy us thirteen days, including two halting days. I do not imagine he will remain long with my division, as he will probably soon be tired of going only three or four leagues a day. He will, I think, make the best of his way to Astorga, and wait there till we come up. We go through nothing but mountains on our road thither.

"Pray tell my mother that I carry my bed with me, as the bugs and fleas swarm, and that every precaution will be necessary to prevent my head being visited with not the most agreeable companions, which I hear thrive in abundance in most parts of Spain. Pleasant! If I catch any I will preserve them in order that she may compare them with the English ones, and she may transmit her observations to the Royal Society."

took us to a 'rout' composed of half a dozen old tabbies. At the colonel's house was a friend of his wife, an exceedingly loquacious sort of lady, in whose company I should very soon have attained the Spanish language.

November 18.—From Betanzos we marched at eight o'clock in the morning, and halted at Monte Salquiero with the left squadron. Captain Treveake's troop with Lord Paget went on to Guitirez.

Nothing could be more miserable than our quarters—in a low house, on a barren heath, to which the Franciscan inn was a palace, and the country about it a paradise. Here I was quartered with three officers and 120 men, all pigging together in the straw.

November 19.—From Monte Salquiero we marched four and a half leagues to Bahamonde, another most miserable village, where I had the good fortune to be quartered in the same house with Lord Paget, and consequently fared very well as to eating; but our lodging was even more miserable than before; ten of us in one little room, and an ante-chamber full of lice, fleas, and all sorts of vermin.

The country through which we passed this day was, in some parts, very beautiful, and cultivated as much as it would admit of. In general, however, it was extremely barren.

At Bahamonde, having heard that there were woodcocks in a wood facing the house. Lord Paget and the major went out, and succeeded in bringing home a couple.

From Bahamonde we marched two leagues to Lugo, a Spanish city, but very inferior in most respects to any English village. In dirt, however, it far surpassed anything I ever beheld. I must do it the justice to say that the cathedral is very fine, and rich in plate, to judge from the massive candelabras and candlesticks it contains.

In Lugo we heard confirmed the report which we had before heard of Blake's entire defeat, and the approach of the French to Astorga; and we received an order to proceed with all possible despatch—not to make the halts at first ordered. In this case it certainly appears to be *more haste less speed.* The horses had already begun to drop off from lameness (owing to their long confinement on board ship.—thirty-seven days—and their being moved off too soon after being disembarked) in a most alarming degree. We had lost twelve; seventeen were lame at Corunna, eighteen at Betanzos, two, three, and four at Salquiero, Bahamonde, and Guitirez, and at Lugo we left thirty-one more.

In addition to the fatigue of the march after disembarkation, the miserable quality of the forage was the principal cause of the falling off as they did, and even those horses that kept on at all were far from being in a fit state for active service.

Between Bahamonde and Lugo we passed the River Minho, at Ponte Ralhado—a most beautiful bridge; and the scenery excellent. The appearance of the country indeed had considerably improved in the day's march. In the Minho are abundance of trout, some even so large as 30 1b. weight I was informed by an inhabitant of the neighbouring village.

In Lugo, we were given to understand, was a strong French party. Whether it was the case or not I cannot pretend to say, but it certainly was most evident to a casual observer that the assistance offered the British army was by no means what an army coming to fight the battle of the Spaniards had a right to expect. Indeed, the difficulty of obtaining country wagons for the conveyance of our baggage, and the impossibility of getting mules to carry the tents and camp kettles, was of the utmost inconvenience to us.

To attempt to describe our sufferings and privations, of men and horses, is beyond my power. No description can be at all adequate to it. It surely would have been reason- able, before the army started from Corunna, for Sir D. Baird to have said: 'We are come to assist you, and before I move a single man I must have so many mules and so many bullock carts attached to each regiment.' Whether this was done, I know not, but at all events I do know that we were without the proper assistance; and daily (whilst we were without the means of carrying our camp kettles except on our troop horses, and actually without tents) did we meet whole droves of mules carrying sardines, the value of the whole cargo of which was not that of a single troop horse. Surely these should have been pressed. 'They manage these things better in France,' but it appears more like asking a favour on our part to be permitted to march through their country, than like the flower of the British army being sent to be sacrificed for the preservation of Spain.

★ ★ ★ ★ ★

In connection with the above strictures on the apparent mismanagement of the commissariat and transport departments, I here quote from Napier's *Peninsula War,* vol. 1. p. 336.

> Sir D. Baird came without money. Sir J. Moore could only give him £8000, a sum which might have been taken for a private loan, if the fact of its being public money had not been

expressly mentioned. But at this time Mr. Frere, the Plenipotentiary, arrived at Corunna with two millions of dollars intended for the use of the Spaniards; and while such large sums were lavished in that quarter, the penury of the English general obliged him to borrow from the funds in Mr. Frere's hands. Thus assisted, the troops were put in motion; but, wanting all the equipments essential to an army, they were forced to march by half battalions, conveying their scanty stores on country cars, hired from day to day; nor was that meagre assistance obtained but at a great expense and by compliance with a vulgar mercenary spirit predominant among the authorities of Gallicia. The *Junta* frequently promised to procure the carriages, but did not; the commissioners had to offer an exorbitant remuneration; the cars were then forthcoming, and the procrastination of the Government proved to be a concerted plan to defraud the military chest.

★ ★ ★ ★ ★

From Lugo we marched four leagues to Constantia. Here I was (quartered on a *señor* who kept a most dirty house and a most miserable carriage, but was very civil indeed, and took me out for a day's shooting, when I killed one red-legged partridge! The men, as usual, were put up in pig-styes.

From Constantia the left division marched to Nogales. I rode a gun, mounted, and, after eleven hours on horseback, joined Major Cavendish at Trebadildos.

During the day we passed through a most lovely country. A bridge between Nogales and Constantia was magnificent—it leaped a valley of immense depth, through which ran a beautiful mountain river. The valley was itself extremely narrow and deep, and the depth of the arches of the bridge, of which there were four, must have been 200 feet at least, whilst the whole length of the bridge could not have been more than 1000.

From the hill a little beyond this bridge to look down on it and the valley, and on an old ivy-grown dwarf bridge which leaped the river on the old road, about half a mile down the valley from the present bridge, was a scene far beyond the pencil of an artist, or the pen of so poor a journalist as myself.

From Nogales is an ascent of six miles—a death-blow to our artillery and heavy-laden wagons. Up this our men walked, being dressed for the purpose in shoes, and we thus saved our poor horses. From the top of this mountain is a magnificent prospect; and the situation of a convent on the height at the foot of it is truly romantic and beautiful.

From hence we descended to Trebadildos, where we halted for the night about a league from Valladolid. On a hill is an old castle, the situation and appearance of which equal any description ever met with in the most romantic novels. In fact, it is a most perfect habitation for *banditti*; and, as these mountains are infested with gentlemen of this description, it is not impossible that it may have been a refuge for them. Our quarters at Trebadildos are pretty much of the same description as our former ones—miserable houses, full of lice, bugs, and fleas!

Our men, fortunately, continue most healthy in every respect, which is wonderful, considering the privations with which the poor fellows have to contend—and which it is but justice to say they experience without a murmur—and the hardships and fatigues they suffer.

At Trebadildos we learnt from an officer of the Greys, going express to Corunna, that the affairs of Blake's army were, if possible, worse than ever, and that the remains of it were expected at Astorga,

From this it seems possible that we may not get so far. If the French succeed in preventing the junction of Sir J. Moore and Sir D. Baird, which they may do by placing themselves at Benavente, the defence of Asturia must fall to the lot of the latter, and Corunna become our only retreat. In this case the cavalry can be but of little use; and those of the finest regiments in England are rendered nearly useless, and for no good reason.

November 24.—Cacabellos, one league in advance of Villa Franca.

From Trebadildos I proceeded two leagues to Villa Franca, and from thence on fresh horses, in advance, to overtake Lieut.-Col. Kerrison with the right squadron. This I succeeded in doing two leagues and a half from the place where I now write this; and, what is rather odd, at the very instant that an order had been received by him to retreat to Villa Franca. The files were just put about, and to my great surprise I found them approaching me! Thus all the evils of a retreating army, through a most wretchedly supplied country, appears to be most likely to attend us.

I undertook to halt the squadron short of Villa Franca in consequence of the approach of night, and took up our quarters here with three guns belonging to the R.H.A.

The army of Sir D. Baird commenced also their retreat from Astorga.

What has occasioned this sudden retrograde movement we do not exactly understand. The defeat of General Blake has been for some time known. It is reported that a column of the French are making their way through the mountains to Ferrol. In this case our situation would indeed be critical. Cut off from Sir J. Moore by the enemy having placed themselves at Benavente, and cut off from England by the enemy having possession of the point of land commanding the entrance to the harbour of Corunna, our only means of escape would be either through the mountains of Oporto; by cutting our way through the French army to Sir J. Moore; or to Cadiz, if provisions for the troops could be obtained on the march. There can be no doubt but that we could effect either of these two latter; and supposing affairs to turn ever so bad at last, the possession of the French and Spanish fleets would recompense to a trifling degree the expense and fatigues of our expedition.

★ ★ ★ ★ ★

It has already been stated that two of the three so called "Spanish armies" had been utterly defeated by the French, but that there still remained the army of Castaños, who had been joined by Palafox with the remnants of his forces.

On November 23, Castaños' army was also defeated by the French at Tudela. The intelligence of this did not, as a fact, reach Sir J. Moore till a week after the event; and it was not therefore because of this further reverse to the Spaniards that the retreat, alluded to by Colonel Vivian, was commenced. It would appear that it was occasioned by a report received from General Blake, who was in the mountains with a few of his defeated forces, that a considerable French force was collecting at Rio Seco and Ampudia, with a view of interrupting the march of the English; and Baird, in consequence arrested the advance and fell back on Villa Franca.

As Sir J. Moore's information led him to believe that Blake's report was false, he recalled Sir D. Baird. In the meantime, however, much valuable time had been lost.

★ ★ ★ ★ ★

November 24.—The country through which we have marched this day was, to Villa Franca, most beautiful; and the situation of that town is truly delightful. The town itself is dirty and miserable in the extreme.

From Villa Franca the country assumes a different appearance—corn lands and immense vineyards; whilst on either side are immense mountains, covered with snow.

The various climates through which we pass day by day are somewhat extraordinary—now pierced with cold, and now drenched with rain, now overpowered with heat, and now blinded with fog. Still, however, the men are healthy in the extreme. In the 7th we left only four men sick on the road before we arrived at this place, and I hear no complaints from the others. This is more wonderful when their fatigues and sufferings are considered.

November 25.—At Cacabellos, on the night of the 24th, I again received orders to advance with the First Division of cavalry, and again retraced the ground we had the day before retreated over, and I personally halted at Bembibre. The division took up its quarters at the little village of Toro—about a league beyond it.

Bembibre is a miserable place on the Nogales road, six leagues from Villa Franca, and five from Astorga.

November 26.—On the 26th the First Division again marched, and reached Astorga that evening. On our arrival there we found that a retreat had actually been determined on, in consequence of the defeat of Blake and advance of the French army on the side of Valladolid, where it was supposed a corps was placed to intercept our junction with Sir J. Moore, who was at Salamanca.

Indeed, no account for some days having been received from him, it was imagined that they had actually placed themselves between the two armies; but Major Temple, A.D.C. to Lord Paget, having on the 26th been sent with despatches to Sir John Moore, and having passed by Benavante and Zamora to Salamanca, and returned on the night of the 29th without having met with any interruption, it was again resolved on to advance; and for this purpose the troops who had retired were again ordered into Astorga from Castaños, Bembibre, Fonteferrada, and Villa Franca.

November 29.—On the night of the 29th, however, despatches having been received stating the defeat of Castaños, and, it was supposed in the army, in consequence of orders to that effect from Sir J. Moore, a retreat was finally determined on, and on the morning of the 30th the infantry commenced retiring.

It would be presumption for me to say how far this was necessary; but my own private opinion, which may perhaps be biased by feelings for the honour of the British name and the credit of the British arms, is that circumstances did not altogether warrant it.

It is true Ministers were deceived as to the state of the Spanish armies; it is true that there appeared a great want of energy in the people; it is true there was a want of cordiality and assistance towards us; but still, having come into the country as friends to their assistance, having, in all probability, in some measure been the cause of their starting their own efforts by leading them to expect great things from us, having most certainly occasioned Buonaparte's having sent a larger force than he otherwise would have sent, calculating upon merely a Spanish army—I say, under all these circumstances, I freely own it was my humble opinion that we should have risked everything rather than retreat.

The enemy had beaten Blake, and it was said that a corps of 10,000—some even said more—were penetrating the Asturias by Oviado to Ferrol. Another corps had made their appearance at Medina del Rio Seco, supposed to be ready to attack us if the attempt were made to join Sir J. Moore, whilst the main body of the enemy were destined to attack Castaños, who was somewhere in the neighbourhood of Segovia, bearing on Madrid.

Our route to join Sir J. Moore was over the bridges of Benavente and Zamora; and the Rivers Esla and Douro were not passable at any other places. It is true that this was a most critical position; if we made the attempt, the enemy from Medina del Rio Seco would probably either at once take possession of Benavente, or admit of our passing that bridge and then attack us between it and Zamora, thus, if they defeated us, placing us in a most perilous situation. But the certainty of the corps stated to be at Medina, and its actual strength, was very ill ascertained; from the enemy never having taken possession of Benavente, or even entered it, the probability was that the French were not in force. Then, if Sir J. Moore had moved from Salamanca for Zamora on the day on which this army moved from Astorga for Benavente, I think there can be but little doubt that the junction would have been effected.

I am aware that by this movement General Hope would have been, in a degree, exposed; but on December 1 that corps was to have joined him; on the 3rd Sir David's cavalry were to have arrived; so that Sir John need not have left Salamanca until the 4th to have arrived at Zamora on the 6th, whilst on the same day we arrived at Benavente. Sir John, however, had, on the 28th, heard accounts of General Castaños' defeat, and he decided on a retreat, and sent orders to that effect to Sir David Baird.

How far the circumstances of the case authorised it, it is not for me to say; but in spite of any French force that was ready to have opposed it, I cannot be but firmly persuaded the junction of the two corps, under the circumstances I have before stated, might have taken place; and with an army of 35,000 he might have moved to his right, and, if compelled to retire, have fallen back upon Cadiz or Gibraltar, instead of disgracefully running into the mammoth mountains of Portugal and Galicia.

Most, however, of this reasoning may be false. I can only speak of the matter as it strikes me. The means of transporting stores were small, and the difficulty of procuring supplies very great. As to what were the means in the country in the rear of Salamanca must be better known at headquarters than I can possibly know it; but I have understood far inferior to those of Portugal and Galicia.

From the Spanish armies we could expect no regular movements, no systematic assistance; but energy on our part would have created energy on theirs; and the probability is that although in the junction we might have suffered much, yet from the losses of the enemy, and from their attention having been drawn off from the Spanish armies, it would have occasioned a very considerable turn in their affairs, and, in all probability, a favourable one.

At all events, anything is better than the horrible disgrace that must attend a retreat such as we are about to make.

★ ★ ★ ★ ★

The defeat of Castaños took place on November 23, but it was not till the 29th that the news reached the English generals.

In the meantime Napoleon, having after the defeat of Castaños a large body of men at his disposal, had marched with them on Madrid.

It was reported to Sir J. Moore that that city would make the utmost resistance, and he was begged to assist their efforts in any way he could.

In ignorance of the defeat of Castaños, his original plan had been to move to that general's support; and with that object he had given orders to Baird to join him.

General Hope, with that part of Sir John's army which had separated from him on account of the badness of the roads, was still *en route*; and it was only by a hasty march that he succeeded in escaping the victorious forces of Napoleon advancing on Madrid.

The news of Castaños' defeat did away of course with all Sir J. Moore's original plans for assisting the Spanish army, and, at the time when Colonel Vivian wrote the above remarks in his diary, the intelligence that was being daily received by the English generals was so alarming that orders were given to the troops to retreat, and Sir D. Baird's forces commenced a retrograde movement.

This determination excited the utmost dissatisfaction in the troops. Officers and men loudly and openly murmured against such a resolution, and declared it would be better to sacrifice half the army than retire from so fair a field without striking a blow for the Allies, who had staked their all in the common cause.—*Alison*, vol. 6. p. 830.

When the news came of the enthusiastic preparations that were being made by the inhabitants for the defence of Madrid, and of their determination to bury themselves in its ruins rather than submit to the invader, these feelings were still further increased; and Sir J. Moore, giving vent to his native courage, eventually suspended the retreat, and resolved to throw himself upon the communications of the French army, hoping, if fortune was favourable, to inflict a severe loss upon the troops which guarded them. If Napoleon detached largely from his forces, Madrid would be succoured; if he did not detach largely, the British would be able to hold their own.—*Life of Napoleon*, vol. 1. p. 448.

Colonel Graham, who had been sent by Sir J. Moore to ascertain what the real state of affairs was at Madrid, returned, on December 9, with the information that that city, in spite of so much boasting, had held out but one day, and was in the hands of Napoleon. That information, however, did not suspend Sir J. Moore's resolution to advance as a diversion in aid of the South of Spain.

★ ★ ★ ★ ★

Astorga is a city situated at the foot of the mountains, on the borders of a vast plain, adapted beyond everything to the movements of cavalry. Not that those of Sir D. Baird, on their arrival, were in a state to act; for, from their horses wanting shoeing, the badness of the forage, &c., the regiments had suffered most severely, particularly the 7th, which was greatly attenuated, having left 160 horses on the road between Astorga and Corunna.

In the month of July, after the battle of Rio Seco, Bessières, with his army, advanced to the heights above the village of St. Justo, about one and a half league from Astorga, and from thence sent to summon the city. The trumpeter was shot from the ramparts, and the Marshal, with all his army retired. Blake's army were then encamped at the miserable village of Manzanal, about three leagues from Astorga, on the road to Villa Franca.

The cathedral of Astorga is most superb; the front gateway high, the sculpture beautiful. The altar-piece is most magnificent, consisting of different Scripture subjects in bronze, surmounted with a very fine figure of our Saviour on the cross. The altar solid silver, and an immense quantity of plate belongs to the cathedral; but, in fear of the arrival of the enemy, most part of it is taken away and hidden.

The painted windows are beautiful, and the colours brilliant to a degree. The pillars of the cathedral are excessively light and elegant, and the whole, for its size (it is but small) I think surpasses almost any building of the sort I ever met with; but it is the case that the cathedrals are excessively handsome and most richly ornamented. That of Leon is, I understand, superb.

I should here mention the sacristy of the cathedral at Astorga, which is a well proportioned, circular room, with a dome painted most beautifully; but the colours are unfortunately damaged by the damp. The subjects I could not exactly make out or have explained to me, but from the number of angels among the figures, we may presume it was a scriptural one. Round the room also are different paintings, one of them representing a martyr on a gridiron; another the Virgin and our Saviour, &c.

Having thus arrived at the end of my travels in Spain, I shall have to return probably by another route. If so I shall continue this journal.

December 1.—I should state that on December 1 the right squadron of the 7th, under Colonel Kerrison, was sent to La Bañeza.

December 5, 1808.—The army commanded by Sir D. Baird continued retiring from the first till this day, with the exception of the cavalry, who kept advancing.

On the 3rd, however, it was decided that 400 men from each regiment of cavalry should march by the mountain road by Ponteferrada to Orense.

On the evening of the 3rd, however, a letter arrived from Sir J. Moore stating that in the event of the regiments of Dragoons not having already gone to the rear, one regiment might march to form the junction with him.

Upon this Lord Paget decided upon marching with the whole brigade, should Sir David Baird not object to his doing so.

On the night of the 4th a message arrived stating that Sir David did not object, and preparations were immediately made for marching this day (the 5th) at 11 o'clock a.m.

The most extraordinary part of this is that Sir John should have thought the junction of the army impossible, until he ordered a regiment of cavalry to effect it.

It is true that cavalry move with less inconvenience than a lot of infantry, but still, if the enemy are in any force, and especially if they oppose the movement at either of the bridges of Benavente and Zamora, it will be impracticable. Not so, supposing the junction had been attempted by the two armies, by a simultaneous movement from Astorga and Salamanca, to Benavente and Zamora. It is, however, understood that the enemy's force between Benavente and Zamora is very small, consisting only of some cavalry. If so, and should we be so fortunate as to fall in with them, we shall, I have no doubt, give a good account of them.

★ ★ ★ ★ ★

Through the kindness of the present Marquis of Anglesey I have been permitted to copy the following letter from Lieut.-Gen. Lord Paget, which gives a vivid account of the state of affairs at this time, and of the steps he took to prevent the retreat of, at least, the cavalry.

Astorga, December 3, 1808.

My dear Father,—I have been so very busily employed since I left Corunna that I have not had time to write to anyone. I will give you a short history of what has happened.

On my arrival at Lugo with the head of the column of cavalry I received an express from Sir D. Baird, stating that he had received very bad news; that he found himself in the most critical situation, and that he wished very much to have me with him. I, of course, set out instantly on post horses, and contrived to ride seventy-four miles in the first nine and a half hours, which, being on tired bidets and over mountains, was no bad work. I was less expeditious in the other part of the journey, but, however, reached Astorga on the next day.

Here I found nothing but long faces. Blake's army had been beaten and totally dispersed. The Estremadurians had shared the like fate. Castaños and Palafox were cut off from Blake, and Sir J. Moore had expressed his determination to fall back the moment the enemy advanced from Valladolid; and he recommended Sir D. Baird to look to his own safety.

Under these circumstances Sir D. Baird had already begun to send back his heavy baggage and a part of the infantry, and all seemed determined to move off. I flatter myself that I very considerably contributed to retard at least this operation, although I acquiesced in the necessity of not advancing into the plain whilst we were without any cavalry at all, or if the enemy should be marching upon us in too great force, or if he should have completely intercepted the communication with Sir J. Moore. In fact, the retrograde movement was stopped, but they soon took alarm again, retired, then advanced, and are now finally gone off. I am in command of the rear guard. It consists of all the cavalry and six pieces of horse artillery, General Crawford's Brigade of light infantry with six guns, and the brigade of Guards. I have kept the cavalry here; the Light Brigade are about nine miles in my rear, in a pass; and the Guards in support of them again.

I really am ashamed of our conduct in Spain. There has been much indecision, and at length the decision come to has been a bad one. I mean for the honour of the country, and for the appearance of things, although I am very ready to admit that the Spanish cause is desperate. The Spaniards have fought ill, are very weak, have no system, do not act in concert, and, as far as I have seen, are totally without the enthusiasm that we were taught to expect in them. Castaños and Palafox have been totally beaten and dispersed, and I know of no Spanish army anywhere. Still, what an ignominious thing it is to go off and embark! I have been stirring heaven and earth to avoid it for my cavalry at least, and I feel sure that you will approve of all I have done, and which I shall now detail.

I have sent in a proposal to endeavour to march to the right by Orense, and so into Portugal, with the most effective part of the cavalry; and I have even determined to take with me four guns, although it is stated to be impossible; but we have so often been taught by the French that nothing; is impossible that I have resolved to try it. The roads will be desperate, and there are several rivers to pass. But as I shall be without infantry, and as the enemy might push a small corps of light infantry across Portugal (and a very small corps would be a desperate annoyance to us), and might even stop our march without a few shrapnel shells to assist us, I shall force through all the difficulties that may occur for the artillery, and, by hook or by crook, get them on.

I forgot to tell you in its place that by desire of Sir D. Baird I went over to Leon to the Marquis de Romana, to endeavour to find out his plans and his means. The latter, alas! were most feeble when I saw him. He had not more than 5000 men, the *débris* of Blake's army, and those are ill equipped in every respect. Since that, however, they have been rallying up a little, and he now talks of being able to bring into the field from 12,000 to 15,000 men.

December 4.—Since writing last night a dispatch arrived here from Sir J. Moore to Sir D. Baird, approving of his arrangements to retire, but desiring that if he has still a regiment of cavalry forward he will send it to him.

I have caught at this, have written to Sir D. Baird, and by every argument that has occurred to me, have shown the propriety of my advancing with three regiments and six pieces of Horse Artillery, and begged and entreated, and begged again, that he will allow me to make this movement with 1200 or 1500 of the Hussars. If he does not consent, or if he prevents *me personally* from going, I solemnly declare that I never will serve again. It will be the finest operation in the world—a rapid march over an immense plain (a perfect sea which has been overrun by the enemy's cavalry), with a compact body of British cavalry and artillery, ready and willing to fall upon almost anything, *in its own way*, that presents itself.

Here I am in a state of the most complete trepidation until I get his answer. He is at Villa Franca. I have sent two orderly officers to him, and everything is quite ready for a start. If it don't take place, *I cut*. It will be the only pleasant thing that can happen to me, if Sir J. Moore retires; for as for assisting in the defence of Portugal, I confess I have no taste for it, and if the French fairly possess themselves of Spain, believe me, Portugal has no chance whatever. It will fall *to a certainty*.

I will leave this open till I know my fate. I shall keep my letters on the subject to show you. I think they must have weight. At all events, I shall feel the happiness of having acted as *you* would like.

Never was any one so well equipped for a campaign as I am. My horses are capital, and in perfect order. My baggage is upon the best of footings, and can keep pace with the Hussars. My staff is very good. I have the best cook and the best set of servants that ever were collected; and I have a little corps of cavalry that cannot be surpassed. With all these *agréments chez moi*, I augur ill of events *en déhors*. Buonaparte is too much for all Europe. He *will* place his brother on the throne of Spain, and he will place *his Imperial Eagles* at Lisbon. 'Tis most humiliating, yet 'tis, I fear, unavoidable.

P.S.—I march tomorrow to join Moore with about 1200 cavalry and six pieces of Horse Artillery.

The news of the fall of Madrid had not at this time reached Sir J. Moore, and it was on December 5 that he sent directions to Sir D. Baird to suspend his retreat; having; then formed the resolve to attack the French communications and thus divert a large detachment (as he hoped) from the French forces before Madrid, and thereby succour that town.

★ ★ ★ ★ ★

On the 5th, at 12 o'clock midday, the cavalry commenced their march from Astorga; consisting; of the 7th, 10th, 15th, and Captain Downman's troop of Horse Artillery.

Our march the first day was to La Bañeza, over a plain country.

The right squadron of the 7th on that day, having previously been at La Bañeza, moved on to Villa Brazaro.

The remainder of the 7th were destined to occupy the villages of Navianos and Aloya, but owing to the darkness of the night and the stupidity of the guide, and the little difference between the roads and the country in general, we lost our way and found ourselves at Puente del Cabroso.

Here then I put up two squadrons, whilst I proceeded myself with the left to discover the village of Navianos, knowing the consequence it might be of the commanding officer not being at the place where orders could be sent to him.

From Navianos I marched at four in the evening of the 6th with Major Paget and the left squadron, and, notwithstanding the experience I had gained during the previous night's march, I found my guide no wiser than my former one, and we again lost our way, and what was still worse, in endeavouring to find a second guide, I myself lost my way and the squadron, and rambled on with a few men of the rearguard, over a miserable plain for three hours, and at length I found myself at Villa Brazaro.

Here I again got a guide, who conducted me to Benavente, and from thence to the bridge over the River Esla—a post where we expected to be very near the enemy, and which is, from the left bank of the river, capable of being made a post of great strength. We could here hear nothing certain respecting the French army; and on the night of the 7th, at twelve o'clock, we again commenced our march for Zamora.

During the two last days I had been extremely feverish and unwell, and under any other circumstances should have laid up; but Lord Paget having done me the honour to say that he should, during the whole march, place the 7th in advance, and that he should trust to me to keep a good lookout, I of course could not think of failing him.

December 8.—At half-past seven on the morning of the 8th we arrived at the village of Riego, five leagues from Zamora. Here the brigade halted in a position about a mile from the village, and remained during the day in the fields; the horses linked, and the men having received firewood from the village.

December 9.—At twelve o'clock at night we again commenced our march for Zamora, where we arrived at 7 o'clock the next morning, and were received with the shouts of the inhabitants, numbers of whom were assembled, crying '*Viva los Ingleses*,' &c.; and here indeed we experienced some attention and were received with greater enthusiasm than in any other town we had been in.

December 10.—On the morning of the 10th we again commenced our march for Toro, where we arrived that evening at 7 o'clock, leaving the 10th behind us at Zamora, having received orders to that effect from Sir John Moore; and thus have we concluded our junction with the greatest facility—a junction which, had it been effected with the whole of Sir David Baird's army, would have placed the character of the British army at least, if not the affairs of Spain, in a very different situation.

We understood that our advance from Zamora to Toro was in consequence of the enemy having drawn the whole of their forces from Valladolid towards Madrid, and of the stand that appeared likely to be made by the inhabitants of the latter city.

★ ★ ★ ★ ★

This was partly the case, as has already been shown—but at the date when the 7th joined Sir J. Moore's forces, the news of the fall of Madrid had reached headquarters; still Sir J. Moore did not abandon his intention to attack the French communications, and Sir D. Baird's army was again moving on to join him.

It was not, however, till December 20 that Sir D. Baird's infantry ultimately joined Sir J. Moore at Mayorga. General Hope had effected his junction after a brilliantly executed march.

The whole of the march from Astoria to Benavente and Zamora was over a flat country, where scarcely any trees were to be seen as far as the eye could reach—nothing but cornfields. Even cattle were very scarce in parts, so much so that milk was quite a treat.

At Benavente is a most magnificent palace, formerly the property of the house of Benavente, now belonging to the royal family of Spain. It is uninhabited and became the quarters of a troop of the 7th. The rest of the town was but shabby. It is enclosed by walls, but is incapable of much resistance.

The bridge of Castro Gonzales, about a league from Benavente, is, from the left bank of the River Esla, a most defensible position; indeed such an one as to forbid the passage of any force, if tolerably defended.

Zamora is by far the finest city we have as yet seen in Spain. It is situated on the River Douro, over which there is a very fine bridge. In Zamora are several very handsome buildings and remains of Moorish architecture; but the fatigues of our marches by night and the duties that followed were such as to put it out of the power of any officer to examine accurately into the beauties of the place.

The road from Zamora to Toro was by the side of the Douro, and through by far the most fertile part of Spain we have yet seen; vineyards in abundance, and fruit trees of every description lined the road; indeed, this part is, we understand, considered the most luxuriant part of Spain.

Toro itself is situated at the extremity of an immense plain, on a level with which it is. On the right bank of the Douro the town stands so high that it is at least 300 feet perpendicular from the water; so that, as a point of defence against an enemy coming from the other side, Toro presents an almost impracticable obstacle. The bridge is immediately under the bank, and the descent to it is by a road cut in the bank and running zigzag up the side of it. Over this bridge, and up this road, no troops on earth could pass against a tolerable opposition; whilst on the other hand, for the left flank of an army, whose right is at Tordesillas, it is far from a position to trust a number of troops in. The advance from Valladolid, Rio Seco, and Benavente, is all over a plain up to the very gates, and consequently offers no advantage to those who occupy the post. The walls being of mud afford no defence, especially as they are very old (Moorish) and nearly level with the ground in many places; whilst a retreat over the bridge, or even to Zamora by the river, would be most awkward, with the town once in possession of the enemy.

Toro contains several beautiful remains of Moorish architecture. The church is perfect of the sort. The name of Toro is derived from there being in the place a figure of a bull which was supposed formerly to have been worshipped by the Romans.

★ ★ ★ ★ ★

December 14.—From Toro we marched on the 14, at two o'clock, for Tordesillas, where we arrived at about eleven at night, and found orders to march again next day to Pedrosa del Rey, our route being along the Douro; but, it being night during the march, we could see but little of it.

Our order to return to Pedrosa was excessively annoying, as the 7th were in advance, and the next morning we hoped to have entered Valladolid, where we were certain of catching some French; but unfortunately we were disappointed, and the 18th did it and took the Intendant General with £20,000.

★ ★ ★ ★ ★

The affair above mentioned would seem to have taken place at Rueda, where a French post of fifty infantry and thirty dragoons were surprised, and either killed or taken prisoners.

Napier says, "Great was the astonishment of these haughty conquerors at finding themselves thus assailed by an enemy who the boastful proclamations of the Emperor had led them to believe was in full retreat for his ships."—*Life of Napoleon*, vol. 1. p. 450. *Alison*, vol. 6. p. 831.

* * * * *

December 15—17.—The next morning the regiment returned to Pedrosa; and the next day halted there; on the following day it marched again for Villa Garcia, a village within two leagues of Rio Seco, where were 600 of the enemy.

December 18.—We hoped at least now it would be our good fortune to fall in with these men; but, alas! the next morning brought us orders to march to the village of San Pedro Zane—about three leagues in our rear.

At San Zane I now write this.

The whole of the country, excepting a ridge of table-land towards Rio Seco, is one dead flat, covered with vines and corn—no grass lands, no milk; plenty of eggs, chickens, and turkeys, which constitute our principal food. The costume of the shepherds is sheepskin, and gives one more the idea of Lapland than of Spain. The weather hard frost and snow.

The whole of the English army is now moving towards the left to join the Marquis de Romana—the cavalry covering the front; but, from the movement at the same time being rather to the rear, I cannot but think it looks rather as though it would end in a retreat; and I really begin to think that the sooner we are off the better.

The Spaniards certainly do not seem inclined to support the cause with that energy which at first it was supposed they possessed. Indeed the spirit of the nation has not been taken advantage of either by us or by themselves. Even had the English general issued proclamations full of energy, and such as were calculated to rouse the spirit of the people, I have no doubt but they would have had the desired effect; and, on the other hand, had the people of property and consequence in the country stepped forward, I am persuaded they might have collected peasantry to any amount. But it is singular that we have never fallen in with any individual man of consequence since our first arrival; nor do I suppose that on the part of the English general any steps have ever been taken to stir up the spirit of the populace.

* * * * *

At Toro, on the 16th, information was received by Sir J, Moore that Romana, with his Spanish troops, instead of co-operating in the advance of the English, had, in consequence of the retrograde movement made by Sir D. Baird some days before (and which has been alluded to), started off" in full retreat towards the Galician mountains.

In spite of this, however, Sir J. Moore did not yet abandon his plan of attacking the French communications. But he had not yet been joined by Baird, and he also realised the necessity for an immediate retreat that would arise should Napoleon send any of his Madrid forces to Soult's support.

★ ★ ★ ★ ★

December 19.—From San Pedro Zane the regiment marched seven leagues to Bolaños, where we fell in with Lieut.-General Frazer's division.

December 20.—From Bolaños the next morning we marched to St. Erbas, where Major-General Paget, and the reserve, joined us.

From St. Erbas we marched the following day to Escobar, one league in front of Grajal, on the road to Carrion los Andes. This was on the 21st December.

★ ★ ★ ★ ★

In order to understand the movements of the troops now taking place, it will be necessary to state shortly the position of affairs, both as regards the English as well as the French forces at this time.

As has been stated, Sir J. Moore, in order to relieve Madrid and succour the South of Spain, had resolved to attack the French forces which were guarding the communications between France and Spain, and had advanced for this purpose.

On December 14, a despatch from Napoleon to Soult was intercepted, from which Sir J. Moore concluded that Soult was ignorant of his movements, and might therefore be surprised and attacked with some hope of success before he could be assisted by Napoleon; and so, though Sir J. Moore felt sure that Napoleon would move from Madrid to Soult's support so soon as he learnt of the British advance, Sir J. Moore did not alter his plans, in spite of Madrid having surrendered and of Castaños' defeat, but moved his troops to Toro and Benavente, making Valderas the rendezvous where he was to be joined by Sir D. Baird.

On December 20, Baird's forces united with that of Moore, and the army then consisted of about 23,500 men, of whom 2278 were cavalry.

On December 16 Soult, who had with him only 16,000 infantry and 1200 cavalry, learnt of the British movements, and, becoming seriously alarmed at his position, commenced concentrating the other French forces which were lying some little distance away from his position.

On December 21, Napoleon learnt of Moore's advance, and leaving 10,000 men to look after Madrid, he instantly started with 50,000 (on the 22nd) against Sir J. Moore, and moved, in spite of the greatest difficulties, with such marvellous celerity that he reached Tordesillas on the 26th. In ten days he had moved over 200 miles of country.

Sir J. Moore's plan was to move on the night of December 23 against Soult, who was at Carrion, so as to arrive there by daylight of the 24th; to force the bridge there, and afterwards, ascending the river, to fall upon the main body of the enemy, which he believed to be at Saldaña. His object was to draw Napoleon away from Madrid; but he knew that Napoleon's advance from there must be a signal for his own immediate retreat, which sooner or later was inevitable.

On December 23, when the troops were in march towards Carrion, Sir J. Moore received authentic information of Napoleon having started from Madrid with 50,000 men. Sir J. Moore's object had therefore been obtained, for he had caused Napoleon to withdraw a considerable number of his forces from that neighbourhood, and now, having the main body of the French forces, amounting to 80,000 men, on his heels, he had practically no alternative but to retreat, the orders for which he immediately issued, and which retreat he commenced on December 24.

It is admitted by the highest authorities that had Sir J. Moore delayed his retreat one day more, he would have been cut off by Napoleon.

December 21.—On this morning, Lieut.-General Lord Paget, with the 15th Regiment of Hussars, marched at one o'clock from Melgar Abaxo, in order to attack a French regiment quartered at Sahagun. He succeeded in arriving there at daybreak in the morning and just as the regiment had turned out, having heard from an advanced post, with which his lordship had fallen in and of whom he had taken six—being half only—that the English were advancing.

He therefore found the enemy prepared for him, and the two regiments, French and 15th, trotted in column alongside of each other for a short distance, until Lord Paget thought he had outflanked them on the side where their retreat lay, when he halted, wheeled into line, and charged. They also formed their line and stood firm, but it was only for a short time; they were soon broken, and a general rout ensued.

They lost in killed and wounded and prisoners about 220; the

English, none killed, fourteen wounded, of which number were Lieut.-Col. Grant, and Adjutant Jones. The number of the 15th was about 500; the French between 600 and 700. Their two Lieut.-Cols. and eleven officers were made prisoners.'

In both Napier's and Alison's histories, the 10th Hussars are mentioned as having taken part in this affair. They describe the engagement as having been a very brilliant one, though it only lasted about twenty minutes.

According to an account in the *St. James' Chronicle* of January 10, 1800, the 10th only came up when the affair was over and helped in the pursuit.—See *Life of Napoleon*, vol. 1. p. 458. *Alison*, vol. 6 p. 832.[2]

★ ★ ★ ★ ★

December 22.—After this affair the position of the British army was as follows:

Right wing: Lieut.-Gen. Hope; at Vallada, with the 18th Hussars and 3rd Germans covering his front.

Centre: Lieut.-Gen. Frazer's division; Grajal, with the 7th Hussars covering his front.

Left wing: Lieut.-Gen. Baird (who had joined with his army from Astorga); with the 10th and 15th Hussars covering his front.

On the night of the 23rd, according; to general orders, the whole army was to move in two columns upon Carrion, to attack Soult's corps, which was stationed there.

The 7th, being detached from the rest of the army, received orders to rendezvous at a particular spot, which I accordingly did; but to my surprise I found no other corps assembled, and I soon received orders to put up the regiment in such villages as I might find near me. I accordingly occupied those of Torremolinas, about two leagues in

---

2. Lieut.-Gen. Lord Paget, in describing this affair in a hastily written letter to his father, says:

"I have but a moment to tell you that I have had an affair with the French cavalry—at the head of the 15th—most honourable to that regiment.

"We attacked about 750 of them with about 400 of the 15th, and an officer and twelve men of the 7th; and the result was several killed, nineteen wounded, about 160 prisoners, 125 horses and some mules taken.

"Immediately after it the regiment insisted upon my accepting two prize horses belonging to officers. One is a strong, low, grey horse, very easy and sure footed in his walk and canter, and perfectly quiet. I destine him for your riding, and will send him by the first opportunity. Coming from your old regiment, and given in so handsome a manner, I know you will ride him with pleasure.

"I have not time to write details."

front of Sahagun, on the Carrion road, and a small village of Lamote, in front of it, was occupied by Lieut.-Col. Kerrison with the right squadron.

At this place I remained the whole of the following day, and in the evening it was reported to me that 600 French were in a village immediately in my front.

The 7th had about 380 mounted men only, having been obliged to send off sixty horses, either on duty or sick, the preceding evening.

The next morning, however, I ordered the right squadron to patrol to their front in search of these gentlemen, and supported it with the remaining share.

Lieut.-Col. Kerrison fell in with their advanced posts at Calcadela, about a league from Lamote, and gallantly attacked them, taking about twelve prisoners, and killing their officer. Unfortunately he had his arm broken on this occasion.

I joined the advance at this instant and found there also a squadron of the 18th, and a field-piece of Captain Evelyn's troop of horse artillery. Learning from the prisoners that the cavalry in search of which I was, was in a village one league in my front, I decided on attacking them, order up the 7th, and assembled the officers to make arrangements accordingly.

It having been reported to me that they had infantry and artillery with them, and considering my force unequal to this, I judged it right to ascertain the fact by a patrol. Whilst the patrol was out Brigadier-General Stewart arrived, and from the lateness of the hour, from the regiment being five leagues from their (quarters, and having eight to march the next morning, he did not consider himself authorised to proceed to the attack.

We accordingly retired to Grajal, this being the commencement of our retreat, which it appears had been decided upon in consequence of information received by the commander-in-chief, of Buonaparte having quitted Madrid with Ney's *corps d'armée*, in order to advance upon us, in conjunction with Soult from Carrion, and Junot from Saldaña. A retreat therefore from so very superior a force became necessary, and that of the most rapid sort. The infantry had previously moved off.

December 26.—From Grajal, therefore, the cavalry marched to Saldaña—eight leagues—where they arrived very late at night.

"On their march, in passing Mayorga, a report reached us of the enemy having arrived there. The 18th Hussars being in front, half of the regiment was ordered immediately to advance against the place.

They fell in with the enemy's advance in the street, and, after a little skirmishing, drove them out of the town into the plain beyond. Here they found a squadron of about 100 formed. Lieut.-Col. Leigh, with a squadron of the 10th, immediately charged and dispersed them, killing, or taking about 80 prisoners. The remainder were taken by a baggage-guard of the 7th and the 18th Hussars, who were marching by another route. These men had marched from Rio Seco the same morning, and were the advance-guard of Ney's force.

*****

On the 24th the general retreat began. General Hope, with two divisions, fell back by the road of Mayorga; and General Baird by Valencia de San Juan, where there was a ferry boat across the River Esla. Romana undertook to guard the bridge of Mansilla.

On the 25th, Sir J. Moore, with the reserve and light brigades, followed the route of Hope's column to Valderas.

On the 26th, Baird passed the Esla at Valencia.

The troops under the commander-in-chief approached the bridge of Castro Gonzales early on the morning of the 20th. The stores and baggage were a long time passing, there was a dense fog, and the scouts of the French were already infesting the flanks of the column, and even carried off some of the baggage. The left bank being high and commanding the bridge, the 2nd Light Brigade and two guns were posted on that side to protect the passage; for the cavalry were still on the march from Sahagun, and Soult, now aware of the retreat, was pressing on vigorously.

When Lord Paget had passed Mayorga he discovered a strong body of horse, appertaining to Ney's corps, embattled on a swelling hill close to the road; the soil was deep and soaked with rain.

Two squadrons of the 10th, riding stiffly against the enemy, mounted the hill, and notwithstanding the superiority of numbers and position, overthrew them, killed 20 men, and took 100 prisoners.

This was a bold and hardy action; but the English cavalry had been engaged more or less for twelve successive days, and with such fortune and bravery that above 500 prisoners had already fallen into their hands; and their leaders being excellent, their confidence was unbounded.—*Life of Napoleon*, vol. 1. p. 463.

*****

December 27.—From Saldaña the cavalry marched six leagues to Benavente.

On the following day the town was alarmed by a report of the enemy's advancing. It proved, however, to be a false alarm. But on the; next day they really made their appearance in force; and, in the face of the pickets, the *Chasseurs à cheval de la Garde Impériale* actually crossed the water, amounting to nearly 600 men, led by General Lefevre, who was considered as one of their best cavalry generals.

Their doing this was a most gallant act, as, from the bridge having been destroyed, they were obliged to ford the river at a place where the water was so deep as to occasion several of the horses to swim, and the current so rapid as to render it impossible they could do it quickly. They, however, succeeded, and occasioned a second alarm in the town, upon which they advanced, the pickets retiring before them.

Lieut.-Colonel Otway, the field officer of the day, who commanded, at length fearing that they should arrive at the town before the regiments were turned out, most gallantly determined on charging them, which he did with 130 men only, and completely checked their advance squadron. The impetuosity of his men, however, was such that in their turn they were checked by the supports, and obliged to fall back.

He was then joined by Brig.-General Stewart and about 100 more men, principally Germans, who again charged the enemy, and checked them so as to occasion their halting, and a skirmish ensued. In this situation of affairs, Lord Paget arrived and ordered them to keep them in check only whilst he brought up the 10th Hussars, who, being nearest the spot, had just turned out. The 10th accordingly arrived, and soon after the 7th and 18th, with two pieces of light artillery.

Upon seeing these the enemy retired at a gallop, closely pursued by the pickets, who chased them to the water's edge, killing hundreds, and making prisoners of about 100 of this elect corps of Buonaparte's, which was never before defeated, and which had in the preceding year in Poland broken through 30,000 Russians. Lieut.-General Lefevre was himself made prisoner by a private of the 7th and one of the 10th.

The artillery arrived just in time to give them three or four shots, which put their columns to flight after they had formed on the other side of the water. Had they arrived even a minute sooner, whilst the French were in the water, they must have been all destroyed or made prisoners.

In this affair the 7th had five killed and sixteen wounded. Of the wounded nine died.

This affair being over, the 7th were ordered to remain on the ground with the two pieces of artillery. The rest of the cavalry returned to Benavente. No movement of consequence took place on the part of the enemy during our stay there, excepting that now and then the head of a column of cavalry would make its appearance, as if intending to cross the water, when a cannon shot or two stopped it.

About the middle of the day a general, with a large suite, made his appearance on the hill immediately above us and reconnoitred our position. From the number of attendants, and more especially from there being some Mamelukes of the party, we had every reason to suppose it was Buonaparte himself.

The officer commanding the artillery wished rather to have given him a shot. Despising a war of outposts, I declined it. I afterwards rather regretted having done so, when I reflected, if it was Buonaparte and should a shot have been successful, on the benefit that would have resulted to the world in general; and I, in consequence, accused myself of having, from motives of humanity, avoided doing that which would have contributed so much to the happiness of mankind.[3]

An opportunity was afforded me, during the time I remained in this post, of seeing and conversing with several of the French officers, they having passed the water with a flag of truce respecting General Lefevre's baggage, &c.

I saw General Davosail, A.D.C. to the Emperor, Colonel Count Grazinsky of the Polish Guards, and several other officers of distinction. Their dress was superb, and their appearance and manners altogether most perfectly that of gentlemen, and their opinions most liberal. They freely abused the Spaniards, and accused them of having deceived us, and spoke in the highest terms of the conduct of our men in the affair of the morning.

From passing the river I had an opportunity of judging of the difficulties the enemy must have encountered. I was mounted on an English horse, considerably stronger and larger than the best of theirs, and in going I found it an operation of difficulty, and several minutes

---

3. A graphic description of the above combat is given in both Napier's and Alison's histories. Napier, however, states that six guns were brought to bear on the French, whereas Colonel Vivian says there were only two. Napoleon, as a matter of fact, was at this time with the French advance; so it is very probable that he was the general seen by Colonel Vivian. The Spaniards indeed afterwards reported that it was he.

on returning my horse swam and was nearly carried down with the current. Count Grazinsky afterwards came to my side of the water, and would have actually been lost but for one of the men of the 7th, who assisted him on shore.

December 19.—At sunset the 7th were relieved by the 18th Hussars, but not before the enemy had brought up some guns, which then opened upon the two left squadrons, firing several rounds of shot and shell without effect.

At seven o'clock both regiments retired to La Vizana, where we bivouacked in a field for a few hours, and then proceeded on our march to La Bañeza, whence, at twelve o'clock, we again marched, and arrived at Astorga the next morning.

December 30.—Here we fell in with the Marquis of Romana and his rabble of an army, who were retiring with all the speed they could on Orense, without ever having attempted or offered to make a stand or afford us the least assistance; nor indeed is it possible to conceive how any one in their senses, who had seen such a force as his was, could have expected to have derived the slightest advantage from their co-operation.

★ ★ ★ ★ ★

On the 30th Bessières crossed the Esla (having been delayed by the destruction of the bridge at Castro Gonzalo), and passing through Benavente with 9000 cavalry, bent his course towards La Bañeza. On the same day Franceschi forced the bridge of Mansilla de las Mulas by a single charge of his light horsemen, and captured the artillery and one-half of the division left by Romana to defend it. The latter then immediately abandoned Leon, which the French took possession of.

★ ★ ★ ★ ★

From Astorga we again retired on the night of December 31, the enemy having pressed our outposts at Celada very sharply.

We marched without halting to Bembibre, where we found the division of the army commanded by Major-General Paget; the other divisions having passed on their route towards Corunna and halted at different villages.

The march from Astorga to Bembibre—eight leagues—was severe, and was over the mountain Manzanal, which had been covered with snow, and which, having been beaten down by the infantry, had become hard, and was so slippery as to make it necessary for the men to lead their horses.

This, added to the impediments that presented themselves from baggage wagons, &c. being left on the road (which, at the village of Manzanal alone occasioned a delay of nearly two hours), caused the march to be very tedious and severe.

January 1.—From Bembibre we again marched the next morning at daybreak for Villa Franca. The rear-guard was composed of the 15th Hussars, two companies of riflemen, two light guns, and the 20th Infantry; the whole under the command of Colonel Ross of the 20th.

The enemy pressed them closely during the march, constantly skirmishing with the squadron of the 15th, who were in the rear.

At Cacabellos, the reserve, with the 3rd German Dragoons, halted. The 15th were halted at a village in front of it. The 10th at two others between that and Villa Franca, whilst the other brigade of cavalry halted at Villa Franca. The other divisions of the army had passed on on their march.

January 2.—On the following morning the enemy again made their appearance and began skirmishing with the advance of the 15th, and towards evening it became more serious, and several of the rifle corps were sent into the village of Cacabellos to fire from the houses, behind walls, &c., and pretty severe skirmishing ensued, in which on our side we lost nearly 100 men in killed and wounded, whilst the enemy lost as many, if not more.

★ ★ ★ ★ ★

Upon January 1, Napoleon took possession of Astorga, and on that day 70,000 infantry, 10,000 cavalry, and 200 guns were united by him. Here, however, he received intelligence of Austria having joined the European Confederacy and of the rapid preparation of her army to take the field. He therefore, on January 3, set out for Paris with his guards, leaving Soult and Ney, with 60,000 men, to continue the pursuit of the English, who numbered about 20,000.

The conduct of the British soldier thus far had, although in some instances very irregular, been in general otherwise; but at Villa Franca it became extremely bad. In order to check such outrages an example was necessary, and on the 7th Hussars it unfortunately fell to afford that example, although, without partiality or prejudice, I declare, upon my honour, I believe no regiment was more orderly in their conduct during the whole of the time they had been in Spain, and very few so much so. Three men belonging to the regiment were, at Villa Franca, detected in the act of stealing some of the wearing apparel of the inhabitants and in the attempt to break open a box. Two were concerned together at one place; the other was at another house.

These three poor fellows drew lots which should suffer death, and it fell to the lot of a man named Day, of Captain Treveake's troop, previously a very steady, good soldier. He was shot in front of the brigade; and in justice to him, poor fellow, be it said that he met his fate with the most undaunted courage—I may say, with the most perfect *sangfroid;* and, if it be of any service to relate it, be it recorded that ten thousand instances of more flagrant outrages occurred than that for which he suffered."

In Villa Franca great excesses had been committed. The magazines were plundered, the bakers driven from their ovens, the wine stores forced, and the commissaries prevented from making; the regular distributions; the doors of the houses were broken open, and the scandalous insubordination of the soldiers proved that a discreditable relaxation of discipline on the part of officers had taken place.

The general immediately arrested this disorder, caused one man taken in the act of plundering a magazine to be shot in the market-place, and issued severe orders to prevent a recurrence of such inexcusable conduct.—*Life of Napoleon.*

★ ★ ★ ★ ★

January 5.—From Villa Franca to Lugo, seventeen leagues (over a most immense mountain, on which several hale men were soon dead from the intense cold and fatigue, and on which guns, ammunition, and money were stuck and were destroyed), the cavalry marched at a rate almost incredible. The 7th were twenty-six hours only completing it, out of which they were halted four; but this rate of marching had the effect of destroying the horses, which never recovered it.

The infantry also began to be fatigued. Hundreds that would not come on either died or were shot on the road; and several hundreds, who for want of shoes had dropped behind, others who straggled to villages for the sake of plunder, and others who were fatigued and in bad health, fell into the hands of the enemy, all together amounting to a very considerable number.

★ ★ ★ ★ ★

Alison thus describes the scenes that took place:

Disorders went on accumulating with frightful rapidity along the whole line, and such was the general wreck of presence of mind, that at Nogales the military chest of the army, containing £25,000 in dollars, having stuck fast in the mud, the treasure was rolled in the cask in which it was contained over a precipice and became the property of the peasantry, who picked it up at the bottom.

All order or subordination was now at an end; the soldiers, exhausted with fatigue, or depressed by suffering, sunk down by hundreds by the wayside and breathed their last; and the army, in frightful disorder, at length reached Lugo late on the evening of January 6.

★ ★ ★ ★ ★

January 5.—At Lugo the commander-in-chief felt it necessary to halt, probably from the great fatigue that the army had experienced; and perhaps also from a wish of ascertaining the actual strength of the enemy that were following, of which, it was stated, he had no accurate knowledge, although in such a country as he passed through it would have been the easiest thing in the world to have counted every man.

January 6.—The day following our halt at Lugo, however, the enemy came up, and a skirmish ensued with the Guards, which occasioned little loss on either side, although both parties fired some cannon shot.

January 7.—The day following there was a second edition of this work, but equally bloodless—sufficient, however, to harass and annoy our army, which was their object; and on the 8th Sir J. Moore expected that a general attack would have taken place, and disposed his army accordingly; General Hope's division on the right, next to the Guards, who had their right on the River Minho, which was impassable from the floods; General Fraser in the centre, and Sir David Baird on the left.

January 8.—The cavalry were disposed of in different parts of the line—the 18th on the main road in rear of the Guards; the 10th and 15th in rear of them (the 10th was afterwards detached to the bridge over the Minho, eight miles in the rear, and the 15th to Sir D. Baird); the 7th and Germans in the fields with General Fraser's division, and in his rear.

The enemy, however, not coming on, at night a retreat was decided upon, and it fell to the lot of the 7th to form the rear-guard of the army, and to supply, by dismounted men, the pickets of the Guards who were close to the enemy; and there to remain at least two hours after the whole army had marched.

This was a delicate and ticklish undertaking, but one which we most fortunately succeeded in without the loss of a man. and without, I believe, the enemy having had the slightest suspicion that the army was in motion.

The scenes of distress and of confusion that presented themselves at Lugo during the halt of the army there are almost incredible, and beyond the power of description.

The weather had been rainy and bad in the extreme; many of our fine soldiers were consequently sick and in such a state as to be unable to get on. For these no conveyances could be procured. The whole of the others were fatigued to the greatest possible degree. Wet daily and miserable, without the means of making themselves otherwise, bread scarce, no linen, and almost all the camp kettles lost, so that there was great difficulty in finding means of cooking; their provisions.

The cavalry, with their horses completely worn out; many of them (especially of the 18th Hussars) standing in the open streets, and dying by dozens. Others of all regiments so crippled as to make it absolutely necessary to destroy them, so that every ten yards you met with a dead or dying horse, and in many places ten, fifteen, or twenty together.

Join to all this the confusion that must naturally be occasioned by 15,000 or 20,000 troops being quartered in one small dirty town, and it is possible some notion may be formed of the scene.

★ ★ ★ ★ ★

At Lugo, on January 8, according to Napier, the number of the French amounted to 17,000 infantry, 4000 cavalry, and 50 guns.

The English had 16,000 infantry, 1800 cavalry, and 40 guns.

For two whole days the English general had offered battle, but the French had not come on.

No sooner had the intention of Sir J. Moore to offer battle to the French been realised by the English army when all disorganisation ceased, and the line of battle was filled with men full of confidence and valour.

There was, however, not bread for another day's consumption remaining in Lugo, and so Sir J. Moore, having by the halt re-organised his forces, broke up his camp at night, leaving the camp fires burning, so as to deceive the French, and resumed his retreat to Corunna.

The ground in rear of Lugo was intersected by walls and intricate lanes, and precautions were taken to mark the right tracks by placing bundles of straw at certain distances, and officers were appointed to guide the columns.

At 10 o'clock p.m. the troops silently quitted their ground, and commenced retiring in admirable order.

A terrible storm of rain, sleet, and wind commenced, however, just as the army broke up from position; the marks were destroyed, and the guides lost their way. Only one of the divisions gained the main road, the other two were bewildered, and when daylight broke the rear columns were still at Lugo.

The line of march was broken, disorganisation ensued, and the main body of the army arrived at Betanzos on the evening of the 9th in a most discreditable state of discipline.—Napier, *Peninsular War*, vol. 4. p, 201.

★ ★ ★ ★ ★

January 8.—From Lugo we retreated on the night of the 8th. The confusion there had not tended to reorganise the army, and the straggling which had before been in a great measure occasioned by fatigue, &c., now became with many systematic; and if I had difficulty in describing the scenes that presented themselves at Lugo, it is almost presumption to attempt to present those I witnessed whilst passing the rearguard of the army during the last part of our retreat.

The commissary stores previous to our departure had been so short as to admit of one day's bread only being delivered, and even this some regiments did not receive. But even still, hunger was the least of the poor soldiers' sufferings; want of rest, want of shoes, wretched roads, and heavy rain filled up the sum of their miseries.

Although I left the advanced posts, which were four miles in advance of the town, full four hours after the retreat of our army, I found the houses on the outskirts of the town full of stragglers. Many of these I succeeded in driving out by force or persuasion. Others were so ill and harassed that nothing could move them.

From this instant the road presented one constant string of stragglers, many of whom no efforts of ours could drive before us; although the certain consequence of their dropping behind was their becoming prisoners, as the enemy would certainly follow early in the morning.

Every house was full (I may say, out of some we drove upwards of a hundred) of these stragglers, and such was the state of carelessness and the total want of spirit occasioned by fatigue, &c., that on being told that the enemy would certainly shoot them, many replied, 'They may shoot us, sir, as you may shoot us, but we cannot stir;' and although there were many instances in which our men actually proceeded to severe measures to force the people on, hundreds remained immovable; of these several were almost in a dying state, and two or three were found actually dead.

Wherever they found straw they rolled themselves up in it, and although our men rode in upon them they would not cry out; and we found the only means was to prick with our swords in order to discover them and make them stir.

The road presented a spectacle even more distressing. Fine fellows, willing and anxious to get on, their feet bleeding for want of shoes, and totally incapable of keeping up; others, whose spirit was better than their strength, actually striving till the last to join their battalions, and several of this description perished in the attempt.

I myself saw five dead on the roadside, and two women, whilst every now and then you met with a poor unfortunate woman, perhaps with a child in her arms, without shoes or stockings, knee deep in mud, crying most piteously for that assistance which, alas! we could not afford her. One poor wretch of this description actually died with two children at her breast, one of whom was also dead, and the second would have shared the fate of its—I may say, under the circumstances—happy little relative.

January 9.—Such was the state of the army that, on the arrival of the reserve at Mobiliano, Sir J. Moore found it necessary to order Major-Gen. Paget to halt in order to ease the stragglers (the first night from Lugo we halted at Bahamonde, in wretched rain, and the whole of the officers of the 7th and 10th in a wretched hovel, the men and horses in a field; we marched at nine with the reserve), and here, the 7th having been previously joined by the 18th Hussars, our halt was between six and seven hours; and during this time, I am certain I speak within bounds when I state that between 4000 and 5000 men who had been left behind passed through us, and a great number must have fallen into the enemy's hands.

January 10.—At length the enemy themselves made their appearance, and immediately in their front a body of stragglers, who, to do them justice, had for the four last miles defended themselves, in rather an open country, against about 400 cavalry who were following and skirmishing with them.

To this succeeded a little skirmishing with us, and we then retreated to a position about seven miles in front of Betanzos—the reserve about two miles in our rear.

From hence we again proceeded at 4 o'clock (the enemy having attacked our advanced posts) to Betanzos, where the 7th passed through the reserve of infantry, having scarcely, since the retreat from Grajal commenced, had the saddles off their horses' backs for above five or six hours at any time, and seldom so long; having been almost constantly wet, without the means of changing; having lost our camp kettles, from the mules which carried them dying or knocking up on the mountains, and consequently having no meat to eat but what was toasted on the points of the swords. Nor were we singular in this respect, for other regiments had suffered nearly, if not fully, as much as we.

★ ★ ★ ★ ★

Napier says (vol. 1. p. 487):
The reserve, commanded by General Paget, an officer distinguished during the retreat by his firmness, ability, ardent zeal, and courage, remained in position during the night of the 9th a few miles from Betanzos.
The rest of the army was quartered in that town, and as the enemy could not gather in strength on the 10th, the commander-in-chief halted that day, and the cavalry passed from the rear guard to the head of the column.
On the 11th Sir J. Moore assembled the army in one solid mass, and from thence marched to Corunna.

★ ★ ★ ★ ★

January 10.—The rear guard of cavalry, after the 7th had passed through, consisted of a squadron of the 18th, under Lieut.-Col. Jones, and eighty men of the 10th, under Major Lord C. Manners of the 10th.

The enemy kept constantly hanging on their rear, and both at the bridge of Betanzos and of Burgo, about two leagues from Corunna, skirmishes ensued, but with little loss on either side.

★ ★ ★ ★ ★

These bridges had been ordered to be destroyed, but the engineers were only partly able to do so, owing to their tools having been abandoned.

* * * * *

January 11.—On the evening of the 11th the whole army marched into Corunna, excepting the reserve, which occupied a position about two leagues in front of Corunna, having the village of Burgo, where a bridge crossed a small, but deep, stream which emptied itself into the bay of Corunna, on their left; and their right at another bridge near the village of Boa on the St. Iago road.

January 12.—On the following day a slight skirmish ensued, without loss on either side, at the bridge of Burgo. And on the next day a more serious one, which appeared to indicate an attack, took place.

January 13.—In the evening Sir J. Moore thought it was advisable to withdraw his advance corps, and occupy a position about three miles in front of Corunna, having his left *appuyéd* to the river, and posted in strong ground, through which the main road ran; his right extending towards some strong hills opened to the sea, but separated from them by some low ground, which made the position far from being an advantageous one; and the more so as the whole front was commanded by hills which were soon occupied by the enemy.

* * * * *

When the troops arrived at Corunna, "all eyes were anxiously directed to the bay in hopes that the joyful sight of a friendly fleet of transports might be seen.

But the wide expanse was deserted, and a few coasters and fishing boats alone were visible in the dreary main.

The sea was in front, the enemy in the rear. The transports had been at Vigo, but had been ordered round to Corunna as being a more easily defended place of embarkation; a head wind, however, had delayed their arrival.

On the 13th two powder magazines, a short distance with- out the walls, containing 4000 barrels of powder, were purposely blown up by the British, with an explosion so terrific that nothing in the whole course of the war approached to it."—*Alison*, vol. 6. p. 843.

On the 14th the transports from Vigo hove in sight, and stood into the bay. Preparations were immediately made for embarkation; the cavalry horses were almost all destroyed, and the greater part of the artillery, consisting of 52 guns, were embarked; eight British and four Spanish guns being alone reserved for use.

* * * * *

January 15.—On the 15th, about noon, a small skirmish began, which lasted till nearly dark, with a loss on our side of Lieut.-Col. McKenzie, of the 79th Regiment, and about sixty men killed and wounded. This skirmish was evidently brought on by the enemy in order to enable them to ascertain our strength and the manner in which we were posted, previous to an attack which was generally expected on the following day.

January 16.—The morning of the 16th, however, arrived without any appearance of an attack; but about noon movements were observed in the enemy's camp, which were immediately reported to the commander-in-chief, who was then in the town of Corunna; and about 3 o'clock a general attack on the outposts commenced, which was followed by a heavy cannonade from some guns which the enemy had posted most advantageously on the high hills on the right and left of their position.

Under cover of the guns of the enemy's left, which severely galled the right of the British, a large column advanced out of a wood, evidently with an intent to turn our right, and the action in this part soon became general and very hot. The regiments principally concerned were the brigade under Major-Gen. Lord William Bentinck, consisting of the 4th, 42nd, and 50th Foot, and the 11th and 26th.

The enemy were most gallantly met and repulsed by these regiments, who, not content with having driven them back, actually attempted to carry their guns, which were posted half-way up the hill. The 42nd and 50th Regiments in particular dashed forward for this purpose, and failed only from the enemy having withdrawn them still higher up the hill.

A village near the foot of the hill was disputed for a considerable time, and several times carried and taken. At length, however, the British valour established itself, and the 42nd and 50th Regiments, supported by the Guards, were finally left in possession of it.

Still further on the right, the Rifle corps and 52nd Regiment actually drove the French riflemen to the top of the hill; and had there been sufficient daylight there is little doubt but that, by General Frazer's division with the reserve, which were not engaged, moving forward in support of these light troops who had carried the height, and then falling on the left flank of the enemy, and at the same time had the British left pushed forward to the village (afterwards taken most gallantly by the 14th), situated half-way between the British and the bridge of Burgo, and from whence the enemy had marched into their position in the morning, a most complete victory would in all probability have awaited us.

As it was, we have to boast only of having defeated their object, which was to turn the right of the British, and thus penetrate into their rear between them and the town; but from the vigour with which, to do justice to the enemy, they made the attack, and from the impetuosity of the British in repelling it and following up their success, this advantage was not gained without a very serious loss on our part.

Sir J. Moore unfortunately fell in the height of the business, wounded in the shoulder and side by a cannon shot, which he survived only a few hours. When hurrying off the field he was anxious only as to the enemy's being defeated, and on hearing that they had been driven back, he said, 'Then it is of little consequence whether I live or die.' He afterwards gave some directions as to his private affairs and his family, and shortly afterwards he said to a friend who was standing by, 'I have always served zealously, and I hope my country will approve of what I have done.' He then said, 'I feel so strong that I fear I shall live and suffer a long time,' and in less than three minutes he expired.

Thus died Sir J. Moore, too late perhaps for his own reputation as a general-in-chief, but to the last supporting that coolness and that gallantry which had always distinguished him, and which led him to his fate by inducing him to expose himself where, as commander-in-chief, he should not have been. He was buried in the great bastion, near to Brigadier-General Anstruther, who had died a few days previously of a fever brought on by the fatigues of the march, and in whom the service lost a most valuable and excellent officer.

Besides Sir J. Moore fell on the 16th Lieut.-Col. Napier, of the 92nd, Majors Stanhope and Napier, of the 50th, and several officers of inferior rank.

Sir David Baird, second in command, was wounded so seriously in the shoulder with a grape shot as to make it necessary to amputate it at the armpit that night.

Lieut.-Colonel Wyack, of the 4th, was seriously wounded, and upwards of 1000 men were either killed or wounded. On the part of the enemy the loss was as great, if not greater.

The party that attacked was commanded, as was stated by the prisoners, by General Laborde. General Junot, it was understood, was commander-in-chief, from a message which was sent by him to Sir J. Moore on the morning by a woman who had been taken and been some time in their camp, to say that he had arrived with the army of Grajal.

It appears certain that on the morning of the 16th a reinforcement of 7000 and 11 pieces of cannon had arrived; and this it was that had occasioned the attack to commence so late. We learnt also from the prisoners that Marshal Soult, who commanded in chief, had been wounded in some of the affairs that had taken place during the retreat, probably at Lugo. The strength of the enemy was stated at from 18,000 to 25,000 men.

From the loss of Sir J. Moore, and the wound of Sir D. Baird, the command fell on General Hope.

On the night of the 16th the whole army, as previously determined on, retired within the walls of Corunna and commenced their embarkation (the artillery and the baggage had been sent on board before), which was completed by the morning, with the exception of General Hill's and General Beresford's brigades.

January 17.—On the morning of the 17th, the fleet of transports continuing in the harbour, the enemy, as had been foretold by many of us, brought some guns to bear upon them; and their masters, who would not be persuaded to get under weigh by all the signals that had been made to them to that effect, most speedily obeyed the orders of General Junot. Perhaps no fleet of transports ever got under weigh so quickly! In less than half an hour the bay was clear!

In the evening the remainder of General Hill's brigade was embarked from a little bay to the north of the citadel; and about midnight General Beresford's, the rear brigade, was, every man, brought off in boats to the men-of-war protecting the embarkation; the others having got under weigh and brought up at a distance from the place of embarkation so far as to render it difficult to embark them on board of them. As soon as these troops were on board they got under weigh, and in the morning they were shifted into other ships; and in the evening the whole fleet bore away for England.

It will naturally be asked what were the circumstances which occasioned so rapid a retreat so very immediately to follow the premeditated advance of the whole army to attack the French at Carrion and Saldaña. And what made it necessary to make such haste through the Galicias—a country so strong by nature?

Without a thorough knowledge of the information received by

the commander-in-chief, it is almost presumption to hazard an opinion—much less to criticise the operations of his army.

But there are some facts that require no such information to ascertain; some circumstances that must strike even the most casual observer.

Of these one fact appears very clear. That previous to the retreat from Sahagun, Grajal, &c., the information received at headquarters respecting the movements of the enemy on the side of Madrid, must have been very incorrect. For had Sir J. Moore been aware that Buonaparte was advancing in person against him, he would never have planned the movement he had in agitation, or remained in a situation where, had he remained one day longer, his retreat, without a general action with a very superior force and whilst almost surrounded by other strong corps, would have been unavoidable.

His movement then upon Valencia with Sir D. Baird's corps, and Bembibre with the right of the army, was certainly well timed; and here let me remark that throughout the campaign, although arrived to assist the Spaniards, and in a country where every man might have been expected to be a spy, the utmost difficulty occurred in getting the smallest intelligence; and even that intelligence was never to be relied on. Unless the enemy was actually at the door of a Spaniard he discredited his being near him; and as to their forces, they never would allow that they had any.

To attempt to state, therefore, what was the certain force coming against us would be ridiculous; but it was understood that Marshal Ney had, with 25,000 men, left Madrid to advance upon us, and that Buonaparte in person accompanied him; his Imperial Guards were with this column, consisting of 6000 infantry and 4000 cavalry.

General Soult was advancing from Carrion by Maintica and Puente D'Orego upon Astorga; and General Junot was supposed to be supporting him, and advancing by Leon, from whence he had driven the Spanish army under the Marquis de Romana.

The probability is that had Sir J. Moore received correct information of the force and movements of the enemy, he never would have altered his first determination of retiring from Salamanca at the same time that a retreat had been determined on by Sir D. Baird from Astorga; for it appears evident that no resistance was made by the Spaniards that could possibly authorise a presumption that they would .succeed in repelling the French, although even to this moment I am fully of opinion that, by a desultory sort of warfare, it is still possible the Spaniards may succeed; at least they will annoy the French so much as to make it necessary for them to keep up an immense army in their country, which alone will be infinitely serviceable to England, and to Europe in general, should other nations take advantage of the circumstance.

The resistance threatened by Madrid probably induced Sir J. Moore to proceed from Salamanca to join Sir D, Baird. Had he been aware of the real truth, this movement would probably never have been made.

The junction having been once determined on and effected, the intended movement in advance from Sahagun, when the enemy had certainly moved for several days from Madrid towards the British army, proves the bad information the general-in-chief received. For had he been aware of their movements he never could have projected an attack, which, had it taken place and even been successful, must have been the precursor of the total destruction of his army; and which attack was fortunately prevented by information (as it was understood in the army) received only on the very evening on which the army was to move forward to it.

The retreat already mentioned upon Astorga ensued, and from the nature of the country and the position of the different corps of the enemy, it was clearly necessary that this retreat should be as speedy as possible.

From Astorga this hurry appeared no longer necessary. The strength of the country—full of defiles, and consequently defensible by a small body against even a very superior force, with the circumstance of its containing only one road passable for artillery—rendered the retreat of our army at its leisure perfectly feasible; the more so as the road leading to Orense, which was the only one by which it was possible for an enemy to advance on our flanks, was defensible by a very small body of light troops.

This circumstance, however, never appears to have entered the head of the commander-in-chief, and perhaps the greatest error committed was the manner in which he hurried his retreat from Astorga.

It is true that to the flank he detached Brig.-Gen. Crawfurd with a light corps; but they retreated as fast as the main body; and from this rapidity of retreat arose that dreadful system of straggling, and that complete state of disorganisation in which, to quote Sir John's own orders, the army was thrown.

Had two or three bodies of light troops been formed into rear-guards, to relieve each other and defend each pass; and had the three days' halt at Lugo been dispensed with and added to the marching days; had every bridge that possibly could have been destroyed been destroyed, instead of having made away with the entrenching tools and placed the engineers in the ridiculous situation of attempting to destroy them, and that without effect; had the passes over the mountains been scarped, which might easily have been effected; the army might have retired at its leisure and have avoided the severe losses it experienced, which amounted to scarcely less than 5000 men.

I am well aware of the difficulties that presented themselves towards the feeding of the army; but a tolerable commissariat would easily have placed provisions for two days in such places that the army never need have had the slightest want; and indeed I am fully persuaded that the rapidity of the march added to the difficulty on this head, instead of taking from it.

By a little arrangement also, shoes, of which there were plenty, might have been supplied to the troops, instead of its being necessary, as was really done, to destroy both provisions and clothing to prevent their falling into the enemy's hands.

The rapid retreat of the army then appears to have been unnecessary, and evidently the cause of the losses that ensued.

The retreat from Lugo to Corunna, instead of to Vigo, is a point on which various opinions have arisen.

When Sir David Baird had at first intended to retire, before the junction, Vigo was the port determined on; and at Vigo the whole of the fleet were assembled for the receipt of the army; and why it was altered is not exactly known.

It is supposed to have been because of the roads to Vigo being almost impassable for artillery; but this might easily have been remedied by sending the artillery to Corunna under an escort, for which purpose the corps under General Alten would have been perfectly sufficient; and the risk that was run by altering the whole arrangements and ordering the transports round from Vigo to Corunna at so late an hour—for the order was sent only from Lugo—and at a time of the year when the winds were most variable, and when a foul wind might have occasioned the most disastrous results, was very great.

I cannot avoid here remarking that the system of taking so much care of our artillery, although perhaps originally founded on the truest principles, is, at least by the French, exploded in their modern art of war.

I have just stated that it was to save our guns that we marched to

Corunna instead of Vigo. A foul wind then might, by stopping the transports, have delayed the embarkation of the army till the French had arrived in such force as to occasion us a loss infinitely of more consequence than that of our artillery.

The same unfortunate attachment to our guns prevented our having, in the action of the 16th, such a force of this description as would have made up for the disadvantages of our position, and been more than equal to that of the enemy; whereas the case was otherwise—nearly all the British guns were embarked, and to supply the place of them some Spanish guns were brought up, and, as might have been expected, some British ammunition was wanting, and these guns badly served.

Now, setting aside all feeling for the animal—man—and taking the man and the gun as two machines of war, calculation alone will convince any one of the extreme impolicy of this over-regard for our artillery.

The soldier requires a growth of upwards of twenty years; the gun may be brought into the field in as many days. It is a maxim with the French that two rounds of grape shot amply repay the loss of a gun. What then to us, who were retiring, could have been the great consequence of saving our guns, when, by running the hazard only of losing them, the defeat of the enemy on the 16th would, in all probability, have been more complete, and our loss infinitely less?

I now come to speak of the last act of the army. I mean the total evacuation of Spain.

On this score I cannot help thinking that Corunna should have been defended even to the last extremity. To me the advantages that would have resulted from this appear very great. Five thousand men would have been equal to defending it for a considerable time. The enemy possessed no heavy artillery; the fortifications of the place, although commanded by the heights within 1000 yards of them, were well supplied with guns, and were in such a state as to defy any attempt to storm them. The citadel was very strong, and in the rear of it was a small bay, from whence the last embarkation did take place, and from whence the troops left might have embarked in the last extremity.

I am aware that the enemy might have, from the heights, most considerably annoyed the town, and that the poor inhabitants would have suffered severely; but the French would soon have wanted ammunition probably.

Be it observed that these very people were most anxious that the place should be defended; and this is one of the reasons why I disapprove of the total evacuation—that I think, in so doing, we deserted those people, who, of all Spain, appeared to be best disposed towards us, and the best inclined to defend themselves.

The other advantages that would have ensued appear to me to be that for a considerable time we would have occupied the attention of the French army, and consequently would have given time to the Spaniards in the South to have made any efforts, if they were so inclined; that whilst Corunna held out, Ferrol would probably do the same; and lastly, that for the honour of the British army the French would not have been able to say that we fled to our shipping with the utmost possible rapidity, and the Spaniards that we had deserted them; and if, after leaving 5000 men for the defence of Corunna, the remainder of the army had been sent to Portugal, against which no army of an equal force could possibly have been marched, it is impossible to say what beneficial results might not have ensued.

To conclude, then, in my humble opinion, the faults of the campaign appear to me to have been the following:—

(1) The advance of Sir J. Moore's and Sir D. Baird's army, after Madrid had capitulated, and

(2) The advance of the army after the movement to the left upon Sahagun, and the intended attack on Carrion.

Bad information, and even the total want of it, certainly in some measure exculpates the General on this subject; excepting that it appears to me that with a proper attention to these points such an apology ought never to have been necessary.

And here I cannot help remarking that from the commencement a general complaint against the information received might be justly pleaded. Before the army was sent Ministers were certainly most grossly deceived by the reports of the officers sent to Spain, who, elevated by the honours and compliments paid them, certainly did not see things in the most correct light; and after the arrival of the army the same want of correct information as to the real position of affairs was severely felt.

As I have, however, before remarked, with the powers that a general officer is invested with, no apology of this sort should be necessary.

The third great error, and that from which all the succeeding evils arose, was the manner in which the army retreated from Astorga; the rapidity, the want of system, the bad arrangements of the commissariat department, the neglecting defending of the strongest passes in the country, the omitting to destroy the bridges, were all faults that might and ought to have been avoided.

The halt at Lugo, made necessary only by the rapidity of the march to that place, might have been followed by the most serious consequences had the enemy come on in such force as to have attacked us with any chance of success. Our stores in this case must have all inevitably fallen into their hands.

(5) The changing the place of embarkation from Vigo to Corunna, and at so late a moment as to make the arrival of the shipping at the latter place very uncertain.

(6) Depriving the army of the great advantage that must have resulted from having a superior artillery in the field, by embarking them previous to the action of the 16th.

And lastly. At once embarking the whole force from Corunna, without attempting the defence of the place.

To these I should have added the not sending a force to Portugal, had not the march of the army placed it in such a plight and state of disorganisation as to make it impossible to send any part of it on a further service without its being again reorganised and reappointed.

If, as an error, I stated the permitting the transports to remain in the inner harbour of Corunna until the enemy had brought their guns on the hills above them, I should not perhaps be wrong; for had we not fortunately had a fair wind, the consequences of their remaining there might have been serious in the extreme. Even as it was, four or five transports were lost. But this error perhaps rests properly with the Navy; and I understand that positive orders for their moving out had been sent early in the morning.

If, in presuming thus to criticise the campaign, I have hazarded opinions not founded on correct information, or sound memory, I am open to correction; and, by thus having encouraged the discussion, I shall have given an opportunity to many others (who at present think with me) of seeing the thing in its true light; whilst the general consequence of all discussions on military matters must eventually tend to the dissemination of information on subjects in which, I fear, we Englishmen have not yet made campaigns sufficient to record us as equal to cope with the enemy in the field in anything else than valour.

These remarks were written, or rather concluded, on board the *Barfleur* returning from Corunna.

In 1819 my grandfather, then Sir Hussey Vivian, added to the above diary these words:

> The brilliant talents of the Duke of Wellington have raised the glory of the British arms to an extent it had not attained, I may say, even under Marlborough; and have occasioned my erasing remarks which were founded on the incapacity which had been displayed by those who, before him, had been placed at the head of our army during the Revolutionary war.

★ ★ ★ ★ ★

With regard to the criticisms made by Colonel Vivian on the manner in which Sir J. Moore conducted the campaign of 1808, it must be remembered that they were made immediately after the events had taken place, and without that full opportunity of making himself acquainted with all the true facts which the exertions of historians have since enabled the present generation to acquire.

In spite of this, however, they are wonderfully apposite, and raise arguments as to which historians, such as Napier and Alison, take different views.

Sir J. Moore's advance was planned in the first place to relieve and support Castaños. After that general's defeat it was continued in order to assist the defence of Madrid, the inhabitants of which vowed they would never surrender; and after the report of the capitulation of that city had reached the ears of the British general, he still did not abandon his advance, in the hopes of succouring the south of Spain, and giving the Spanish both the time and the opportunity of defending themselves against their enemy.

Levelled against the enemy's communications. Sir J. Moore's advance paralysed the movements of Napoleon, and by drawing him with his legions into the northern extremity of the Peninsula, it gave time to the southern provinces to restore their armies and arm their fortresses.

Napoleon, however, with 70,000 chosen troops, was speedily sweeping round the audacious enemy who had thus interrupted his designs; and but for the celerity and skill of the retreat to Astorga the army which achieved this must speedily have been consigned to destruction.

As to whether or not the army had necessarily to retreat from Astorga with the celerity it did, Napier and Alison differ.

Napier says there was such necessity—that had not the retreat been executed with the greatest speed, the flanks of the British would have been turned, and the French, but for the jealousy that existed between Soult and Ney, even as it was, might have been manoeuvred so as to cut off the English at Corunna; besides which, though there were some positions on the route which were easily defensible by small bodies of men against superior forces, yet anything but a permanent defence would have been useless; and such permanent defence was impossible, owing to dearth of provisions and the poverty of the land.

Alison, on the other hand, says that, admitting that the celerity of the retreat to Astorga was unavoidable and saved the army from destruction, there was no necessity for the subsequent forced marches to Lugo. It was admitted that there were provisions for fourteen days' consumption at Villa Franca and Lugo; and even if there had been nothing but the resources of the country to be had, events proved that they were sufficient for the maintenance of the army, inasmuch as the French found enough to live on, though following in the rear of the British. There was no danger of being turned on the flank, for Ney's corps was several days' march behind Soult's, and the rugged nature of the country rendered it impossible for his troops, worn out by the rapid march from Madrid, to attempt any threatening-movement against the British flank.

The alteration from Vigo to Corunna as the port of embarkation was made in consequence of reports that were made to Sir J. Moore by officers of the Engineers, detached for the purpose of making inquiry as to which of the two was best. From them it appeared that Vigo, besides being further away, offered no position to cover the embarkation, whereas Corunna and Betanzos did.

With regard to Colonel Vivian's criticisms on the great attention that was paid to ensuring the safety, of the artillery, and on the disadvantage in which the British were placed at the battle of Corunna through the guns having been embarked previous to the battle, there can be no doubt that had the British then had artillery the repulse of the French would have been turned into an utter defeat.

On the other hand, it should be pointed out that, during the whole of this disastrous campaign, the only guns lost by the British were six three-pounders, which had been landed at Corunna without the general's knowledge—which never went past Villa Franca—and which, never having been horsed, were thrown down the rocks when that town was evacuated by the troops.

As to whether the British should have defended Corunna, or at all events not have deserted Spain by sailing direct for England, Alison says:

> If the British could not have maintained their ground behind the strong battlements of Ferrol, or the weaker fortifications of Corunna, that might have afforded a good reason for bringing the troops round to Lisbon or Cadiz; but it was none for setting sail to England with the whole expedition, abandoning the contest in the Peninsula as hopeless, when the South was still unsubdued, and leaving 10,000 English still in Portugal to their fate.

General Jomini, the great Swiss historian, writing of Sir J. Moore's retreat, says:

> The road from Astoria to Corunna traverses a long defile of 30 leagues, bounded by high mountains on either side. A slender rear-guard would have defended that *chaussée*, and it was impracticable to manoeuvre on either side of it. That rendered it impossible for Soult to get at the enemy; and Ney, entangled behind him in the defiles, could do nothing. This was the more unfortunate, as the English army, having prepared nothing on that line, stood in want of everything, and was in a frightful state of disorder in consequence of the forced marches it took, for no conceivable reason. He (Sir J. Moore) cut the traces of their horses, and abandoned 3000 or 4000 stragglers or dying men when their line of operations was never menaced. It is impossible to conceive why the English did not defend Corunna. It is not, indeed, a Gibraltar; but against an enemy who had nothing but field-pieces it surely could have been maintained for some time, the more especially as they could at any time throw in succour by sea. I could never understand their haste on that occasion, which the nation, it is true, have well wiped off in subsequent times, but which was inferior to no other of the same description.

The losses during this campaign were, according to Napier:

Lost at, or previous to arrival of army at Lugo, 95 cavalry, 1302 infantry; total, 1397.

Of this number 200 were left in the wine vaults at Bembibre, and nearly 500 were stragglers from the troops that marched to Vigo.

Lost between Lugo and embarkation, 9 cavalry, 2627 infantry; total, 2636, making a total loss of 4033. Of these, however, 800 escaped into Portugal.'

The disasters of the army did not end on its embarkation for England at Corunna; for the fleet, on its way to England, was caught in a terrific storm. Many ships were wrecked, and the remainder, driving up Channel, were glad to put into any port; and the soldiers, thus thrown ashore, were scattered from the Land's End to Dover.

Their haggard appearance, ragged clothing, and dirty accoutrements—things common enough in war—struck a people only used to the daintiness of parade with surprise. The usual exaggerations of men just escaped from perils and distresses were increased by the uncertainty in which all were as to the fate of their comrades.

A deadly fever, the result of anxiety and of the sudden change from fatigue to the confinement of a ship, filled the hospitals at every port with officers and soldiers; and thus the miserable state of Sir J. Moore's army became the topic of every letter and the theme of every country newspaper along the coast. And the cry was raised that England was no match for France on land, and that the only rational policy for the prosecution of the war was for her to withdraw entirely behind her wooden walls.

Yet the campaign had been more calamitous to the French than to the Allies.

The Spanish armies, it is true, had been dispersed; Madrid had been taken, and the British, after a calamitous retreat, had been driven to their ships; but the Peninsula was still unsubdued. Saragossa was again preparing to defend its bloodstained battlements; Catalonia was in arms; Valencia and Andalusia were recruiting their forces; Portugal was untouched; and the British troops, though in diminished strength, still held Lisbon.

What had happened in the same campaign to the hitherto invincible arms of France? One whole corps had laid down its arms with unheard of disgrace; another had capitulated and surrendered a kingdom to purchase its retreat; the Imperial arms had been driven from Madrid, and only regained their lost ground by denuding Germany of its defenders, and exposing the Rhine to invasion; and Austria was preparing to renew the struggle against France on a scale of unprecedented magnitude.—*Alison*, vol. 6. p. 855.

One of the transports conveying the troops on their return from Corunna, the *Despatch*, with a detachment of the 7th Hussars, consisting of Captain Treveake's and Dukinfield's troops, on board, was wrecked on the Manacle Rocks, off the coast of Cornwall. In this disaster Major Cavendish, Captain Dukinfield, and Lieutenant Waldegrave were drowned, besides 8 non-commissioned officers, 60 men, and 35 horses.

Out of the 751 horses which the regiment took to Spain, the 7th brought back only about 70.

For his services in this campaign Lieut.-Col. Vivian was awarded the Peninsular gold medal for the actions of Sahagun and Benavente.

On February 20, 1812, Hussey Vivian was promoted to the rank of colonel in the army, and was shortly afterwards appointed Equerry to H.R.H. the Prince Regent, afterwards George IV,

CHAPTER 3

Campaign of 1813

I have no letters from Colonel Vivian subsequent to the Corunna Diary until the letter dated August 19, 1813, quoted later on, when he was on the point of starting with his regiment—the 7th Light Dragoons (Hussars)—for Spain, to join the forces under the Duke of Wellington.

In the notes to the Corunna Diary it has already been stated that Napoleon, who had left Madrid in order to assist Soult against the English, had been obliged to return to Paris because of Austria having joined the Allies and declared war against him.

With his usual rapidity Napoleon marched upon Vienna, gained a decisive victory at Wagram, and in October dictated terms of peace to the Austrians. During this time an expedition which the English sent to the Scheldt came to a disastrous ending at the Island of Walcheren.

Napoleon practically was now master of Europe; Russia was his ally; Prussia and Austria almost his vassals; Germany at his feet; his brother-in-law, Joachim Murat, was on the throne of Naples; while his brothers, Joseph and Louis, reigned in Spain and Holland.

England alone defied him, and resolved to continue to support Spain in spite of Sir J. Moore's disastrous retreat. Accordingly, Sir A. Wellesley again landed in Spain at the head of 25,000 men in 1809; he crossed the Douro in the face of Soult's army and defeated the French at Talavera.

He was, however, subsequently obliged by the numerical superiority of the French forces to retire into Portugal, where he prepared the celebrated lines of Torres Vedras, behind which he retired after checking the pursuit of Massena at Busaco, in October 1810.

In the spring he again advanced, when he gained victories at Fuentes D'Onoro in May 1811, Ciudad Rodrigo in January 1812,

Badajos in April 1812, and Salamanca in July 1812. He advanced to Burgos, but retreated from thence to Ciudad Rodrigo for the winter. In the spring of 1813, however, he again moved forward, and gained a decisive victory over King Joseph and Marshal Jourdan, at Vitoria, on June 21, 1813.

In the meantime Napoleon had quarrelled with his old ally, Russia, and had advanced with French, German and Austrian forces as far as Moscow, where he was stopped by the inhabitants setting fire to the town, and was compelled to make that awful retreat in which, from the intense cold and the *Cossacks*, he left nearly half a million of men dead on the route. In 1813 he was in Germany, fighting against the forces of that country, Austria and Russia, all of whom had combined against him after the retreat from Moscow.

After landing; from Corunna, Colonel Vivian's regiment was for some time quartered at Guildford. In May 1809, Colonel Vivian acted as second to Lord Paget in a duel that was fought between that nobleman and Captain Cadogan, the brother of Lady C. Wellesley, wife of the Honourable Henry Wellesley. Captain Cadogan fired at Lord Paget, but the latter discharged his pistol in the air, and as he declared his intention of doing so again were the duel continued, the seconds refused to allow a second shot. In June 1809, Captain Edward Keane—a relation of Colonel Vivian—was transferred from the 23rd Foot to a troop of the 7th, and later on he acted as A.D.C. to Colonel Vivian.

During 1809, the 7th went to Ireland, where they remained for the next three years, and seem to have been known as "Paget's Hussars."

In September 1810, Lieut.-Col. Vivian, together with several other officers, was given the medal for Spain and Corunna. He also obtained the rank of full colonel in the army, and was made an A.D.C. to the Prince Regent. In February 1811, a detachment of the regiment went to Spain, and on the 7th of June in the same year 200 of them went to Sheffield, to take the place of the 6th Dragoons, who were ordered on foreign service.

In August of 1813 Colonel Vivian was ordered with his regiment to take part in the Peninsula campaign, and in the middle of that month the 7th, who mustered 800 men, sailed for Bilbao.

★ ★ ★ ★ ★

At this period Colonel Vivian's letters begin again, most of them being written to his wife.

Portsmouth,
3 o'clock, Thursday.

My dearest Eli,—Captain Gordon of the *Magicenne* has written me that he sails at daybreak tomorrow if the wind suits. He is our convoy. Under this expectation I must sleep on board; but if it is decided otherwise and the wind contrary, you will see me nearly as soon as this letter. If not, may God protect and comfort you is the sincere wish of your ever affectionate husband. Tell Richard if the wind is doubtful to come down tomorrow to Spithead, and look for No. 619, *The Lord Wellington*. I want to send 'Lackless' and the puppy to you.

★ ★ ★ ★ ★

The above letter is not dated, but from the one that follows it obviously was written when Colonel Vivian was setting out for the Peninsula. August 19 fell on a Thursday in 1813, which further corroborates the inference.

★ ★ ★ ★ ★

On board *The Lord Wellington*,
Under weigh at St. Helens,
August 20, 1813.

My dearest Eli,—Here we are off, with a famous breeze. All my hopes of again seeing you, my ever dear wife, before sailing are at an end—perhaps so much the better.

If the wind continues as it is now, we shall reach our destination in about six days."

Lord Wellington Transport,
Bilbao Bay, August 29, 1813.

My dearest Eli,—Half of the regiment is arrived here safe. The other half I expect tomorrow, I hope all well. Some few horses only lost—none of mine. I am quite stout, thank God, but was dreadfully seasick.

I have just been up to Bilbao for orders, and land tomorrow. No chance of any work for the cavalry, or infantry either, I expect; but I know very little.

The river from hence to Bilbao is quite beautiful. However, I have no time for description. I have but an instant to write, or would say more."

The next letter appears to have been kept by Colonel Vivian until he had written a later one (quoted further on), dated September 11, and to have been then enclosed in that later letter.

Bilbao, September 4, 1813.

My dearest Eli,—You will probably expect me to give you some account of the place in which we now are quartered.

Its situation is beautiful, as I have already told you; on a river in the midst of magnificent mountains; and, in peace, when things are neat and settled, I have no doubt it is a delightful residence.

The *alameda*, on which my mansion stands, is on the banks of the river, planted with rows of trees, with handsome stone seats, and is the rendezvous of all the *beaux* and *belles* of the place every evening at six o'clock; but somehow or other I have hardly ever contrived to walk in it—I have so much to do.

There is also a famous lounge here at the coffee-house, where we generally all go about eight o'clock, and stay until half-past nine or ten. We get punch, lemonade, coffee, &c. &c.; and the room—a large one—is always completely full. I forgot to tell you we smoke cigars at this place, and I get on famously, notwithstanding you say I can't smoke.

As to messing we have lived hitherto at a Spanish *posada*, and had plenty of garlic and oil. I have once attempted to give a dinner *chez moi*, and succeeded very tolerably well. I find Higgins really a most useful and excellent servant; he was our steward on board ship, and I never saw a better one. Mrs. Jarvis was our cook, and a very tolerable one; and she is now mine. I give her a dollar a week for everything—cooking, washing, &c. I find soap, of course. I hope to live cheap in this country, at least to live upon my pay; but everything is very dear here. We have paid as yet for our mess seven shillings a head, besides wine.

I am sorry to say that two of our transports are not arrived, having on board Roberts and Uniacke, and 51 men and horses. It is a sad loss to us. I very much fear, if they are not put into Falmouth, that they are taken, as they have never been seen since we lost sight of old England.

You must not expect me to give you much news of the army. We know much less here than you do in England, and it is even still worse with the army; you know nothing but what is going on just where the regiment is stationed.

You will of course have heard of the fall of St. Sebastian, and of poor Leith being wounded, and also the particulars of an attack on part of the army which was defeated with considerable loss on the part of the French. The Spaniards, they say, behaved well. Such are the reports here.

The fall of St. Sebastian completely secures our left flank, and my opinion is that the campaign is at an end. Everyone here is in fact completely tired of the war, and longing for peace, and I assure you no one more so than your humble servant.

I was fortunate enough to bring all my horses out safe, and since their arrival here I have sold two for two hundred guineas—the cream and the one that was sick at H. Court. This will pay for my mules, I shall even sell another if I can, for four are ample enough for a winter campaign. I have bought four mules at one hundred and forty dollars each, and a pony for one hundred and ten, for Mrs. Jarvis to ride; and if I can sell another horse, I shall buy another mule for Higgins to ride. They require less care and are hardier than the horses.

I am now going to breakfast with old Thornhill, so I must conclude this for the present.

★ ★ ★ ★ ★

St. Sebastian was besieged by the English in July 1813, but, owing to Soult's advance and the battle of Sauroren, the siege was for a time abandoned.

It was renewed in August, and on the 31st of that month the place was stormed and taken by Sir Thomas Graham. Sir James Leith commanded the column of attack, and was severely wounded. He had only joined two days before.

On the same day the French, under Soult, crossed the Bidassoa and attacked the Spanish and English forces near San Marcial, with the object of preventing them establishing themselves on the French frontier. The French were entirely repulsed.—See *Alison*, vol. 9, pp. 797, 823, 828. *St. James' Chronicle*, September 16, 1813.

★ ★ ★ ★ ★

September 8.—I left off three days ago, just as I was going to breakfast with Thornhill. Since that nothing has occurred worth adding to my letter. I shall therefore now conclude.'

Bilbao, September 11, 1813.

My Dearest Eli,—No opportunity having until now offered of

sending the enclosed, I take this advantage of Colonel Roberts' going to England (sick) to let you know that I am quite stout and well.

I have as yet not heard a syllable from headquarters as to our movements; but as mules for the carriage of provisions, &c., have joined the regiment, I take it it will not be long before we start.

I shall write to you regularly by every post, but if you are ever any length of time without hearing do not be alarmed; it is very possible, from the irregularity of posts, &c., that I may not be able to send letters so often as either you or I could wish.

I have not, up to this moment, since I left England, heard a syllable from anyone, and seldom seen a paper, even. The last I saw was of August 19, at Portsmouth; but Shakspeare writes me word that there are papers with the army of the 27th, which state that Austria has declared for the Allies, and that the armistice is broken. If so I expect we shall attempt to advance into France; but it will be only an attempt. Be assured of it, there will not be much fighting this campaign. For my part, I do not believe we shall fire a shot.

I am sorry to hear from the army that Colonel Grant is dangerously ill with a liver complaint; so much so that if he recovers it will be necessary for him to go to England. This will, I expect, put me into the command of a brigade. I shall go to headquarters as soon as I can, and see what is to be done. I do not like leaving the 7th; but the emoluments of a brigade are not to be refused.

September 13.—All well.

Bilbao, September 15, 1813.

My dearest Eli,—I have this instant heard that Roberts is not gone, and I shall therefore send an orderly with this to him, just to say that we are all quite well and stout. That is, Ned and myself. Higgins has had a little touch of a complaint in his bowels, which frightened him most infernally. He is now much better, and indeed well.

In a day or two I start for headquarters. Our destination is Tafalla, to join the Hussar brigade under Lord Edward Somerset; but I expect to be sent to the command of the brigade of either General Alten or Colonel Grant, who, they say, are both going home ill. If either goes I step into his shoes.

Bilbao, September 18, 1813.

My dearest Eli,—I am just getting upon my horse to ride off to Lord Wellington's headquarters at Yrun, and propose returning here in about a week or ten days.

I shall leave this with Edward to send by any opportunity that may offer, just to inform you of my being quite stout and well; and here I must observe to you that you must not expect from me always very long letters. I often have so very many things to do as to be unable to write long epistles, though at the same time I may wish just to let you know that I am as stout and well as any man in the army.

I have written to my father to beg him to send me out hams, tongues, butter, cheese, and wine. The hams and tongues I wish you to send him for me; four hams and eight tongues.

I expect the regiment will march to Tafalla, about midway between Pampeluna and Tudela, when I return. The whole of the cavalry are obliged to be near the Ebro for the sake of getting fed; and even there, I fear, it is short commons. We are in clover here, and if they do not want us they might as well let us remain here during the winter.

As soon as Pampeluna falls we shall move either to the front or rear, for Lord Wellington will certainly not remain in the mountains all the winter. I expect we shall be in quiet quarters on the Ebro. Pampeluna is expected to fall about the beginning of October.

I will write again, if I hear any news from headquarters.

Fraser is going up to Yrun with me.

★ ★ ★ ★ ★

Pampeluna, like St. Sebastian, was one of the fortified towns into which the French had retreated after the battle of Vitoria, and which they still held, although besieged by the English.

Like St. Sebastian, also, it had been momentarily relieved by the battle of Sauroren, by which it had been enabled to obtain a fresh supply of food.

It finally surrendered from starvation on October 31.

★ ★ ★ ★ ★

Legacia, September 24, 1813.

I was delighted, my dearest Eliza, on my arrival here yesterday, to find a letter from you, dated both inside and out the 9th of August, but of course meaning September. Be more careful, if you please, in future on this head, and always let me know in each letter the date of your two or three last, in order that I may know whether I receive all your epistles; and I will do the same in mine to you.

I arrived here yesterday [*September 23*] after a delightful journey of six days, through the most romantic and beautiful country I ever saw.

September 18.—The first day from Bilbao I slept at Durango, an excellent inn, much better than any in Ireland, excepting Dublin. The road, part of it, very tolerable; the rest, stony and bad. The whole through the mountains five leagues.

From Durango to Azpeytia (seven leagues), through the villages of Ermua, Eybar, Elgoibar, and Azcoytia, I think one of the finest rides I ever took. The country beautiful, the mountains covered with vineyards or forests of chestnuts or walnuts; the valleys were narrow defiles, through which was tumbling over rocks just such a river as that by Ivybridge, only much more wild and magnificent, and abundantly larger. The villages I have mentioned were beautiful beyond conception; the houses excellent, and in general that of the *Señor* quite a palace. The villages have but little felt the effects of war.

September 19.—I dined this day with Lieut.-Gen. Sir Stapleton Cotton, who was excessively civil and kind. He expressed his regret at there being no brigade vacant for me, and added that he hoped very soon there would be one by General Alten's return to England, which is expected very shortly.

September 20.—From Azpeytia, the day following, I went to Andoain, on the road from Tolosa to Oyarzun. Part of this day's journey was also by mountain roads, impassable for anything but horses and mules, and scarcely passable for them,

At Tolosa, a large but dirty town, I got into the great road—a very good one, but very stony and rough.

At Andoain I dined with my old friend, Colonel Ross, of the Horse Artillery, whom you may remember at Ipswich. From Andoain, the following day, I went by way of St. Sebastian to Oyarzun.

I shall not attempt to describe to you the horrible state in which the town of St. Sebastian is. Never did I see such an example made of a place. It cost both parties very dear. In short, from the effects of the fire I am only surprised at any one, on either side, being alive to tell the tale. The last assault cost us 2300 killed and wounded.

I saw General Leith, and Robinson: the former suffering, but doing well; the latter quite well.

★ ★ ★ ★ ★

St. Sebastian was unsuccessfully stormed on July 24. On August 31 it was again stormed, and after a most sanguinary fight, was taken by the English troops, supported by a most furious bombardment.

An immense fire also broke out which destroyed, nearly all the houses that were left standing, and, to add to the horrors of the scene, both the English and Spanish troops, in the exultation of victory, gave way to the most horrible debaucheries and atrocities.

The siege of St. Sebastian cost the Allies 3800 men, 2500 of whom were killed in the final assault.

★ ★ ★ ★ ★

September 22.—At Oyarzun I dined with Sir Thomas Graham, and on the following morning rode with him to Yrun, to see the ground where the last action was fought with the Spaniards, and to take a peep into France.

The Spaniards behaved very much better than they have ever done before; but they began by giving way and allowing the enemy to get possession of a hill which ought to have been impracticable. On the other hand, the French committed themselves very much, and, but for the fog which came on, would have been well trounced.

★ ★ ★ ★ ★

On August 30 Soult again made an attempt to relieve St. Sebastian and Pampeluna, and attacked the Allies near San Marcial, where the forces were chiefly composed of Spanish troops. The latter behaved with considerable gallantry, and Soult was driven back over the Bidassoa.—*Alison,* vol. 9. p. 828.

★ ★ ★ ★ ★

The country of France for some distance appears much the same as here—mountains, &c.; but beyond them, at a distance of two or three leagues, it appears flat. They talk of our soon going to see, but I doubt it. No movement will, I apprehend, be made till Pampeluna falls, and then I think we are more likely to go into Catalonia than anywhere else. The French do not appear to be strong in front of this; their camps are on the hills exactly opposite, and we can see every man.

* * * * *

Wellington looked to the security of the Peninsula as the main object of his efforts, and was desirous that his troops should be turned against Suchet, in Catalonia, in order that, during Napoleon's absence in Germany with the greater part of his forces, an effectual barrier against France in the east might be recovered to the Spanish monarchy.

The English Government, however, looking to the general interest of Europe, and the probable effect on the Allied sovereigns on the Elbe, decided otherwise; the invasion of France, even before Pampeluna had fallen, was decided on; and Wellington, like a good general, set himself to execute, to the best of his ability, an offensive campaign which, on military principles, he deemed premature.—*Alison*, vol. 9. p. 845.

* * * * *

September 22.—But I am wandering from my journey. I slept again at Oyarzun on the 22nd, for the sake of dining with my old friend, Colonel Delancey; and yesterday I came over here, through one of the most impracticable roads I almost ever passed, but through mountain scenery beyond anything beautiful.

I dined yesterday with the great Lord; he but made his bow, and said very little.

September 24.—Today I dine with Sir Lowry Cole; and I am just now going to ride one of his horses two leagues to Echalar, to see Colonel Hawkins.

Friday evening, September 24.—I returned too late from Echalar to write before dinner, and now sit down to say a few words to you before I retire to my bed to be bitten to death by fleas, for, *nota bene*, in this country the fleas have not that respect for me that they have in England, and there are myriads of them!

A mail is just arrived without a letter from you. What can this mean? Pray write often. I am always too happy to hear from you for you ever to disappoint me so.

I start tomorrow on my way home. I cannot find much news here. Many reports about advancing, and moving into Catalonia. I expect the latter, if either; but nothing will take place until the fall of Pampeluna, and that will not happen time enough for us to move.

I forgot, in my account of my journey up, to tell you of a most beautiful convent between Azpeytia and Azcoytia that I saw, founded by Ignatius Loyola, the famous Jesuit, built of marble, with the most magnificent altar I ever saw, of inlaid marble; but the whole has never been finished.

I hope it is Roberts and Uniacke in Falmouth; it cannot be Pipon's squadron.

Fraser accompanied me to Oyarzun, where he is with his friends of the Guards.

All well.

On board the Surveillance frigate,
Passages Harbour, September 27, 1813.

My dearest Eli,—Although I wrote only two days ago from Legacia, I cannot miss the opportunity now offered of the *Dwarf* sailing for England, to tell you I am alive and well; indeed, I never was better in my life.

I start tomorrow on my way to Bilbao, where I shall arrive in about four or five days."

Passages is near St. Sebastian, and, being at this time in the possession of the English, was used by them as their chief harbour. It will be seen from the date of the next letter that though Colonel Vivian only left Passages on September 28, and then expected to be four days on his journey, yet, as a fact, he reached Bilbao in two days.

Bilbao, September 30, 1813.

My dearest Eli,—I found on my arrival here your two letters of August 22 and 30. As your last was of later date they of course contain no news.

In reply to the questions you put me on the matter in dispute between Sir John and Richard, I can only say, on the first, that I have never known an instance of a junior captain in a regiment getting a majority of that regiment in preference to the senior captain, because he was senior in the service.

In reply to the second, I should say that, in a battalion composed of detachments, the majority, if it went in it, would go to the senior captain of the detachments; but there is no fixed rule on such occasions—kissing goes by favour, and so do majorities: they are often given away out of the regiments, without even reference to seniority.

I found all here on my return pretty well the same as when I left it. On October 2 we shall commence our march for Durango, where we shall halt for some days (two or three) and then march to join the Hussar Brigade at Tafalla and Olite. The latter will be our headquarters.

★ ★ ★ ★ ★

Soult at this time had taken up a strong position on the northern side of the Bidassoa, near Bayonne, and between Yrun and St. Jean Pied-de-Port, on the summit of a ridge of mountains overlooking the valley of the Bidassoa.

Wellington intended to attack him in September, immediately after the fall of St. Sebastian; but the excessive rains which came on had swelled the Bidassoa into a raging torrent, and made it an impossibility to attempt to cross it till October.—*Alison*, vol. 9. p. 846. *Life of Napoleon*, vol. 6. p. 249.

★ ★ ★ ★ ★

I have just heard that our fourth squadron is arrived at Passages together with our missing ships. I hope it is true.

Tell John I wish he would come over and see us. It is not above three days' sail to Passages in the packet, and three days' march afterwards to Olite. I will send horses, mules, &c., for him, and in the winter will accompany him to Madrid. He must bring a cloak, and portmanteau and uniform. Young Bankes is here, travelling all over the country. He is now started for the south, having travelled alone from Portugal all over the north of Spain to this.

★ ★ ★ ★ ★

On October 9, Wellington determined to cross the Bidassoa at Yrun, San Marcial, and Vera.

Soult, not expecting that Wellington would venture to attack him in his strong position, was surprised, and obliged to retreat into France, where he took up a position on the Nivelle. The Allies lost in the engagement 1600 men.

* * * * *

Olite, October 20, 1813.

My dearest Eli,—I was delighted at the receipt of two letters from you—one of the 16th, and the other of September 22. These complete the five you mention having written.

Higgins and William both do very well; the former is cook, &c..; in fact he is a most useful fellow, and very attentive. Henry Walker is my valet, and an admirably good one he is, but he has been very ill. Mrs. Jarvis is scullion and washing woman. Foxlow takes care of my mules, and I have a German who helps him, and takes care of the goats—an excellent fellow. Antonio turned out sulky and good for nothing, and on the march here he deserted because I would not give him a mule to ride. I was rejoiced at his going.

We are now in a totally different country to that we have just left—an open town, in the midst of an immense plain covered with vineyards and olive gardens.

Johnny, if he was here, would kill himself with eating grapes. I was out shooting yesterday with old Thornhill in the vineyards, and we killed three brace of red legs, and I think ate about twelve pounds each of the most delicious grapes you can imagine. Tell Johnny only to imagine himself panting for breath on a hot day in Sussex, having laboured after a covey of birds for six hours, planted in the midst of the finest possible hothouse full of the finest possible grapes. This was precisely our case, only that the day was October, and rather hotter than one of yours in September.

The olives are still green, and are as nasty as the grapes are good; but every species of fruit and vegetable, and the wine and mutton, in this country are quite delicious.

I wrote to ask my father, amongst other things, to send me some wine. If it is not sent off I would now rather have hams, cheese, tongues, &c., in greater abundance; for if we remain in this country I would rather drink its wines than any port. If we move it will perhaps be into a country where we had better not carry much luggage; for everything now seems to denote a crusade into France even beyond the Garonne, as soon as Pampeluna falls. If this really takes place, the 7th will have the honour of showing the way; so you will perhaps, soon hear of our having had a brush with the *Gendarmerie Française*.

If Pampeluna holds out to the middle of next month, any movement of this sort will be out of the question; and in that case we, the cavalry, shall have to retire to the Ebro in order to find wherewithal to feed upon.

I shall lament leaving this, for the quarters I now occupy are most excellent ones, with admirably good civil creatures, but *no pretty girls*, which I lament, as it assists me in learning Spanish, in which, however, I have attained great proficiency, and I am sorry only at my having left my grammar and dictionary behind me. Pray send me one of each.

I should tell you that to make up for the want of pretty girls in my house, the cousins of my patroness (for that is the proper name for the mistress of the house in this country), *two most beautiful creatures*, pay me a visit every morning at breakfast-time, and sit and chat an hour or two. Tell my mother one of them is the very picture of . . . . only rather taller, and about seventeen years old. Don't be jealous; you need not.

The patron of the house is an Irishman, and like many others of his countrymen, is a great vagabond. His name is Murphy. He came here and married, about sixteen years ago, the daughter of this house. He very soon left her and a little girl he had by her, and went to America, where he now is. Here I have mother, daughter, and grand-daughter, constantly at my elbow. I am in so much favour with them because I talk and laugh with them. Grant, who was here before me, would never speak to any of them; indeed he could not, and they disliked him very much.

Throughout the whole of this country are visible the ravages of war. Just here it was that Mina was eternally ravaging the enemy, and they were obliged to fortify convents, &c. &c., in order to maintain themselves at all in any degree of safety; the consequence has been that Mina, whenever successful, has invariably destroyed all these strongholds, by which many of the most beautiful buildings are now in ruins. In this very town an old Moorish castle, the residence of the Kings of Navarre, was last year totally destroyed. From the remnants of columns it must have been a most magnificent building.

All your old friends in the regiment are quite well and stout. Most of them have had a little touch of a complaint in the bowels prevalent in this country, excepting myself. I grow fat and saucy.

The men are all well. they get sadly drunk now, and then, for which I have tickled a few of them; but in general they have behaved admirably well. Wine is so cheap it really is no wonder that they get drunk. It is sixpence a quart only, and very strong.

Other articles, however, are as dear as wine is cheap. Eggs, three pence each; chickens, one dollar; sugar, three and sixpence a pound; wax candles (no tallow), six shillings a pound; beef, mutton, &c., from a shilling to one and three pence a pound. However, we contrive to live very well. I generally have soup and fish (salt), with a joint of meat, or a brace of birds, or a hare, and an apple or rice pudding, for dinner, with a dessert that would grace the table at Carlton House, and which costs about three pence.

I wish my father would inquire whether any captain of a packet would bring me out six couple of hounds, and if so get them for me (old, steady working ones), and send them out, letting me know first that they are coming, in order that I may have a man at Passages waiting for them. This country is delightful for hare hunting, and there is just game enough. Pray try what can be done for me.

Tell my father I have received his letter. This must for the present serve you all; when you separate again I will write to each. Tell Johnny to come out and see the country. From Tolosa to Pampeluna is through the most magnificent and beautiful mountain scenery in the world.

I shall send this to Torrens, because I want to write to him.

Old Thornhill is just come in from shooting, and desires his kind regards. Ned is well, and sends his love. Thornhill desires me to say that the key he gave you of his portmanteau is not the right one, so you must have the lock picked in order to air the things.

★ ★ ★ ★ ★

Mina was one of the many Spanish guerrilla chiefs who kept harassing the flanks of the French during this campaign.

At the time when the next letter was written the 7th had joined Lord Edward Somerset's brigade. Olite is near Tafalla.

* * * * *

Olite, October 25, 1813.

Your two letters of September 30 and October 9 reached me, dearest Eliza, this morning.

If Victor Alten returns to England I shall certainly have his brigade, and nothing prevents his return but the chance of having something to do; but, as they still talk of an advance into France, he cannot of course go until it is decided one way or the other; and if I get a brigade I shall of course return it when a Major-Gen., and in this case there is no chance of my returning in January; but, of course, if I have no brigade, and am then made a Major-Gen., I shall not remain here.

Believe me, my dearest Eli, I shall most truly rejoice when that day arrives that shall restore me to you, to my dear boy, to my kind parents, and to all my friends; but if the war continues I am afraid there is no prospect of that day soon arriving. My prospects are in my profession, and if I am to get a regiment, or a staff appointment in England, &c., by-and-bye, I must do my duty for it now. Besides which, it really is not worthwhile to run to and fro for a few months; so, barring accidents, I shall stay out here, and when I do return, I hope it will be to sit down in peace and quiet by a good and happy fireside, with you and my dear boy, and all those I love best in the world.

October 27.—I left off here in consequence of being interrupted, and, as the post does not go until tomorrow, I have delayed writing again until this day, supposing something might turn up.

There is no longer any doubt of an advance into France as soon as Pampeluna falls; in fact our orders are arrived to move forward the instant it does; but I conclude if it holds out till the middle of November that any forward movement will be out of the question. The Pyrenees are already covered with snow.

If we do go into France it will, I hope, be in earnest, I have no notion of doing things by halves; besides which, nothing but a good and complete thrashing will secure us quiet winter quarters; not, indeed, that I expect these under any circumstances, for, in my mind, a British army, even on the Garonne, would be pretty much in the same situation that a French army would be at Exeter—surrounded by a hostile population who would not give them a moment's rest.

Our advance into France will be the signal for the union of all parties to resist the invader; and when this is the case a military nation is not easily beaten.

I think it very possible that, in the first instance, our success may be very considerable, and, if Lord Wellington pushes it, there is no saying how far we may not proceed; but it is as to the ultimate consequences that I have any fear; and I have seen too much of winter campaigns, and retreats in frost and snow, to wish for another edition!

We are all ready for a move. Our horses at first suffered considerably from change of food and climate, &c., but they are getting about fast, and we are nearly in as good order as at Hyde Park barracks.

Our men are very healthy in general. We have lost two, and have eight sick. The officers' private servants are failing most. Vernon has lost his, and two or three others have been very ill. William was, at one time; he is now better. Poor Walker is, I am sorry to say, very ill indeed; I fear, going into a consumption; at least he looks so. If we advance he must remain behind.

Of our officers most have been a little amiss. Grenfell was left sick at Bilbao, Mr. Moffatt at Hernani, and Hamlyn is now in bed here with a very considerable degree of fever on him, but nothing at all alarming. *Pour moi*, thank God, I never was better in my life; seldom so well.

My stud also is in excellent force. Tell my father that little 'Dragon' is just as fat as he was at Truro, and just as well. Poor 'Dash' had his thigh broken by a kick from a horse at Bilbao, and was left in hospital there after Irvin had set it. He is a sad loss to me; he would have done nicely for the red legs. However, 'Jane' does just as well. We have, amongst other game, immense flights of bustards; but they are so wild that neither Thornhill nor myself, with all our ingenuity, can get at one.

We are now here in the midst of the vintage, and such a dirty operation as is the making of wine you cannot conceive. The grapes are brought in in large tubs on mules' backs, and sprinkled with fine lime—they say, to make the wine high coloured; they are then thrown on a floor of dirty bricks, that has never been cleaned for centuries, probably. These floors have a gradual slope to the centre, where there is a funnel which conveys the juice of the grapes into immense vats below; and when the floor is covered with grapes, four or five dirty, filthy wretches, without shoes or stockings, and their feet covered with every species of dirt that abounds so plentifully in the streets of a Spanish town, walk in, and begin treading away. After having thus for some time pressed the grapes, they are collected, and, by a very simple operation, their stems are extracted from the fruit. The fruit is then put into a press which extracts all the juice, and which runs into the funnel already described. The skins of the fruit are then taken from the press and carried to the still to make brandy. The wine is fit to drink in eight or ten days, the brandy at once.

Since I wrote last I have had my general—Lord E. Somerset—to dine with me; and I must tell you my dinner, in order that you may not think we starve. N.B. I never have more than six.

First Course.	Second Course.
Salt fish and potatoes (*i.e.*, "*chowder.*")	Roast partridges.
	Apple stewed.
Removes.	Rice pudding.
Roast saddle of mutton.	Tart
Stewed beef, roast potatoes.	Mushrooms.
Steaks.	Omelette.
Boiled chicken.	
Soup removed.	
Ham.	

This, you will say, was a very good dinner. As to dessert, I could beat all the grape-houses in Truro, tell my father.

The order of the day in the army is now for everyone to live as well as he can; and a very wise plan it is. In the first campaign it is certain that many officers died from poverty of food; now it is *toute autre chose*. I am badly off only in my canteens. Instead of those abominable leaden dishes, &c., which I brought out, all these things should have been plated. I was penny wise and pound foolish on this head, for the plated last ten times as long, and cost very little more. My leaden dishes are now all shapes; in short, no one who has been here any time has anything but plated dishes, cups, &c., and what provokes me most is that several of our officers were wise enough to bring out plated articles—Kerrison, Lowther, Wildman, Vernon, and many others. It is astonishing, besides, how much better a dinner looks on them. But we do very well altogether.

If we get to Bordeaux, tell my father I will send him home two of the best hogsheads of claret I can pick up; and when we dictate peace at Paris I will return *via* Calais, and drink it. One, to my mind, is pretty nearly as possible as the other; but, to hear these crusaders talk, we are already at Paris and the Palais Royale! A short time now will decide it.

There was a report yesterday that Pampeluna had fallen, but I sent an officer there to learn, and he tells me that they only offered to surrender on condition of being allowed to return to France with their baggage. That is the sort of proposal that comes often long before a surrender; but it is certain that they are short of provisions and have for some time been eating their horses. I gave Thornhill yesterday five guineas to give me a guinea a day until they surrendered, and my opinion is that I shall make money by it.

★ ★ ★ ★ ★

This Colonel Vivian did; for Pampeluna did not surrender till the 31st.

★ ★ ★ ★ ★

The governor is well aware of the consequence it is to the army being detained even a few days, and therefore will not—dare not—surrender till the last moment; he can have no hopes of being relieved.

Pray order the hams, tongues, and butter, &c., that I wrote for, to be sent to the packet, write to me by the packet to say that they are coming, so that I may be prepared to send for them,

"I have now written you a long letter, full of nothing, but I know you like to have plenty of reading! I shall send this by the packet. I sent my last to Torrens because I wanted to write to him.

P.S.—*October 28.* All well. No news of Pampeluna.

Olite, October 31, 1813.

My dearest Eli,—Pampeluna has fallen, and I have this instant received an order to march tomorrow morning; so this must be a short letter.

We go tomorrow to Salines de Pampeluna and Noain. The next day to Berrioplano. The next to Arraix. The next to St. Estevan;

and thence we shall *enter France* by the pass of Maya. How long we shall remain there I cannot pretend to say. My opinion is that our quarters will not be very pleasant ones.

I shall have to send about fifty-six horses, and ten sick men, to the rear; and I regret to say that poor Hamlyn is amongst those who will be sent; in fact, I have just seen him off to the hospital at Vitoria, and I very much fear whether I shall ever see him back again. He is very seriously ill, with every appearance of its ending in a typhus fever; in short, he is precisely in the same state that Vernon's servant was, and the dragoon that died.

★ ★ ★ ★ ★

Pampeluna surrendered on October 31, and 3000 men were made prisoners.

During the delay caused by Pampeluna holding out, Soult had been strengthening his position on the Nivelle.

★ ★ ★ ★ ★

Buenza, November 3, 1813.

After making two forced marches which has nearly knocked up all our horses and almost killed my mules, &c., I reached this last night, and was preparing to proceed this morning to St. Estevan, when, thank God, I received an order to halt; so here I am, in the clouds, with Edwards' and Robins" troops.

I say 'thank God' we halted, because another such a day's march as we had yesterday and the regiment would have been *hors de combat*. No description that I can give you, nor can the worst roads that you ever heard of or saw, at all enable you to form an idea of the mountain paths we climbed yesterday. The worst goat path in all Wales is a garden walk compared to it; and they tell me that we have eight leagues more into France of still worse roads! When I tell you that we were yesterday on horseback from seven till past six, and only accomplished three leagues of good roads (from Pampeluna until we turned into the mountains), and three leagues of bad afterwards, you may suppose what a march we have in view. After we get into France I hope, at least, that the roads will be better.

We are now in a village situated most romantically in a country which is beautiful, and which in happier times must be a delightful residence. The villages are exceedingly good, and the peasantry admirable people; but, alas! the men and the houses are all that are left.

We are almost in a state of starvation. What little our horses have to eat is the wheat taken by force from these poor creatures; and when you imagine that this has been going on by the French first, in their retreat; then by ourselves; then again by the French, in their advance; then by us; and since constantly by British cavalry and infantry marching to and fro, you will not suppose much is to be had here.

I have this instant heard that an order was sent to Olite to stop us in our quarters, but we had marched before it arrived. The movement into France is for the moment suspended, and my opinion is that Lord Wellington will be wise enough to suspend it altogether. If he does not I very much fear he will lose more credit than he has gained.

I had the good fortune to arrive at Pampeluna just in time to see the garrison march out and lay down their arms; and a finer body of men I never saw. they looked a little pale or so, and when we considered that they had been for six weeks living on cats and dogs and rats, with four ounces of horse flesh and four ounces of bad bread each per day, it is not to be wondered at their looking so. There were about 3500 of them. They marched past 12,000 Spanish troops that had blockaded the place, and very respectable looking soldiers they were.

Pampeluna is a beautiful city—by far the finest I have seen in Spain; a remarkably fine cathedral, a very handsome *plaza* with a public walk, and altogether very neat and clean; but the poor inhabitants were in a dreadful state. They had been driven, as some of them most pathetically told me, *al ultimo*; and a few days more and many must have died from starvation. But for this the garrison would not have surrendered, for they might have dragged on a little longer; and Buonaparte will say that they *ought* to have dragged on a little longer, I expect.

I am in daily expectation of letters from you. We know there is a mail up to the 22nd arrived, but where our letters are the Lord knows!

Thornhill is here with me, and has just been paying me a visit in my *casa*, which is what in Cornwall would be considered a good farmhouse, situated almost at the top of a range of mountains, enveloped in clouds, with one of our worst Cornish—I should say Pendarvis—days; a driving rain, with a gale of wind;

windows to which glass is unknown; the wind at N.W., blowing right in; William below, swearing at the country and the bad food for the horses; Higgins cutting up a sheep that we have just caught off the mountains; and your humble servant writing to his darling; and you will, when you take all this in, have a true picture of my present situation.

The regiment is (quartered in the villages about. I will tell you their names; but I fear you will hardly find them out in any maps you have. Lopez's provincial maps are the only ones that are of any use, and they are not to be purchased in England. Our villages are Buenza, Ciganda, Borasain, Aristigue, Musquiz, Garrons, and Erize; all within about two miles of each other.

I forgot to tell you that I was one of the first officers that entered Pampeluna. You have no conception of the joy that appeared on the meagre countenances of the poor people. Kerrison was with me, and they gave us plenty of '*Viva Inglaterra*,' '*Viva los Ingleses*.'

We remarked that in the whole town we saw but one poor mangy dog alive, and one cat, dead, which had probably been killed that morning for dinner, but thrown away in consequence of the gates being opened and other food admitted. The sufferings of these poor people, and the battered state of St. Sebastian, have together fully determined me never to build a house in a fortified town.

★ ★ ★ ★ ★

The blockade of Pampeluna had been carried out with such vigilance that during the three months it lasted the garrison never once received even a letter from their comrades.

On October 26, when the garrison was subsisting only on the most revolting reptiles, and unwholesome plants which grew upon the ramparts, negotiations were entered into for a surrender; but Wellington declined to accede to any terms except a total surrender. Hostilities were then renewed, but three days more of hunger compelled the garrison to surrender at discretion.

★ ★ ★ ★ ★

November 5, 1813.

I was last night rejoiced at the receipt of your four letters of the 11th, 14th, 16th, and 22nd. I will in my next answer any parts of them that require it.

I shall be most happy to receive the wine, &c., as nothing is to be had here of that sort, and I hope that my order to countermand did not arrive before it was sent off.

If the French tell truth, they have thrashed the Allies; at least they have sent word to Lord Wellington to say so; but they only say they have completely defeated them, taking 3000 prisoners. No cannon, &c., are mentioned, so I hope it is not much.

No order to march. Just going to seal up.

St. Estevan, November 7, 1813.

After having scrambled for six hours over mountains and roads, if possible ten thousand times worse than when I last wrote I attempted to describe, I arrived here about half an hour since, with about half of my regiment.

You may guess what the roads were when I tell you that in one troop alone upwards of twenty horses lost their shoes; and so full of rocks and loose stones are they that without a shoe it is impossible to move an inch; so the farriers are hard at work in the rear, and the road from here to Arraiz is full of the 7th, and I am here with about half the regiment.

Tomorrow, I expect, we shall start again very early.

★ ★ ★ ★ ★

Allured by some fine weather, Wellington moved his forces on the 6th to attack Soult, but subsequent bad weather setting in caused him to postpone doing so till the 10th.—*Life of Napoleon*, vol. 6i. p. 331.

★ ★ ★ ★ ★

They do say that tomorrow is to be the day when the British flag is to wave triumphant on French soil. I trust with all my heart it may be so; in fact, I have very little doubt as to the success of our troops in a general action; what I doubt is the policy of entering France at all, at least at this time of year.

If the battle is fought tomorrow, we shall have no concern in it; for the position of the army is now full seven leagues from hence, and seven leagues in this country would go well to tire the best horse in England.

★ ★ ★ ★ ★

The position of the army was at Sarrè, in front of St. Pè; and the expected battle was that of the passage of the Nivelle.

★ ★ ★ ★ ★

If the poor horses could but admire the prospect as we do, then indeed they would have been compensated for their labours; for I really cannot describe to you the beauty of the scenery through which we passed. I think it even surpassed anything we have yet seen. Mountains rising to the clouds, covered to the summit with trees, some of them magnificent oaks; the valleys full of the most delightful villages—to look at—but, alas! to enter, the miserable ravages of war are everywhere to be seen.

Bread, straw, and wheat are scarcely to be had, and we and our horses shall starve if we do not soon get into quarters that have been less subject to the passing and repassing of troops.

If we move on tomorrow it will be on the road towards Vera, where headquarters now are. I expect either Echallar or Lesaca will be our headquarters—or perhaps both.

From hence to Echallar and Vera we follow the stream of the Bidassoa, and consequently our road will not be mountainous as today, but as rough as you can well imagine anything.

The town from which I now write has been an exceedingly good one. It is about half as large as Truro, and contains several very good houses, but completely destitute of furniture, excepting here and there an old broken chair or table.

Lesaca, you know, is the village where headquarters were so long; and Vera is where they now are. From Vera to the position of the army is about two leagues, and from their position they look over France, and a country that appears to contain good quarters and fit ground for us to act in. I shall be able to tell you more about it when I finish this epistle. At present I must break off to go and look up my regiment a little.

November 8.—Still here, without orders to advance, but in hourly expectation of them.

The attack commenced this morning, it is said. It is distant eight leagues from us, and as the wind blows from hence we do not hear the firing. As you may imagine, we are all anxiety to know the result.

Our orders to advance will, I have no doubt, arrive tonight—that is if the army is successful; if otherwise, we shall have to retire to the Ebro; for, however unsuccessful the grand lord is in the action, I apprehend nothing can compel him to retire from his lines on the Pyrenees, nor do I conceive the French can attempt taking them.

I cannot imagine what can be the object of this movement. Besiege Bayonne he cannot, I think, during the winter; at least, if he does, his losses will be dreadful; and if he does not take it his advance can be but trifling, and will not, in my mind, secure us quiet winter quarters. *Nous verrons.* Tomorrow I shall be able to tell you more; at present I am all anxiety, as you may imagine.

★ ★ ★ ★ ★

Although Colonel Vivian"s regiment was at St. Estevan, some distance away from the scene of the battle that took place at the passage of the Nivelle, yet he himself seems to have gone forward and to have been present at that battle, as the following letter shows.

★ ★ ★ ★ ★

St. Pè, November 12, 1813.

My Dearest Eli,—As I promised you, I took especial care to keep clear of the shot in the attack of the 10th, and, being present only as an amateur, I had an opportunity of witnessing the whole of the battle, at least, the whole of that part of it where it was most severe.

Lord Wellington's despatch will give you a better general account than I possibly can. I can only speak as an observer.

The position of the enemy was taken up with great judgment on a line of small mountains, extending from near St. Jean de Luz on their right to St. Jean Pied-de-Port on their left. Of course it was so extended as to make it impossible so to connect it throughout as to prevent there being weak points; but everything had been done to secure it by chains of redoubts, covering and supporting each other, some containing cannon and others only for infantry, and these again, connected by intermediate breastworks, made it altogether a most formidable attempt to drive the enemy from it. To British soldiers, however, nothing is impracticable.

The attack commenced at daybreak; Sir Rowland Hill, on our right, with the 2nd and 6th Divisions, and some Spaniards under Morillo. Marshal Beresford commanded the centre, composed of the 3rd, 4th, 7th, and Light Divisions, with some Spaniards under Ghiron; and Sir J. Hope commanded the left, composed of the 1st and 5th Divisions, with some Spaniards under Frere. The attack on our left was not intended to be carried to any extent. The principal object was to force with our centre, where was supposed to be the principal strength of the enemy; and it was with this part of the army that the lord himself was.

Nothing could be more beautiful than the day, at the very point of which was fired the first shot.

It is impossible for me to describe the particular attacks of each division. They all had in their front different batteries and breastworks; and they were all carried in the handsomest possible manner.

The resistance was by no means such as I expected to have seen, or such as the position authorised. One after another the different works fell into the hands of our gallant fellows, with a loss infinitely less than ought to have been occasioned; but it is possible it was never the intention of the enemy to risk the loss of any number of them by engaging in a general action; for certainly this can hardly be called a general action, although it was a general attack, everything almost having been carried by our light troops before the supporting columns could come into action.

Nothing could be more beautiful than the manner in which the French retired from one height to another; they never stood long enough to be severely pressed, and consequently never had any difficulty in re-forming on one hill after having been driven from another.

The severe part of the action, I believe, fell upon the 3rd and 7th Divisions. John Keane's brigade suffered severely. I saw him about five o'clock in the afternoon. He then told me he had lost about 400 men, and he was then again immediately under fire, but I apprehend did not suffer much, as the action entirely ceased with the day. I have not since seen him, but he is, I understand, very well out of it.

We have advanced about three leagues, not, I think, much to our advantage as far as obtaining quarters for our men goes. In the villages few inhabitants are left, and those few have been so plundered as to render it impossible for us to get any assistance from them; and the roads are so dreadfully bad that I fear the difficulty of provisioning our people will be extreme, and nothing but a very considerable advance into a better country can, in my mind, save us having great distress.

If (as I conclude was the case) the object of Soult was to draw us on without committing himself, and to keep harassing us in our winter quarters, he has done his business well.

We shall, I expect, move on again in a day or two, and if we can manage to drive the enemy beyond the Nive, and get a good road from St. Jean de Luz to the right of our position, we may be able to maintain ourselves; but even in this case I fear the troops must pass the winter in camp.

What is to become of us I do not know! Nothing but an advance that would enable us to extend away towards Pau, into a country where there is forage for us, would save us serious Josses. A day or two will show; and in a day or two I will write again.

The 7th are today at Sarrè and Vera.

I take it the British and Portuguese loss in the action was about 2000. The French could not have lost so many. They lost about 1000 prisoners, 500 of them very clumsily.

Sarrè, November 12, 1813.

My letter of this morning, from St. Pè, will have told you of the action having taken place on the 10th (having been postponed from the 8th in consequence of the badness of the roads from wet weather) and of the result.

I now write from the quarters of my advanced squadron, (Colonel Kerrison's); three others being at Vera. This village is in the most dreadful possible state. It was one of the points most hotly contested (if indeed any may be said to have been hotly contested), and the consequences are dreadful.

The inhabitants, of course, from the fire, were compelled mostly to desert their homes; and the soldiery, on entering, completely despoiled them. In addition to all the other miseries, it is now full of wounded men; and the very house in which I am now writing contains three officers of the 68th severely wounded—Captain Gladstone, Lieutenant Clark, and another.

I have fortunately been able to afford them some small comforts, such as tea, &c., which has delighted me. That regiment has again been most unfortunate. Captain Irvin and another have been killed, and six wounded.

But to quit such melancholy subjects. This country is less mountainous than that we have left, but still infinitely impracticable for cavalry to act in; nor do I apprehend it is otherwise on this side of the Adour.

The inhabitants are but half French, Their language is Basque—perfectly unintelligible. Here and there we meet with those who speak French; but all the better classes are gone, and most of the lower.

Sarrè, November 13, 1813.

No movement; nor is it possible to move, for such a day of rain I never yet witnessed. I cannot do better, therefore, than sit down to answer *seriatim* all your last letters.

First, with respect to the things to be sent to me. They would now be truly acceptable; for nothing is to be had here for love or money. I send you some general regulations as to the conveyance of baggage to officers. If my things are not sent off, pray have the goodness to let them be sent to Plymouth, to be forwarded as therein directed.

You are become a prodigious politician, and enter most heartily into the affairs of the North! Boney, it now seems, has truly got himself into a scrape. He has gone to Paris, we hear, to call out 800,000 men! Will they come at his call? France has no longer the assistance of other Powers either in feeding or paying her armies. The Allies are, I conclude, now beyond the Rhine; and men, money, and provisions must all now come from France, whilst all the North will, with one heart and soul, be united against her.

I hope, for my part, that the Allied Powers will be content to find France driven within her original boundaries; I am not satisfied to say her 'natural' one, the Rhine; for that would leave her Holland, and that I am not disposed to do.

As to H——, he is absent, sick; he is not quite what he ought to be at bottom in any way, I fear. You know what a fuss he made about coming out, and yesterday I received a letter from him, saying that his fever was gone, but that his *constitution was so shattered* that it required the care of his friends in England to restore it, and begging me to make application for leave! Only conceive this at the moment when the regiment is just commencing upon active service! If he was half dead he never should have asked such a thing. There are hundreds of officers in the army who are now serving, having had the similar fever without going home; but there is more vapour than anything else about that young man! I said, before I left England, that he would be the first to wish to return; you see what a true prophet I am.

*****

After the battle of the Nivelle, the English were situated in a very contracted space, and Wellington was anxious to extend his cantonments, and gain possession of more fertile districts by pushing his way across the Nive and throwing the enemy entirely back under the cannon of Bayonne.

But the heavy and long-continued rains rendered the roads impassable for artillery, and prevented his taking advantage of his passage of the Nivelle, and indeed of his making any offensive operations until the end of the first week in December.—*Alison*, vol. 9. p. 874.

Colonel Vivian was now promoted to a brigade, and had appointed Captain E. Keane (a relation of his wife) his A.D.C.

*****

St. Jean de Luz,
November 26, 1813.

My dearest Eli,—Although I have not a word more to say than when I last wrote, I cannot let the packet sail without giving you a few lines.

I have, since my last, been staying in this neighbourhood with my different friends. Sir S. Cotton, Waldegrave, Ponsonby, &c. I am just now going to join my brigade, which is between Ustarits and Cambo, on the river Nive. I shall today dine with Sir L. Cole, on my way.

I assure you it makes me very miserable to part with my old friends, the 7th. Not a soul shall I have about me but new faces, excepting Edward, to whom I have written to desire him to join me as soon as possible; but that I expect cannot be for a week.

As it is necessary now that as colonel on the staff, which gives me about 28s. a day, I must keep a somewhat better table than usual, I was yesterday extravagant enough (or rather, in short, I was obliged, in order to put myself on a level with my brother brigadiers) to give Lord Waldegrave £200 for his canteens. I shall sell my own, I hope, for about £60 or £70, and I have Waldegrave's a great bargain; for they cost near £300. Most of the articles are silver. I wish, by-the-bye, you would get from Thompson the bills for the whole amount of the canteens, in order that I may know how to sell them.

I will write again as soon as I get to my brigade and see how things are going on. There is an idea that we shall shortly have something to do, but I rather doubt it just at present.

The weather is now more beautiful than anything you can imagine; and, strange to say, we are all complaining of colds, headaches, &c. &c. Amongst the others I am rather an invalid with one of my old feverish attacks, but very trifling; not, in fact, worth mentioning.

I suppose you may have seen Grant. He sailed in the last packet and was not only, I hear, most wretchedly unwell, but very homesick; and so, to tell you the truth, is the whole army, and peace would delight everybody, and no one more than your ever affectionate husband.

★ ★ ★ ★ ★

Laressore, the place from which Colonel Vivian wrote the letter about to be quoted, is on the Nive, between Ustarits and Cambo.

Colonel Vivian was at this time in command of the cavalry posted between Cambo and Laressore, with General Hill's division. See *Alison*, vol. 9. p. 876; and *Life of Napoleon*, p. 371.

★ ★ ★ ★ ★

Château de St. Martin, Laressore,
December 2, 1813.

Here I am, my dearest Eliza, in the midst of my brigade—in the midst of the enemy! Out of the very window of the room from whence I now write this I can almost converse with the French sentries! Nothing but a narrow river (the Nive) separates us; and it is fordable in many places; but they are very quiet, harmless neighbours.

We have agreed not to fire at each other; and they are too much afraid of an attack from us to make it at all probable that they will molest us in our quarters. If they chose it would not be a very difficult matter to walk into my bedroom any night. There is, however, a brigade of infantry in the village, under General Pringle, and they would hold them. We could do nothing, for it is nothing but hill and dale!

You can have no conception of anything more magnificently

beautiful than the situation of my *château*, which is on the point of a hill overlooking a beautiful mountain river, and looking up a most delightful valley, through which runs the river, the hills rising from the valley on either side crowned with timber; villages in abundance, bordering on the river.

But it is to the eye only that it is now delightful. The ravages of war have depopulated these otherwise charming residences; few, if any, of the inhabitants remain, and what few do remain are almost starving from having been eaten out of house and home by the soldiery, with whom their houses are literally crammed. General Hill's division, of which I command the cavalry, is posted in the villages of Cambo, Espelette, Souraide, and Laressore— altogether about 12,000 men within a space of three miles of each other.

On our left, at Ustarits, is the 6th Division, Sir H. Clinton, about a mile off. I am just going there to dine and sleep at General Pack's.

Beyond Ustarits, at Arauntz, is the third division, with which John Keane is. He came here yesterday to see me, and I expect him tomorrow to stay a day or two.

They talk of an advance soon, but I do not think it possible; for the roads are in such a dreadful state from the constant rain we have had that it is perfectly impossible for troops to move.

I have just received your two letters, Nos. 13 and 14. No. 12 has not yet come to hand. It is, I conclude, gone to the 7th, from whence Edward will bring it. What has become of that man I cannot imagine! He ought to have joined me a week since.

Here I am in a great *château*, with no soul about me I ever saw before. I have, however, a pretty good sort of a Brigade-Major—a Scotchman—Captain Dunbar; and Harvey, who commands the 14th, together with all his officers, has been attention itself, and when Ned comes I shall be very comfortable; but I never shall forget the loss of the dear old 7th.

I send you, for your amusement, a copy of a letter I wrote to K [Kerrison] after being appointed to the command of the brigade. I wrote it in a hurry, and it is but a scrawl. I have had no answer to it as yet. I think if they do not write me a very handsome epistle in return they are very unhandsome fellows; for they never will have any one at their head who will take half the pains about them—and, though I say it who should not—

will do half as much for them as I have. No regiment out here was in half the order they were when I gave up the command of it. Every one said so. How long it will last so I cannot pretend to say, but I hope some time, for the officers are all most anxious, and there is a good system which is not to be lost in a day. Keep the letter I send you. I will send you also the answer.

Many thanks for the articles you have sent me. They have not yet arrived—at least, I have not heard of it. You, like a *stupid* woman, do not mention the name of the man or the ship; so I must send to Passages on a wild-goose chase. Oh, Eliza, after having been married to me for nine years and a half, to be so very thick! Jarvis goes off tomorrow to search for the packages. The contents, I assure you, will be most acceptable, for we are starving here, man and beast. If you had but sent a little hay also it would have been most acceptable. Candles are articles dreadfully in request, and you have sent none! Tallow are not to be had, and wax are three dollars a pound; and as I am obliged to keep a regular table every day for my A.D.C. and my Brigade-Major, these matters are of consequence.

The wine, too! I would have given the world for it! What we purchase is poisonous to the palate and ruinous to the pocket. I hope your man 'going out upon speculation' will not speculate with my goods, and sell them all! I should not wonder! Only think of you not even giving me his name, or saying what ship he went in, &c. &c.! 'A man'—as if *he* was the only man in the world! Oh, fie, Eliza! Now you must admit you *are* very stupid!

I hope, as my mother does not like John coming out, that he will give it up; if not, I will soon send him back again. I do confess I should like to receive the old gentleman in my *château* on the Nive, and show him how we soldiers live on active service. I want a livery jacket, two waistcoats, and two pair of breeches, for Walker. I wish you would get them made up ready to send out. I must also, if we remain here, have a blue and gold pelisse, jacket, &c., &c. I will, however, give you orders about all this.

John Keane is just arrived, and is making such a bother that I must conclude. He sends his love to you all. He is quite stout and well.

Château de St. Martin,
Laressore-on-the-Nive,

December 3, 1813.

My Dear Mother,—As Eliza has by this left Cornwall, and my letters can no longer be considered *pro bono publico* of the whole fireside, I take the earliest opportunity of letting you know how I go on.

You will have received a few lines announcing my appointment to the command of a brigade, since which I have been put in orders as a Colonel on the staff of the army, which gives me 20s. 9d. a day and 9s. 6d. a day battalion and forage, when they choose to pay it; but as the staff is eight months in arrear, and the army six, I must for some time to come live upon my means, which as yet (fortunately, from the cash I brought out, and the sale of two horses) are very good.

I have been obliged, in order to start my establishment for a regular table, &c. (which I am obliged to keep, having an A.D.C. [Keane] and a Brig.-Major, a Captain Dunbar, a very good sort of Scotchman) to be at some expense in canteens, &c.

"I fortunately met with a set of very good ones with Waldegrave, for which I have given him £200, and three more mules have cost me £100; and I shall do very well now, I take it. For about £600 or £700 a year I shall manage, and as my pay altogether as Lieut.-Colonel, A.D.C, Equerry, and Colonel on the Staff, is little short of £1500, I shall manage, if I stay here long enough, to save some money, for the *first time in my life*.

I am now here in the midst of my brigade, on the banks of the Nive, and the enemy is quietly opposite me; so near that I can certainly make them hear out of the room where I now write; but they are in a great fright that we should advance, and we are really very good friends, and they do not molest me, or prevent me sleeping in perfect safety and comfort.

I have a capital *château*, delightfully situated, &c. I only wish it were in England. I could sell about £10,000 worth of timber without doing any harm.

They talk of an advance very soon. I hope so, for we are terribly off for forage, and we shall get that in front. Otherwise I see no great advantage that is likely to arise from the movement. They say the army is to place its right on the Adour, and invest Bayonne; but this they cannot do without crossing the river, and it will ensure a winter campaign in a wretchedly muddy country.

* * * * *

Wellington's object in his advance across the Nive was to place his right on the Adour, whereby the enemy, already distressed for want of provisions, would lose the means of communication with the interior by the river, and be compelled to fall back to other, and more distant, quarters from which to draw his resources.—*Alison*, vol. 9. p. 877.

* * * * *

We gentle cavaliers are to cover the rear towards Navarrenx, Oloron, and Pau, where the French cavalry are. There are only three weak brigades of ours up—Vandeleur's, Alten's, and mine—altogether about 2000. If the country will suit we shall soon have some more up. My old regiment, the 28th, are here in the village with me; but very few of my old friends are left.

Château St. Martin, Laressore,
December 8, 1813,

My dearest Eli,—Your dear letter of November 26 has just arrived. I have only a few minutes to write and thank you for it, having many arrangements to make in consequence of an order to march tomorrow to the attack that is to take place on the enemy's left. God send us a good day of it. I hope we shall be amongst them. I will take care of myself for your dear sake.

John Keane has been staying with me for the last two days, and Ned has joined me; so I have been quite *en famille*—only wanted you and dear Cresp. I am glad John has given up the idea of coming out here, as it fretted my father and mother—dear people, they are too good to be fretted.

What glorious news from Holland; surely there never was such a scrape as Boney is in. They do say that the people of France are all ready to rise. These hereabouts abuse little Nap terribly.

What stuff and nonsense it is about the papers and the duty; it is no such thing; there is not an officer in the army who has not a regular paper. Tell Huntley to send me the *Globe*. Ned joins in love.

Excuse this scrawl. I have some excuse; you have none, and I cannot read half of your letter!

Jeys, jun., is just returned from Passages. No accounts of the prog!

* * * * *

On December 7th, orders were issued for forcing the passage of the Nive on the 9th. Hope was to attack the French and keep their troops in check, whilst Beresford and Hill crossed the Nive. Beresford, with the 2nd and 6th divisions, was to cross at Ustarits; whilst Hill, with the 3rd Division, Hamilton's Portuguese, Vivian's and Victor Alten's cavalry, and fourteen guns, was to ford the river at Cambo and Laressore; and to cover Hill, on the right, Morillo's Spaniards were to cross at Itzazu. Foy was in front of Laressore, and Paris and D'Erlon were nearby on the heights.

On the 9th, Hill forced the passage above and below Cambo with slight resistance, though the fords were so deep that several horsemen were drowned, and the French strongly posted at Halzou.

Hill placed a brigade of infantry at Urcurray, to cover the bridge of Cambo, and to support the cavalry, which he despatched to scour the roads towards Lahoussoa, St. Jean Pied-de-Port, and Hasparren, and to observe Paris and Pierre Soult; whilst he himself marched to the heights of Larmenthoa.

The greatest danger now was that Paris, reinforced by Soult, should have returned and fallen either on Morillo or the brigade left at Urcurray in the rear, whilst Soult, reinforcing D'Erlon, attacked Hill and Beresford in front. It was to prevent this that Hope and Alten pressed the enemy on the left.

The Allies were now divided by the Nive; and Soult determined to attack their left on the 10th. In order to do so, he abandoned the heights in Hill's front. Wellington directed Hill to occupy these, and at the same time moved the 3rd, 4th, and 7th Divisions to the left to oppose Soult, who was then repulsed.

On the 11th there was a thick fog, but Soult sent his cavalry over the Nive at Mousseroles, to check the incursions of Hill's horsemen.

On the 13th, Soult marched against Hill, and drove the Allied posts from Hasparren. Colonel Napier, in giving an account of this day's proceedings in his history, says:

Colonel Vivian, who commanded there, immediately ordered Major Brotherton to charge with the 14th Dragoons across the bridge; but it was an ill-judged order, and the improbability of succeeding so manifest, that when Brotherton, noted throughout the army for his daring, galloped forward, only two men and one subaltern—Lieutenant Southwell—passed the narrow bridge with him, and they were all taken.

Vivian then, seeing his error, charged with his whole brigade to rescue them, yet in vain; he was forced to fall back upon Urcurray, where Morillo's Spaniards had relieved the British infantry brigade on the 11th.

This threatening movement induced General Hill to put the British brigade in march again from Urcurray on the 13th, but he recalled it at sunset, having then discovered Soult's columns passing the Nive by the boat bridge above Bayonne.

In the night of the 13th the rain swelled the Nive, and carried away the Allies' means of communication. It was soon restored; but, on the morning of the 13th, General Hill was completely cut off from the rest of the army, and while seven French divisions approached him in front, an eighth, under Paris, and the cavalry division of Soult menaced him in the rear.

To meet the French in his front he had less than 14,000 men; and there were only 4000 Spaniards and Vivian's cavalry at Urcurrav.

The battle of St. Pierre on the 13th resulted in Soult being repulsed by Hill. Yet the French maintained their line towards the Adour, for Sparre's cavalry, passing out that May, rejoined Soult on the side of Hasparren.

During the day Soult and Paris menaced Morillo's and Vivian's cavalry at Urcurray; however, not more than thirty men of a side were hurt, and when Soult's ill-success became known, the French retired to Bonloc."

It will be seen that whilst Colonel Napier describes the order given by Colonel Vivian on the 13th, as an "ill-judged one," and "improbable of success," yet Colonel Vivian gives a very different account of it in the letter copied post.

According to his account (and as he was on the spot, and wrote immediately after the event, he ought to have known what actually occurred), his object was to "drive the enemy out of the town," and he says nothing about an order to charge the bridge: but he states that the two officers were taken prisoners "in consequence of their extravagant gallantry;" which, even according to Colonel Napier's statement about Major Brotherton, appears extremely probable.

The above is not the only occasion in which Colonel Napier thought fit to attempt to disparage Colonel Vivian's abilities as a soldier, as will be seen hereafter.

Napier's account, founded on the evidence of Major W. Brotherton, who commanded the 14th Light Dragoons on this occasion, was, as he subsequently admitted, 'in some measure wrong,' and he promised to set the matter right in any future editions of his work.—*Royal United Service Journal*, October, 1896.

Among the preparations described by *Alison* as having been made by Wellington for the passage of the Nive was this:

> On the right Sir Rowland Hill, with the 2nd and Portuguese divisions, Vivian's and Victor Alten's cavalry, and Rosses horse artillery, was to put himself in motion in the night between the 8th and 9th, so as to pass the Nive by the fords of Cambo at daybreak on the latter day, and advance by the great road from St. Jean Pied-de-Port towards Bayonne.
> The main attack was to be made by the centre and right.
> Hill's troops, on the 9th, under cover of the artillery, forced the passage on the right above and below Cambo, and drove the French left wing back on the great road to Bayonne. With such vigour was the onset made that Foy, who commanded in that quarter, was separated from his men and driven across the fields towards Hasparren.
> Hill shortly after noon attacked D'Armagnac's troops at Villefranche and the heights adjoining, and, after some sharp fighting and one repulse, drove them out of the former, and established themselves in strength on the latter, the French retiring in heavy rain, by deep and almost impassable roads, towards Bayonne.
> During the night Soult drew back his forces into the entrenched camp at Bayonne, and early on the 10th issued forth with 60,000 men to assail one-half of the Allies, not mustering more than 30,000, on the British left, many of whom, not thinking of an attack, had retired to their cantonments, some miles in the rear.
> The French were at first partly successful, but ultimately were repulsed.
> On the 11th more fighting took place, when about 600 on each side were killed.
> On the 12th a severe cannonade killed about 400 on each side, and on the night of the 12th Soult again attacked Hill, and by daylight of the 13th had placed 35,000 men in front of him, while 7000 menaced his rear.
> Beresford's bridge over the Nive had been swept away, so that Hill was unsupported; but, though his position was at one time

extremely critical, he held his ground till Wellington arrived with other divisions of the army and drove the enemy back into their entrenched camp.

★ ★ ★ ★ ★

Hasparren, December 14, 1813.

After five hours' fighting, and a prospect of five more, here we are, not much advanced; nor shall be until the lord gets Bayonne—and that is not the work of a day or week!

Soult is determined to die hard. He has attacked three days following, and always with great loss. We cover the right flank, and have not had much to do.

The French have two brigades of cavalry opposed to me, and Lord Wellington having called for one of ray regiments, I was left with the 14th alone—about 350—to look after them. This has worried and harassed me much. For four days I have never undressed; but last night Alten's brigade arrived to my support. I then determined to avenge myself for the impertinence of the enemy, and advanced with the 14th to drive them out of this town, in which I succeeded, making some prisoners, and killing and wounding a few others; but, I am sorry to say, with the loss on our side of Major Brotherton and Lieutenant Southwell taken prisoners.

The officers were taken owing to their *extravagant gallantry*. They rushed so far into the French that one had his horse killed, and the other was taken away in the crowd.

Urt, December 18, 1813.

My dearest Eli,—Ever since the crossing of the Nive on the 9th I have been so constantly in sight of the enemy, and so constantly on the alert, that I have not had time to sit down and write to a single friend, excepting only the few minutes I found for your service the other day. I am now but little more quiet. On my flank is the Adour, with Foy's division of infantry on the other side; and in my front is the 5th regiment of *Chasseurs-à-cheval*. I have with me 200 infantry only, so that I must look out! The 5th Chasseurs are nearly as strong as my brigade!

This is the most infernal country' to campaign in I ever met with. For ten days I have been covered with mud. You can have no conception of the sort of lanes—I can't call them roads—that we have here; up and down stiff hills, knee deep in mud.

From head to foot we are all covered, and, being without our baggage, you may imagine we are pretty figures.

In every other respect the country is good. In spring it must be beautiful. The houses are good; the inhabitants civil; and plenty of everything to be had; that is, plenty of chickens, eggs, &c..

They all are, or pretend to be, rejoiced at our arrival. It certainly has saved their sons from the conscription—they say to the amount of 1500 in the country we now occupy; but I do not anywhere observe a spirit of resistance to the conscription. They all say: 'We are rejoiced you are arrived as it has saved us;' but they do nowhere say, 'We would not have gone.' However, an ensign who is believed to be an agent of the Royalist party yesterday came to us to say that the people in the interior were everywhere disposed to rise, and that we have nothing to do but cross the Adour; but I fear the Adour is not so easily crossed, for the roads here are so tremendously bad that it really is quite out of the question endeavouring to advance with an army and supplies, &c.

I have no conception how we get on even now, and I shall be much surprised if all our baggage animals do not die under it. In the event of any reverse I am confident that the immediate consequence would be the entire loss of all our baggage; but I do not like to anticipate misfortunes. I hope the reverse will happen; but if Buonaparte is able to call out the conscription, and assemble 100,000 men at Bordeaux, we can advance but little further.

How admirably things go on in the north. I long to hear the Allies have crossed the Rhine, and to know the result. If the French have any spunk in them they will assuredly follow the example of Holland and get rid of the tyrant. Nothing but his fall can restore peace to Europe; and the sooner the day comes the better.

★ ★ ★ ★ ★

At this time, Russia, Austria, and Prussia, had combined together and were pre paring to invade France; but they had not yet crossed the Rhine.

The object of both generals, at this period of the war, was to nourish their armies and circumvent their adversary in this respect. Soult aimed to make Wellington retire into Spain; Wellington to make Soult abandon Bayonne, or so reduce his force in the entrenched camp that the works might be stormed. At Urt, the stream being narrow, the navigation could be interrupted. Soult therefore ordered Foy to build a fortified bridge there, but Wellington menaced him with a superior force, and made him recross the river.

Soult, embarrassed by Foy's failure, reinforced him with Boyer's and D'Armagnac's divisions, and transferred his headquarters to Peyrehorade.

★ ★ ★ ★ ★

Urt (on the River Adour),
December 23, 1813.

Tomorrow, my dearest Eli, is the birthday of my darling boy. I shall commence the day by offering a prayer for his happiness and that of the dear woman who gave him birth; and I shall end it by dining oft' a roast turkey and drinking the largest bumper of wine I can get to both your dear healths. Thornhill and Fraser I have written to, to come and partake of the cheer my house affords, both for tomorrow and Christmas day. I have a turkey one day, and a goose the next, stuffed with potatoes.

I am now quartered in the country house of one of the best and dearest women in the world. Don't be jealous now, Eli; for observe, she is upwards of fifty years old, and is a widow with daughters as old as you; but, alas, the daughters are absent. So to return to my widow; never did there exist a better woman. Poor soul! she is frightened out of her wits, and she considers me her guardian angel. She cannot do too much for me; her house, and everything belonging to it, is at my service, and Madame Genevoit is never happy unless she is conferring some act of kindness on me. Stewed pears, stewed apples, jellies, preserves, and wines, are daily furnished for my table, together with the nicest napkins and table-cloths I ever saw.

Her property is small, but delightfully situated, consisting of vineyards and garden ground. She has two boys and two girls, and her house is a little outside the town, beautifully situated on the magnificent river Adour. We occupy a very comfortable parlour (only a stone floor), two capital bedrooms, a good kitchen, and excellent stables, farmyard, &c.; and altogether we could not, on this side of the water, have found better Christmas quarters.

I very much fear, however, I shall not remain here long, for Alten is going home, and they have desired me to take his brigade. I have begged to decline and keep that I have, which I like very much; and I hope my prayers may be heard. If not I must go off to Hasparren, which is now full of infantry, and which consequently I have no fancy for; for it is the devil to be so situated! We are now stuck fast in mud and water; no possibility of moving, either for the enemy or us; nor do I suppose either party wish it. We all want a little rest!

I expect General Fane here tomorrow, to take charge of I know not what besides my brigade; but to please him, they must, forsooth, call him a general of division! There is nothing here but Spaniards and myself. However, I shall do very well with him, I have no doubt.

The 7th are now at Hasparren. From Fellows I hear that they have already been three days without bread—literally starving—and two men have shot themselves. They will want me back soon I expect!

You have no conception of anything so abominably cold as the letter I received from —— in answer to one I wrote him taking leave of the regiment. My letter was dictated from my heart, and I spoke my feelings towards the regiment. I know not what dictated the answer: but I should feel excessively sorry if I thought any officer of the regiment approved of it. In short, it was by no means such a letter as I had a right to expect, and in fact did expect, from them; but *n'importe*! I cannot help liking them still, and have applied to have them, if I may, in my brigade.

I am a stupid man! I made up this letter and directed it to Lord Uxbridge, so I must now put it into an envelope, which will cost you something for nothing.

I will now tell you the news of my family. Higgins goes on admirably; he is really a most excellent servant; always ready, always good humoured. William also is very good. Jarvis and his wife are most useful people. Walker is so ill that he must go to England. Edward Walker was taken prisoner with my mules, as I told you before.

My horses are all well. 'Dragon,' still fat as a beast; and so is the horse you rode—'Johnny.' 'Jane' and 'Slasher' quite well. Poor 'Dash' still at Bilbao.

I have just heard that Grant was taken, going home. Poor fellow, he was very ill. I am truly sorry for him. In the packet were letters for you, Sharpe, Hodge, and Lord Uxbridge. Pray write to the two former to explain my silence. Two mails have now arrived without a letter from you. How is this?

★ ★ ★ ★ ★

Colonel Vivian was now transferred from his former brigade, of the 10th and 14th, to that of General Alten, consisting of the 18th and German Hussars, who were quartered at Hasparren. He, however, did not take over the command of them till January 1, 1814.

Just before Colonel Vivian took command of this brigade, the 18th Hussars, whilst on a foraging expedition, had a severe skirmish near Mendione and Macaye, during which the Spaniards, under Morillo, who were with them, withdrew, without informing Major Hughes, who commanded the 18th, of their intention. The cavalry were consequently turned, and escaped with difficulty, having had one captain killed, and two others (Hughes himself and a lieutenant) wounded.

The unfortunate issue of this affair was attributed to the bad conduct of the 18th Hussars, against whom Wellington was, by a malicious misrepresentation, previously prejudiced; for at Vitoria they had been unjustly accused of being more licentious in plundering than others.—*Life of Napoleon*, c. 6. p. 414.

★ ★ ★ ★ ★

Urt, December 29, 1813.

My Dearest Eli,—It is now upwards of a month since the date of your last letter. What in the name of mercy can occasion this long silence? I hear there is another mail at headquarters; but as the post goes tomorrow, I shall write you in order that you may not be disappointed in the manner I have been.

I desired Edward this morning to write to you, thinking it possible that I might not return from the outposts in time. However, I have a quarter of an hour to dinner, and I cannot employ this time better than by assuring you, myself, of my health, &c. Edward will, I have no doubt, have told you how we go on in every way. I am sorry to say that I have left my dear old widow's house. General Fane, as a senior officer, turned me out! However, I am by no means in an uncomfortable house, appertaining to *Mons. le Medecin*, who, with his young wife, has fled to Dax, leaving his house all to me. Of course he fled before I arrived, or, I flatter myself, the *young wife, at all events, would have remained*!

We are in very comfortable quarters, and, as yet, have plenty to eat and drink, and, thank God, Edward and myself are as well as any fellow in England. I cannot say so much for my household. Poor Walker gets worse daily, and is of no use whatever. Higgins is far from well; William still worse. Blofield, my *famille* orderly, goes into general hospital with a fever. Old Foxlow and Hubbard in great force. My horses and mules in great force. So much for family concerns.

I am appointed to the command of General Alten's brigade, consisting of the 18th and German Hussars. I would much rather have kept the one I had, but Fane is to have it, as Grant does not return. I hope in my new one to change the Germans for the 7th, and then I shall be happy. I saw Thornhill two days since at Hasparren. He tells me the 7th are going on very badly. K—— has no management, no arrangement; in short, they want me back, so he says; and this is, he tells me, the wish of the majority of the officers.

However, I suppose the men do not think so; for he lets them do pretty well as they like, and after he had made them a speech, on my going, they gave him three cheers. He is always courting popularity, you know. I never cared a damn for it. I did my duty. Those that pleased might like or dislike me. However, I cannot help thinking, if it were put to the vote of both men and officers, I should have the majority. I am sure I should of all those worth commanding.

Pray write constantly, and long letters. No news of my things from Falmouth!

Hasparren, January 5, 1814.

My Dearest Eli,—I arrived here on the 1st of the month to take charge of my new brigade, the 18th Hussars and German Hussars. I assure you I do not like them half as well as the last. I shall see tomorrow what they are made of, for these impertinent fellows, the French, have of late been disturbing us considerably; and we mean therefore to make them pay for it.

I have for the last two days had my old friends, the 7th, under my command, and I assure you I was delighted to see them; and for the last two days also I have had the pleasure of giving my old friends, Thornhill, Fraser, Kerrison, and Lowther, a good dinner, when they otherwise would have starved. Fraser and Thornhill are now in the room with me, and desire to be most kindly remembered.

We have had no mail from England since that of the 9th, and we are consequently in a very considerable state of anxiety as to the proceedings of our Allies in the north. There is a report that Switzerland has joined us; if so, it is a great thing for the Imperial army in Italy.

I hope after tomorrow we shall have a little peace and quiet for some time; but, to tell you the truth, I do not much expect it. I shall, however, be better able to tell you how this is likely to be after we have settled the business with these impertinent fellows who are now annoying me.

January 8.—I have just time to tell you that both Ned and myself are alive and well. The French, on the 6th, ran like merry fellows; and we ran after them; but they had the heels of us. We will now, I hope, have a little peace and quiet for a week or ten days.

We fully expect a peace here, at which I shall be delighted; although it will lose me about £1000 a year, if I am not on the staff.

No things yet arrived at Passages. Sugar 3s. 6d. a pound; hams 2s. 6d.; fowls 12s. a couple; and everything else in proportion; and I have to feed four people—A.D.C., Brigade-Major, and Quarter-Master-General Campbell! My B.-M. is a nice young German, Claudt.

★ ★ ★ ★ ★

Wellington had intended to fall upon the enemy at once, but the swelling of the small rivers prevented him.

However, on January 5, the Portuguese marched against the French right; the 4th Division against their centre; the 3rd, supported by cavalry, against their left; the remainder of the cavalry and the 7th Division, under Sir S. Cotton, were posted at Hasparren to watch Paris on the side of Bonloc.

Soult was at Bastide de Clarence, and a general battle appeared imminent; but the intention of the English general was merely to drive back the enemy from the Joyeuse; and the French gen-

eral, thinking the whole Allied army was in movement, directed the troops at La Costa to retire fighting upon the Bidouze,
The affair terminated therefore with a slight skirmish on the evening of the 6th, and the Allies resumed their old positions.—
Life of Napoleon, vol. 6. p. 417.

* * * * *

Hasparren, January 11, 1814.

I have received your letter, my dearest John, of December 24. A thousand thanks for the good wishes it contains, which I return to you, and to all the house of Vivian, with tenfold interest.

We are pretty much in the same position as when I last wrote to Truro. Covering too much ground, we are liable at any moment to be harassed by the enemy; and they daily take advantage of it. A day seldom passes without my being roused out to the outposts, to stand like a crow to be shot at for half an hour!

When this is over we are all the best friends possible, and ride down to the river and talk across it as affectionately as if we were sworn allies! I should tell you that the river is precisely such a stream as runs at the bottom of our garden (neither more nor less), fordable in ten thousand places, but an excellent line of demarcation; and such it is understood to be.

This morning at half-past four I was roused out of my bed by a considerable firing of musketry. I galloped down to the advance and found that the enemy had attacked a hill on their side of the water, on which I had a sergeant and six, and a sergeant and twelve infantry.

They came on with about 150 men. Of course they soon drove us beyond the river; but, the firing still continuing, I went down and holloaed to the French to cease firing and to send an officer to me.

In a very short time an A.D.C. of D'Armagnac's came to me, and I asked him if his only object had been to carry the post. If so, I told him, he should have had it by asking for it, without the loss of two or three poor fellows' lives on each side; to which he replied he had done; it was their only object to gain the bank of the river, and he concluded that I would admit that they had a right to it as the proper line. I assented. The firing ceased; and we talked together for half an hour.

I mention this to show you how we go on. A forage, or any

trifle, brings on a skirmish daily; but it ends in our all being the best friends possible; and this I expect will be the case for some weeks to come, when we shall either have a peace, or advance, or retreat. A peace I scarcely look to; there is so much to settle. Nothing but Austria positively saying *"Je le veux"* will do, to my mind. As to Lord Castlereagh's mission, I view it more as a warlike than as a peaceable embassy.

Advance we cannot, without more troops; and you are sending them all to Holland. Retreat we will not, whilst we can feed where we are. We have now about 45,000 effective British and Portuguese, and the army is very healthy, but dreadfully reduced from hard blows. Divisions that were 6000, 7000, and 8000 men, are now 3000 and 4000; none exceed 5000. Some regiments that left Portugal 900 strong have not now 200 effective—many, I may say.

We have nothing but hard work, so we keep up very well. My brigade is 800, as you will see by the return I send for your amusement and information.

We have a report that the grand Allied army have marched upon Basle, and from thence are to advance to Lyons and cut off Italy. It would be a bold move if it takes place. More extraordinary things have occurred than that we should give them a hand; but I can scarcely look to such an event.

What stuff and nonsense the papers talk about Bayonne being blockaded, &c.! We have not a man across the Adour, and the French have just as free an exit to Bordeaux as you would have from Bodmin to Truro if the enemy were at Chevala and Calenick. We have no chance, in my mind, of getting Bayonne without a siege; and then it will be a work of six weeks or two months, with the loss of at least 5000 men in the siege, and with the certainty of a general action. You may judge from this what prospect there is of our advancing much.

At present we are much crippled also by a want of forage; but when the grass begins to grow, the valleys of this country are so fertile that they will afford us excellent green forage, and get up the horses that are not starved between this and then; and we shall then, I conclude, think of moving on. I expect it will be by marching towards Dax; but much is to be done between this and then.

Instead of saying we are crippled for want of forage, I should have said that our cavalry are literally starving; neither hay nor corn! The country is exhausted by the number of troops that are feeding on it. My horses are as yet doing very well. If the brigadier commanding the advanced cavalry cannot take care of himself, who should? 'Dragon' is as fat as butter.

I wish to heaven you had come out to me. I do not keep the worst table in the world, I assure you; but had you come, I should have purchased the pleasure dearly at the expense of the feelings of our parents; so all is for the best!

Since I commenced this I have been to the advanced posts, and agreed with the French not to fire on each other but in cases of a serious attack; so we now ride along, side by side, within five yards of each other, without any more danger of being shot than you are in when hunting on the town burrows. This is doing as gentlemen should. They really are devilish civil, honourable fellows, and know how to make war. They behaved admirably to the two officers of the 14th made prisoners.

If we have a peace I shall return through Paris, if I can, to save the misery of the sea.

★ ★ ★ ★ ★

In the sixth volume of Napier's *History*, p. 422, several instances are given of the friendly intercourse that at this time existed, by mutual agreement, between the French and English outposts.

★ ★ ★ ★ ★

Hasparren January 14, 1814.

My dearest Eli,—Ned will have told you all the news here, how we go on. &c. &c. He has more time than I have, for he is never happy but 'over a fire of wood,' or, I must do him the justice to say, 'under a fire of shot,' or in bed! He is a good creature, but *entre nous*, the very indolentest (to coin a word for the occasion) young man I ever met with,

We are precisely in the *statu quo* as when I last wrote you, and so I expect we shall remain for some time to come—a week or ten days. By that time, if we do not move on, I expect Mr. Soult will think of trying to make us move back,

John Keane is quartered close to us, and we see a good deal of him. He is a very good fellow, a very good officer, and very much liked,

We are all very anxious here for news from the Austrian army that is advancing upon Lyons. We hear from the French themselves of their having arrived at Besançon. I wish to God we could give them a hand, and advance with them; but the bad roads and the want of transport will completely prevent our moving for some time,

We are most anxious to hear also the result of Lord Castlereagh's embassy. For my part, I think he is principally gone from an alarm lest the Allies should make a peace and leave us in the lurch. I am not one of those Quixotes who calculate upon marching to Paris, unless well seconded by the French themselves; and therefore I think that the best way will be to make a good peace whilst we can. By a 'good peace' I mean an honourable and liberal one to all parties. It will not do to screw any one too tight; the consequence would be a renewal of the war on the first opportunity; and, for my part, if I once sheathe the sword I do not wish again to unsheathe it.

So much for my speculations on affairs. By-the-bye, clearest Eli, I am always delighted to have yours in return; but I wish you would not half fill your letters, as you do sometimes, with news from the papers, the whole of which I see. Your paper is too small, and you have so many other things to write about, that I can spare this! As to papers, I am almost the only officer in the army who has them not. Once more I beg you to desire Huntley to send me the *Globe*. Ned grumbles terribly at their non-arrival. I tell him it is all your fault!

I hear there are several ships lost near Passages. I am in a great fright for my hams, tongues, &c. I shall send again very soon after them.

Poor Walker was so ill that I was obliged to send him off last week for England; and poor old Foxlow was, last week, also left in general hospital at Cambo. William has also been very ill, but is now much better. All the rest stout and well. I have now an excellent establishment, but in the event of advancing into France I shall send all my valuables to the rear, so I shall not yet part with my old canteens.

Hasparren, January 21, 1814.

My Dearest Eli,—I again return to my weekly duty of announcing to you my being perfectly well, &c.

Nothing whatever worth mentioning has occurred since I last wrote, except that poor Higgins, two days since, was severely wounded whilst on a foraging expedition. The ball went through his arm into his side, and ran round the muscles of his back, lodging almost close to the bone, from whence it was extracted, and he is now doing as well as possible.

My old friends, the 7th, have been great invalids for the last week. Churnside, I am sorry to say, is seriously ill still. Lowther has been in bed for six days, but writes me word this morning that he is better. As soon as he is able to move he is to come to my house to stay; their kindness to you demands some return from me. Pipon has been very ill, and still looks dreadfully so. Uniacke is in hospital in the rear, and Kerrison and Thornhill have been ailing. Old Irvin is more altered than any man I ever saw. Ned and your humble servant were never in more perfect preservation, and if a comfortable house and good living will keep us so, we shall have, I hope, no reason to complain.

The French and ourselves remain exactly in *statu quo*—all quiet and likely to continue so. I yesterday talked for a considerable time to a French officer. He told me Turkey had declared war against Russia and us, and that Buonaparte had gone from Paris at the head of 100,000 Imperial Guards for Lyons, where he would find 350,000 of the *levée en masse*, with the magistrates at their head. I told him I thought they would be well *commanded—that the magistrates would make good generals, no doubt*! But, in truth, I believe not a word of what he said. Buonaparte has not 100,000 Imperial Guards, nor have the people risen *en masse*. We have reports of insurrections at Nantes, Toulouse, &c., but I believe not half the reports I hear.

★ ★ ★ ★ ★

Napoleon had ordered a levy of 300,000 conscripts; but it was not till January 25 that he set out from Paris; on the 29th he defeated Blucher at Brienne.

★ ★ ★ ★ ★

Lord Castlereagh has, I have no doubt, gone to prevent a separate peace; and I should not be surprised to see a general one take place. Austria must have some little feeling for Marie Louise. A very few weeks will let us into the secret. We shall soon see how things are likely to go!

It is a great pity that we cannot stir from here to assist the Austrians; but we cannot move. The impossibility of transporting provisions, Sec, with us, precludes all hope of our going on.

I write to Hodge by this post, and have sent him my letter to the regiment on leaving it, and answer, with directions to send it to you. You will, I am sure, see that I have reason to complain. I have never said a syllable to anyone but Thornhill on the subject, and I hear from him that several officers disapproved of it, but did not like to speak.

We are in expectation of a mail. Our last is only up to the 31st. There is a report that the brevet is stopped on account of the expectation of peace. If so, I hope it will be stopped altogether; for to be a major-general, unemployed, all peace, would make me poorer than ever by taking from me my A.D.C.'s pay. However, we shall be able to do very well by living quietly in the country on what we have. I will see it fairly out, this war, come what will; and then, having once sheathed my sword, I hope never again to draw it, but to pass the remainder of my days in peace and quiet with my Elizabeth and her boy, and all those that I love best in the world about me.

If the war continues I wish you to pack up and send out for me my two A.D.C's coats, six shirts, four pair of net pantaloon drawers, four under-waistcoats of the same, twelve pair half stockings (thin worsted), six black neckties, six of the white waistcoats I have at home, and half a dozen pairs of the nankeen overalls and white trowsers, some of each, for summer wear.

I have written to Hodge about some other things he is to send; among the rest some hams, &c. He will send all together. Communicate with him and settle between you; but send nothing till peace or war is decided.

Direct your letters *France* not Spain.

Hasparren, January 28, 1814.

Another week, dearest Eli, and nothing has occurred to disturb us in our quarters; and the weather is now so dreadfully bad as to prevent either party from moving for some time to come. In fact, before it is possible for us to do so, I expect something very decided will have occurred; for, if report speaks true, the Allied army is rapidly advancing into France; but I confess myself I expect a peace. The Emperor of Austria seems so disposed, and all the other powers must of course say aye.

★ ★ ★ ★ ★

At this time the whole country was a vast quagmire. It was with difficulty that provisions, or even orders, could be conveyed to the different quarters; December and January were thus passed by the Allies.—*Life of Napoleon*, vol. 6. p. 423.

★ ★ ★ ★ ★

Your two letters of December 31 and January 4 arrived together. I do not expect a brevet, because, if there is peace, they will be obliged to give another; and therefore, notwithstanding all reports to the contrary that we have had, I think that they will hardly give us one just yet. It makes very little difference to me. In fact, if there is a peace, it would be worse for me being a Major-General; for in that case I should be off the staff, and lose my A.D.C.'s pay; for I certainly would not go to the East or West Indies from choice, and I could not expect to be employed in England. So I should take a house, and sit down quietly in the country, and keep a pig—a horse, I fear, I should not be able to afford, unless times changed.

You must have been in a sad fuss about us during your suspense, before the official documents arrived. But be assured of it, we, the cavalry, can have but little hard fighting until we advance considerably out of this country. It is by no means adapted for mounted gentlemen!

What possibly can make you suppose that I shall be quietly settled at Bordeaux? Depend on it there is no chance of that! If there is peace, we shall move back into Spain to embark; if there is a continuance of the war, we shall not be quietly settled at Bordeaux.

If the war goes on send me the things I mentioned in my last, but no wine; we shall do very well with the wine of this country. It is not claret, but very like it.

My horses, goats, servants, and dogs, all well; excepting poor 'Dash' who has not yet returned from Bilbao. 'Slasher' and 'Jane' as fat as butter. Higgins was tipsy yesterday for the first time, but he is greatly ashamed of himself. I gave it him properly, both with my tongue and hand; for I pushed him head first into his room and locked him in! I never saw a fellow so penitent, and he is in truth an excellent servant. It was an old fellow-servant of his that he met with who gave him some brandy-and-water before dinner, and he was overtaken he knew not how! Lowther is better; he is living in my house. I sent my last letter by Colonel Hawkins of the 69th. He will call on you if he can.

Hasparren, February 3, 1814.

My dearest Eli,—Your letter of the 17th has just this instant reached me. . . .

I have no idea but that we must shortly have a peace, let the advance of the enemy be what it may. My opinion is that, notwithstanding their talk of peace, the Allies mean, if they can, to walk to Paris and upset Boney. They know there is no safety for Europe else, and they think that by giving out that peace is likely to take place, the people of France are more likely to remain peaceably at home in their houses, than if they were at once to declare that they would march to Paris and overthrow the present Government. I only lament that we cannot move on and assist them in this operation, but, alas! the weather gets worse and worse here, and there is not the slightest chance of our being able to move for a very considerable time; so I cannot get my head knocked off if I would. There is no hope for you at present!

You will, ere this reaches you, have seen my letter to ———, and his answer. I do not believe the man dislikes me. I believe he was jealous of me, and was not anxious that the officers should pay me any particular mark of attention on leaving them. You will observe that in ———'s letter, there is not one expression of regret at my quitting the regiment. I blame the officers for allowing this letter, for it was a reply to one from me addressed generally.

They should, if they disapproved of ———'s answer, have said so. However, I have had several messages on the subject, all very gratifying; and if ——— dislikes me, I heap hot coals on his head, for I have been invariably civil to him ever since, and in two or three instances have had the pleasure of giving him a dinner when he would not otherwise have had one.

I hear you correspond with Thornhill! Robbins told me he saw a very *handsome* letter of yours on the subject of my leaving the regiment. The old sinner did not show it to me! He generally dines and sleeps at my house once or twice a week, and so does Fraser. He is now by my side and begs to be kindly remembered.

John Keane also has just called in, and he desires to be kindly remembered. He is an excellent fellow and, as I told you before, no man more liked, and no better officer.

No news yet of the hams, which I much regret; for my housekeeping is now most ruinous. Sugar and butter 5s. a pound! My last week's bills are 62 dollars. This is ruination!

I have just had an order to be in readiness to move on with my brigade in about a fortnight, I am to have the advance guard of cavalry; so I shall, in about six weeks, write from Paris.

* * * * *

The advance actually commenced on February 13. On that day the Anglo-Portuguese army numbered about 70,000—10,000 being cavalry—and with the Spaniards it amounted to 100,000.

The English general's first design was to threaten the French left, and turn it by the sources of the river with Hill's corps.

On the 12th and 13th, Hill's corps was concentrated about Urcurray and Hasparren.

On the 14th they marched in two columns. One by Bonloc, to drive the French posts beyond the Joyeuse; and the other against Harispe, who was at Hellette.

On the 15th, Hill marched upon Garis, and Beresford sent a brigade of the 7th division to the Bastide de Clarence. The front was extended from Urt towards Garis—a distance of twenty miles—and was too attenuated.

The fight near St. Palais alluded to in the following letter is described in *Life of Napoleon*, vol. 6. p. 529.

* * * * *

Ayherre, February 16, 1814.

At last, my dearest Eli, we have had a week's fine weather, and we have made a forward movement, hitherto without any opposition.

The day before yesterday, the 2nd Division, under Sir R. Hill, with the 3rd, a Portuguese, and Morillo's Spaniards, in all amounting to about 18,000 men, advanced from Hasparren upon St. Palais. They reached Hellette the first night. Last night they skirmished rather sharply near St. Palais, and this morning, I hear, they have entered it, the enemy having retired.

My brigade is at Bardos and this place. We have not fired a shot, but I have been very considerably harassed, riding about from morning till night.

The country here is by no means as rich as what we have left. The mountains, or rather, large ranges of heathy hills, do not abut in fertile valleys; and what there was the French have exhausted; in short, they have *abîméd* (to anglicise a French term) the country. Forage and provisions of all sorts are not to be had for love or money, and unless we soon move on and get into a better country we shall literally starve. Bread is not to be had, nor are chickens, sheep, &c. Bad beef and biscuit, and my Cornish tongues, constitute our dinner food.

I expect we shall find considerable opposition in crossing the Gave de Pau, and still more the Adour; but I suppose the lord has some plan in his head by which he thinks suddenly to pounce upon these *monsieurs*; and they will find him on the other side of the Adour before they know what he is about! They talk of his crossing at the mouth of the River Adour. I almost doubt it. I rather suspect his preparations for so doing are all sham, and that he will cross somewhere about Urt or Urcnit. However, there is no saying; he is a close sort of chap!

However, if he is right, we shall not cross at all; for I heard him take four to one in *dubloons* that we heard of peace being made before the 21st of this month. *Eh, bien*! If so, old girl, I shall have the pleasure of hugging you in my arms before I am many months older; but still, I cannot help believing that the Allies have no intention of making peace with Boney. I am persuaded they consider him a troublesome dog that is better out of the way, and therefore will set him aside if they can; and all this talk of making peace with him is humbug, in order that he may not have a handle to move the people by.

The Allies must now be pretty near Paris, if it is destined that they are to get there at all.

I have sold the pair of canteens that I purchased from Lord Waldegrave for £200 to Lowther, and have sent the money to the agents. My pay and allowances will, I hope, more than cover my expenses here, although lately things have been most exorbitantly dear. I paid, last week only, 82 dollars! You see I have to keep a daily table for four, both breakfast and dinner; and this is the very devil! However, I must try and get on as well as I can. I am afraid I am going to experience a sad loss (certainly for some time, at least) in the services of the horse that was John's; his leg has for some time been dreadfully swollen and inflamed, and now it has gathered and broken, and he can scarcely walk. However, we must rub on as we can.

'Dash' has joined me from Bilbao with his leg quite recovered—only a little lame. All the rest of my family are in high preservation. I have got a beautiful cock turkey, which I mean to bring to England with me, if I can. I never saw so tame a bird, or so handsome an one. I have two goats, and that is all my animals in addition to those with which you are already acquainted.

Ned is blooming, but as lazy, and not more talkative, as ever. I ought not, I think, to say 'as lazy' quite; for I do now and then get him out a little early, and to bustle a bit!

I must now shut up my epistle to send to headquarters tomorrow, so *adieu*.

★ ★ ★ ★ ★

On February 23 Colonel Vivian was with Beresford's divisions, who held the line of the Bidouze down to its confluence with the Adour.

Apparently to distract the enemy, Beresford threw a battalion over the Adour at Urt, and collected boats there as if to form a bridge.

In the evening he recalled this detachment, yet continued the semblance of building a bridge until late on the 23rd, when he moved forward and drove Foy from Overgave and Hastingues into the entrenchments near the bridge of Peyrehorade. The Allies lost fifty men, but Soult's right and centre were thus held in check; for Beresford, having the 4th and 7th Divisions and Vivian's cavalry, was strong enough for Foy at Peyrehorade, and Taupin at the Bastide de Béarn. The rest of the French army was distributed at Orthez and Sauveterre.

On February 24 Wellington put his troops in motion to pass the Gave d'Oloron. The ford at Villenave, about three miles below Doguen, was where Wellington intended to cross the Adour at this part of his position; but he made feints of passing the river at Monfort, Barraute, and Sauveterre; and Vivian's Hussars, coming up from Beresford's right, threatened all the fords between Picton's left and the Bastide de Béarn; and below this some detachments were directed upon the fords of Sindos,

Castagnhede, and Hauterive.

Beresford, during this movement, kept Foy in check at Peyrehorade with the 7th division, and sent the 4th towards Sordes and Laren to seek a fit place to throw a bridge over.

Thus the whole of the French front was menaced on a line of twenty-five miles; but the great force was above Sauveterre.

The first operations were not happily directed on the side of Sindos, for the columns there missed the fords.

Picton opened a cannonade against the bridge-head at Sauveterre, and made four companies of Keane's brigade and some cavalry, pass the Gave in the vicinity of the bridge. They were immediately assailed by a French regiment, and driven across the river, with the loss of ninety men and officers, of whom some were drowned, and some made prisoners; whereupon the cavalry returned to the right bank, and the cannonade ceased.—*Life of Napoleon*, vol. 6 p. 547.

Colonel Vivian alludes to this affair in the next letter, and he explains how it occurred.

On the 25th Lord Wellington was near Orthez with the 2nd, 6th, and Light Divisions, and five regiments of cavalry.

The 3rd Division and a brigade of cavalry were in front of the broken bridge of Bereux. The 4th and 7th Divisions, with Vivian's cavalry, were in front of Peyrehorade, from whence Foy retired by the great Bayonne road to Orthez.—*Life of Napoleon*, vol. 6. p. 549.

★ ★ ★ ★ ★

Bastide de Béarn,
On the Gave d'Oloron,
February 25, 1814.

My dearest Eli,—Since I last wrote from Ayherre I have been so constantly on the move that I have not had a minute's leisure to write.

We are arrived thus far without any serious opposition, and the weather has favoured us excessively. It has not rained now for upwards of a fortnight, and in consequence all the rivers are fordable, and the roads passable; and if it only lasts fine for a few days longer, we shall, I hope, succeed in passing the Adour.

Lord Wellington yesterday passed the Gave d'Oloron above Sauveterre with the 2nd and Light Divisions, and a Portuguese and Spanish division, and my old brigade of cavalry. He had no fighting.

At Sauveterre was the 3rd Division, with Lord E. Somerset's brigade of cavalry, with orders to threaten a passage there, but not to cross. Somehow or other, however, either through Sir S. Cotton or Picton, the Light companies of John Keane's brigade passed, and, not being supported, they were driven back with the loss of five officers and forty men, killed and wounded. John's horse was wounded, and I only wonder at his getting back at all! There were very high words between Picton and Cotton on the disaster happening, and I expect some inquiry will follow. Thank God, John is not blamed, as far as I can learn; he received positive orders to cross.

I must tell you how gallantly our friend Fraser behaved; and I beg of you to write the account to Lady Fraser, from me. It will so delight her—Sir William, at least.

Sir S. Cotton called for a subaltern and six men of the 7th to lead the way across the river in order to show the ford to the infantry; and, no subaltern being immediately in front of the regiment, there was the trifling delay of sending to the rear of a squadron for one; upon which, Sir S. Cotton reflected on the slowness of the Hussars, and said he wished he had one of the old brigades there.

Fraser was by, and heard this, and he most gallantly said, 'Subaltern or captain, it is no matter which, I will take the six men over, and lead the way across. And this he did through a most difficult and deep ford (so bad that several infantry were drowned), and under a very severe fire of the enemy's infantry from a house on the other side, and he was the first man that landed. As God's mercy would have it, neither he nor any of his men were touched. How they escaped is wonderful!

Now to return to the position of the army. My brigade was (and is now) on the left of the 3rd Division, with orders to threaten the fords over the Gave between Sauveterre and Peyrehorade.

On my left is Marshal Beresford, with the 4th and 7th Divisions, opposite Peyrehorade.

The 6th Division is at Bardos, and the 5th and 1st, under Sir J. Hope, are watching Bayonne. What they have been doing

I know not; but there was a very heavy firing there two days since. Whether they have passed the Adour there, or not, I cannot say; but there is a report that such a plan is in contemplation."

Sir J. Hope crossed the Adour below Bayonne on the 23rd, which would account for the firing heard by Colonel Vivian.

We are now getting into a country where the houses begin to look French, the furniture neat, most admirable beds, the people all understanding a little French, and everything to be had excepting tea, sugar, and butter, and I am sorry to say that my stock of the two latter is nearly exhausted.

I fear there may be some delay in sending your letters, as the post is now irregular.

February 26.—Puyoo. Near Peyrehorade. All well.

Puyoo, February 27, 1814.

My dearest Eli,—I finished a letter last night by dating it and saying ' all well." From this time I shall write you a sort of journal of our movements, &c., by which means I shall be able, day by day, to devote some little time to it, and also have a letter ready to be despatched by every opportunity.

February 25.—We marched from Bastide de Béarn on the 25th to Sorde, Cassabe, and Carivo, villages on the banks of the Gave d'Oloron, and I was quartered in a capital *château* belonging to the ancient Comte de Berieux, at Cassabe, where we found every comfort, and which put us in mind of a good old English nobleman's house. The count was himself absent; but his *aumônier* and his *homme d'affaires* did the honours.

The corps of General Hill was opposite Orthez; and Beresford, with three divisions, was between the two Gaves, near me: Sir J. Hope, with two divisions and the Spaniards, covering Bayonne; Sir J. Hope himself having passed the Adour by landing the 1st Division at Cape Le Breton.

February 26.—Marched from Cassabe, &c., and crossed the Gave de Pau with four squadrons at Hointon, and with two, with the infantry, at Sorde.

On arriving in the great road leading from Peyrehorade to Pau (which, by the way, is more admirable than any road I ever beheld), I found that a party of the enemy's cavalry were in the village of Puyoo, and having selected twenty well-mounted men, with them and the patrol of about as many I charged them, supported by the squadron.

After a chase of two miles as hard as we could race along the road, we overtook them and cut down and took about half a dozen, and were, I thought, in complete possession of the rest; but they, having fallen back on a small party of their supports, and our troop horses being all almost blown and tired from their bad condition, the enemy in turn halted upon their support, and charged us. The men deserted their officers, who were in front, and Ned and Hughes of the 18th were very nearly taken. Ned jumped over a hedge and saved himself. I was not far from it. The enemy chased us for about five hundred yards, when I got the fellows a little together and again turned upon them; but by this time the horses were so blown that nothing more was to be done, and we remained in quiet possession of our prisoners, without the loss of a man. One fellow made a cut at Ned, and Ned cut again and passed on; the fellow then turned upon me and gave point, but I cut at his elbow and disarmed him and left him to a man of the 18th.

After this we quietly put up here, in a very comfortable house of a Mr. Rheinhardt, a West India planter formerly, with a wife and eight children—some daughters beautiful!

The 3rd and 4th Divisions passed us on the great road towards Orthez.

The Hussar Brigade put up at some villages on this and the other side of the Gave de Pau, and the corps under Hill is marching from Orthez towards this place to cross.

★ ★ ★ ★ ★

Napier describes the events of this day (so far as they concern Vivian's Brigade) thus:

On the 26th, Beresford, finding that Foy had abandoned Peyrehorade, passed the river. He had previously detached the 18th Hussars to find a ford higher up, and, this being effected under the guidance of a miller, the Hussars gained the high road about halfway between Peyrehorade and Orthez, and drove some French cavalry through Puyoo and Ramous.

The French, rallying on their reserves, turned, and beat back the foremost of their pursuers, but could not await the shock of the main body, now reinforced by Vivian's Brigade, and commanded by Beresford in person.

In this affair Major Sewell, an officer of the staff, happening to be without a sword, pulled a large stake from the hedge and with that weapon overthrew two hostile Frenchmen in succession.

The negligence of the French officer who had suffered Vivian's Hussars to pass at Puyoo without making any report, enabled Beresford to make the movements he did in safety, when otherwise he might have been assailed by at least two-thirds of the French army.

It was not till three in the afternoon that Soult received intelligence of this movement; and then Beresford's columns were close to Baights, on the right flank of the French army; his scouts were on the Dax road, and at the same time the 6th and Light Divisions were seen descending by various roads from the heights beyond the river, pointing towards Berenx.

In this crisis Soult hesitated whether to fall upon Beresford and Picton, while the last was crossing the river, or to take up a defensive position; but he finally decided on the latter, and took up his position at Orthez.

★ ★ ★ ★ ★

February 27.—We shall probably not move today.

The enemy are said to be in force at Orthez, but I believe they have no idea of waiting for us.

We have with us six divisions of British, one Spanish, and altogether are about 35,000 men.

The enemy have nearly as many. Our heavy cavalry are marching up. At present we are short of cavalry, having only seven regiments, averaging about 350 each. The 7th are stronger. The enemy, however, are not stronger; but their horses are in better condition.

★ ★ ★ ★ ★

On the 27th, the 6th and Light Divisions, having crossed the river, were on the road of Peyrehorade.

Beresford, with the 4th and 7th Divisions, and Vivian's cavalry, had meanwhile gained the ridge of St. Boës, and approached the Dax road beyond.

Hill menaced the bridge of Orthez; and between Beresford and Picton there were no troops, but an old Roman camp, on which Lord

Wellington surveyed the enemy's position immediately before the battle of Orthez.

Lord Wellington determined to assail the French chiefly on the side of St. Boës, with the intent to overlap their right and seize the St. Sever road, while Hill passed the river at Souars and cut off the road to Pau, and in this way to enclose the French in Orthez. The village of St. Boës was strongly fortified.

★ ★ ★ ★ ★

Mont Marsan, March 2, 1814.

I was completely out in my reckoning as to our not moving, and the enemy not waiting for us! I had scarcely finished my paragraph before I received an order to march immediately, we found the enemy in position, waiting for us on some strong heights covering Orthez, and the whole British army was marching to attack him.

General Hill, with the 2nd and 15th Light Divisions, attacked their left.

The 3rd and 6th Divisions, with Lord Wellington, attacked their centre.

The Light, 7th, and 4th Divisions attacked their right.

The attack commenced about eleven o'clock, and the 4th Division met with great resistance in the village of St. Boës, which was taken and retaken three times.

After about three hours' very severe fighting the enemy began to give way on every point, but still retiring regularly and defending their ground from position to position until towards five o'clock, when they were completely *en déroute*!

The ground was altogether excessively unfavourable for cavalry; but towards evening our old friends the 7th were fortunate enough, with three troops—Heyliggen's, Lowther's, and Elphinstone's—to get in among their broken infantry. Kerrison and Thornhill were of the party. Nothing, I understand, could have behaved better than the dear old regiment.

Thornhill charged an officer with a colour, who, with the pike at the end of it, struck him in the stomach, but not severely, and he secured both the colour and the officer, and walked back (for he was in too much pain to ride) with his trophy, and met Lord Wellington, who was much pleased; and I hope it will secure him the rank of lieut.-colonel. Poor Heyliggen is again wounded severely, in the thigh.

I, unfortunately, could not all day get into action with my brigade; that is to say, I could not get amongst them. I was almost all day under a cannonade, but I kept my men under the hedges, hills, &c., and so saved them. The country was completely intersected by deep ditches and enormous enclosures, and it was only by getting into the fields in small parties that the 7th got at them. Douglas had his horse killed, and Robbins his wounded. The loss of the British during the day was about 3000 men; that of the enemy much greater, besides a considerable number of prisoners and guns, &c.

On the night of the 27th I bivouacked my brigade at Bonnegarde, near Sault de Navailles. My baggage and everything was in the rear, and we had to exist on what we could find in a miserable farmhouse.

★ ★ ★ ★ ★

Napier says the British lost 2200; Soult, 4000 in killed and wounded and six guns.

With regard to the charge made by the 7th Hussars, and alluded to by Colonel Vivian, Alison says:

> Cotton charged on the only occasion that presented itself, at the head of Somerset's Dragoons and the 7th Hussars, three battalions of the enemy, which he broke, and made 300 prisoners; but although 2000 more threw down their arms in an enclosed field, the greater part contrived to escape across the river, which was not far distant.

At the battle of Orthez Colonel Vivian's Brigade was, as has been seen, with the 4th and 7th Divisions on the heights of St. Boës. Napier says that this village was carried five times, but Taupin's supporting masses had on each occasion forced the shattered columns back again.

On the other side of the battlefield also the 3rd and 6th Divisions had made no progress.

Some Portuguese troops, sent to assist the attack on St. Boës, gave way in disorder, and the French pouring on, the British retreated through St. Boës with great difficulty, and Soult felt confident of victory.

Wellington, however, now changed his plan of battle. Supporting Ross with Anson's Brigade, which hitherto had not been engaged, he backed both with the 7th division and Vivian's cavalry, now forming one mass, towards the Dax road.

He threw the 3rd and 6th Divisions on Foy's flank, and sent the 52nd from the Roman camp to assail the French flank and the rear, engaged with the 4th Division at St. Boës.

With a mighty shout and rolling fire the 52nd dashed forward between Foy and Taupin, throwing everything before them into confusion. Foy was dangerously wounded, and his troops got into disorder and retreated.

The narrow pass beyond St. Boës was thus opened, and Wellington, seizing the critical moment, thrust the 4th and 7th Divisions, Vivian's cavalry, and two batteries of artillery through, and spread a front beyond.—*The Life of Napoleon*, vol. 6 p. 561.

The victory was thus secured. The 7th and 3rd Divisions continued to advance, and the wings of the army were united.

Hill had forded the river at Souars and now menaced Soult's line of retreat by Salspice, on the road to St. Sever, just at the time when the Allies" wings were united; and Soult immediately determined to retreat, but the French yielded step by step and without confusion.

As the danger of being cut off by Hill at Salspice became more imminent, the retreat became more hurried.

Hill, seeing this, quickened his pace, till both sides began to run violently, and the whole country was covered with scattered bands.

Sir S. Cotton then, breaking with Somerset's Brigade, through a small covering body opposed to him by Harispe, cut off about 2000 men. The 7th Hussars cut them off in an enclosed field, but some confusion occurring, the greatest part, recovering their weapons, escaped. The pursuit ceased at the Luy de Béarn.

The vigour of the pursuit after this battle would probably have been greater but for Lord Wellington having been struck by a musket-ball just above the thigh, which caused him to ride with difficulty, though he was early on horseback on the following morning.

Soult, in his retreat, abandoned his magazines at Mont-de-Marsan, and on the following day Wellington detached Beresford, with the Light Division and Vivian's cavalry, to seize them, whilst he himself continued in pursuit of Soult, during which time a combat took place at Tarbes.

In his observations on the operations that had been taking place since the advance on the 13th February, Napier points out that on the 15th and 16th Soult, by rapid and well-digested combinations, might have united four divisions of infantry and a brigade of cavalry to attack Beresford between the Nive and the Adour; when, if successful, the defeated English, pushed back on the 6th Division, must have fought for their lives, with the rivers on their flanks, Soult in front, and the garrison of Bayonne in their rear.

Again, he says that before Orthez Soult's original design was to assail the head of the first column that should come near him, and Beresford's approach to Baights on the 26th furnished the opportunity.

It was true that the French cavalry gave intelligence of Beresford's march too late, and thereby marred the combination; but there was still time to fall on the head of that column while the 3rd Division was crossing the river and entangled in the narrow road leading from the ford to the Peyrehorade road.

It was not till the morning of the 27th that Wellington discovered that Soult meant to fight, and that he himself was in a false position. Instead of hesitating, or assuming the defensive, which would have drawn Soult's attention to his ticklish position, Wellington confidently sent Picton forward as if to assail the French left, and put Beresford in movement against their right, with all the coolness imaginable. The success was complete.'—*The Life of Napoleon*, vol. 6. p. 577.

A full account of the battle of Orthez is given in *The Life of Napoleon*, vol. 6. p. 555, and *Alison*, vol. 10. p. 320; but perhaps the best account of all is that contained in Lord Wellington's despatch, from which the following is extracted:

> On the 24th Sir R. Hill passed the Gave d'Oloron at Villeneuve; while Sir T. Picton made demonstrations of an intention to attack the enemy's position at the bridge of Sauveterre, which induced the enemy to blow up that bridge.
>
> Sir W. Beresford likewise, who since the movement of Sir R. Hill on the 14th and 15th, had remained with the 4th and 7th Divisions, and Colonel Vivian's Brigade, in observation on the lower Bidouze, attacked the enemy on the 23rd in their fortified posts at Hastingues and Oyergave, on the left of the Gave de Pan, and obliged them to retire within the *tête de pont* of Peyrehorade.
>
> Immediately after the passage of the Gave d'Oloron was effected, Sir R. Hill and Sir H. Clinton moved towards Orthez and the great road leading from that town to Sauveterre, and

the enemy retired in the night from Sauveterre across the Gave de Pau, and assembled their army near Orthez, on the 25th, having destroyed all the bridges on the river.

The right, and the right of the centre of the army, assembled opposite Orthez; Sir S. Cotton, with Lord E. Somerset's Brigade, and the 3rd Division, under Sir T. Picton, was near the destroyed bridge of Berenx; Sir W. Beresford, with the 4th and 7th Divisions, under Sir L. Cole, and Colonel Vivian's Brigade, towards the junction of the Gave de Pau with the Gave d'Oloron.

The troops opposed to Sir W. Beresford having marched on the 25th, he crossed the Gave de Pau below the junction of the Gave d'Oloron, on the morning of the 26th, and moved along the high road from Peyrehorade towards Orthez, on the enemy's right.

As he approached. Sir S. Cotton crossed with the cavalry, and Sir T. Picton with the 3rd Division, below the bridge of Berenx; and I moved the 6th and Light divisions to the same point; and Sir R. Hill occupied the heights opposite Orthez and the high road leading to Sauveterre.

On the 27th I ordered Sir W. Beresford to turn and attack the enemy's right with the 4th division, and the 7th Division and Colonel Vivian's cavalry; while Sir T. Picton should move along the high road leading from Peyrehorade to Orthez, and attack the heights on which the enemy's centre and left stood, with the 3rd and 6th Divisions, supported by Sir S. Cotton and Lord E. Somerset's Brigade.

Sir W. Beresford carried the village of St. Boës with the 4th Division, after an obstinate resistance by the enemy; but the ground was so narrow that the troops could not deploy to attack the heights, and it was impossible to turn the enemy by their right without an excessive extension of our line.

I therefore so altered the plan of action as to order the immediate advance of the 3rd and 6th Divisions, and I moved forward Colonel Bernard's Light Division to attack the left of the heights on which the enemy stood.

This attack dislodged the enemy from the heights, and gave us the victory.

In the meantime Sir R. Hill had forced the passage of the Gave above Orthez, and, seeing the state of the action, he moved immediately with the 2nd Division and Fane's cavalry direct for the great road from Orthez to St. Sever, thus keeping on the enemy's left.

The enemy retired at first in admirable order, taking every advantage of the numerous good positions which the country afforded. The losses, however, which they sustained in the continuous attacks of our troops, and the danger with which they were threatened by Sir R. Hill's movement soon accelerated their movements, and the retreat at length became a flight, and their troops were in the utmost disorder.

Sir S. Cotton took advantage of the only opportunity which offered to charge with Lord E. Somerset's Brigade in the neighbourhood of Sault de Navailles, where the enemy had been driven from the high road by Sir R. Hill. The 7th Hussars distinguished themselves upon this occasion and made many prisoners.

The whole country is scattered with the enemy's dead, and their army was in the utmost confusion when I last saw it.

We followed the enemy the day after to this place (St. Sever), and we today (March 1st) passed the Adour.

Sir W. Beresford, with the Light Division and Colonel Vivian's Brigade, marched upon Mont-de-Marsan, where he has taken a very large magazine of provisions.

The charge made by the 7th Hussars, under Lord E. Somerset, was highly meritorious.

Colonel Vivian's conduct in the battle of Orthez earned for him the approbation of Sir W. Beresford, and he was awarded a clasp to his gold Peninsular medal.

Vivian continues his account thus:

★ ★ ★ ★ ★

February 28.—At daybreak commenced our march in pursuit of the enemy; but the roads were so bad that the left wing, with which my brigade was, could not get to St. Sever in time enough to co-operate in an attack on the enemy, who had been obliged to halt in position there in order to cover the retreat of their artillery, &c., over the bridge of the Adour, which is behind that town. Had we got up I have no doubt but that the principal part of Soults army would have been destroyed. As it is, they are completely disorganised.

My brigade halted this night at the village of Mauntot, on the Adour. Fortunately, in the house of the mayor, I got for myself and staff a very tolerable dinner, or we must have starved, as my baggage was still in the rear."

The combat alluded to above was one that took place at Caceres, when a charge of cavalry was made and a few men and officers hurt on each side.

March 1.—We marched at daybreak, as we thought, to attack the enemy in position at St. Sever; but Soult was too wise! His halt had answered his purpose. He had secured his retreat, and, at one o'clock in the morning, had quitted St. Sever and marched upon Grenade towards Aire.

We then received orders to ford the Adour and march upon this place (Mont-Marsan), and here, at last, we have had a day's rest from our fatigues, and here, at last, I have had the good fortune to be joined by my baggage, after having been as uncomfortable and as dirty a pig, for two days, as ever existed!

We are now got into the department of the Landes, a sandy desert just getting into cultivation; but beyond this, towards Bordeaux, a complete desert altogether.

This town in which we now are is the capital; and a very delightful one it is. Situated on the Midouze—a stream navigable for boats from Bayonne—it has the means of procuring from that port every sort of French luxury, so that we are admirably off for a few days, and I hope that we shall stay here for a little to refresh, and then, I conclude, we shall march again to the Garonne, behind which Soult's army is retiring.

I reckon Agen will be our point. Some say we are to go to Bordeaux; but I expect Sir J. Hope will go there after having taken Bayonne, which he is, I believe, now besieging.

I think that the thing must be settled either one way or the other before we again come to blows. If the Allies have met with any reverses, of which we find Buonaparte boasting in his Paris journals, they will be disposed to make peace; if, on the other hand, they are successful, the French will certainly declare themselves.

Here they are well disposed towards us; but the absolute dread they have of Napoleon is such that they are afraid to move. They, however, prevented the Prefect from blowing up a beautiful new bridge here before his departure, which there were orders for doing; and they now mount guard for the protection of the peace of the town in conjunction with our soldiers!

March 2.—Mont-Marsan. We have delicious wine here. *I can never drink strong wine again!*

The poor little Major! How mad he will be when Thornhill gets his lieutenant-colonelcy!

* * * * *

The following letter is written on paper at the top of which is printed the official heading of the "*Préfecture de Marsan.*"

* * * * *

Mont-de-Marsan, March 3, 1814.

Paper running short, my dearest Eli, I cannot do better than take advantage of a good stock found in the house of the Prefect, who has absconded!

We are still here, in comfortable quarters; and thank God we are so, for such a dreadful day I never witnessed—hail, rain, snow, thunder, lightning, and wind!

In this town everything is to be procured. It is situated at the commencement of the sandy desert that runs from the Garonne to the Adour and up to the sea on the west; but this place, being on a navigable river (the Midouze), receives all sorts of supplies from Bayonne. I believe I told you this before!

We have found some remains here of our ancestors; the bridge and the church were both built by the English; but Buonaparte has just built a most beautiful new bridge which, on our arrival, was not yet opened for passengers. I think it is by far the neatest piece of architecture I ever saw. It must be admitted that, with all his iniquities, the Corsican has done much for this country. He has built a new prefecture also, not yet inhabited.

My landlord—M. Barrère—has supplied me with excellent claret and brandy, gratis. This is a nice country to make war in! Whilst I am now writing, an order has arrived to march immediately; so I must shut up.

March 4.—I now write from the most miserable habitation, in the midst of a pine forest. My brigade around me dispersed over ten miles of ground. What a change from yesterday!

We moved, it seems, to attack the enemy who had taken up a position near Aire, near Barcelone, and where they had had a brush with Hill's corps; but, whilst on the march, an order came for us to halt where we were as the bird was again flown towards Nogaro. Consequently two divisions and my brigade, marching in the most tremendous weather, and up to our necks in mud and quicksands, were halted and ordered to put up as well as we could. Late at night I found out the wretched hovel I am now inhabiting, after having put up my brigade as well as circumstances would admit.

I have just returned from a ride to Mont-Marsan to see my excellent host and his wife. I have never met such kind people, and I was compelled by the husband at parting to salute his wife, and, what was worse, I was obliged to submit to being myself embraced by him, in spite of garlic, &c.

Villeneuve, on the River Midouze,
March 5, 1814.

I have just marched into this place with my brigade, to look out towards Roquefort, St. Justin, Cazaubon, &c.; but there is no enemy to look after! They have retired from Nogaro towards Plaisance; I suspect with an intention of drawing Lord Wellington away from Bordeaux, and probably also of joining part of Suchet's force at Toulouse; but I do not think it improbable that Lord W. will, with the 2nd, 3rd, 4th, and 6th British and Portuguese and Spanish, and two brigades of cavalry, follow Soult, whilst he sends Beresford, with the 7th and Light Divisions, and my brigade, towards Bordeaux.

I think this is just possible, because it is certainly an object to get as fast as possible to Bordeaux, where we shall find friends; whereas the enemy is collecting there an army of National Guards, &c. I believe the original plan was that Sir J. Hope, after Bayonne fell, should proceed to Bordeaux. I understand also that the army from Holland is to land somewhere about the mouth of the Loire.

We have heard nothing from Paris since February 21, when it appeared that Buonaparte had obtained some successes over the advanced guard of Swartzenberg.

The town from whence I now write is small, but a very nice little place. I am of course very comfortably lodged in the best house in the town; my host, a very kind old man, with a kind old lady for a wife, and a family of four sons and four daughters, all grown up.

The country about, immediately on the banks of the river, is pretty; otherwise it is all sand and pine forests. The produce of the banks of the river is corn and wine. From the pines they collect quantities of turpentine by cutting down the bark and allowing the turpentine to run into a small excavation made at the bottom for its reception.

March 6.—No orders yet received to move again. No enemy near me.

My patrol has just returned from Roquefort, St. Justin, and Montguillem, and can see or hear nothing of any French troops. I have now sent off an officer and twenty men to a village near Gabarret, to take possession of an immense store I am told there is there.

March 7.—Still at Villeneuve. Nothing extraordinary.

★ ★ ★ ★ ★

On March 3 and 4 Soult retreated by Plaisance and Madiran to Rabastens, Marciac, and Alaubourget, where he halted, covering Tarbes, to await the development of his enemy's plans.—*Life of Napoleon*, vol. 6 p. 581.

★ ★ ★ ★ ★

Roquefort, March 8, 1814.

My prophecy was right. I last night received orders to march at daybreak to this place, where I have met with the 7th division marching towards Bordeaux. We are, I understand, to have with us the 4th Division, and Marshal Beresford is our commander-in-chief, and no bad one either.

★ ★ ★ ★ ★

On the 8th Beresford marched towards Langon with the 4th and 7th Divisions, Vivian's horsemen, and some guns; he was joined on the road by some of Vandeleur's cavalry from Bayonne, and he had orders to observe the enemy's movements towards Agen; for it was still in Soult's power, by a forced march on the side of that town, to cross the Garonne and enter Bordeaux before him.—*Life of Napoleon*, vol. 6 p. 593.

★ ★ ★ ★ ★

This town (Roquefort) is situated on a small stream, in the midst of a sandy desert. It has the remains of a castle which was taken three times in one day by the Black Prince; so you see we are only treading where Englishmen have trodden before. We have found throughout this country bridges castles, and churches, built by the English.

March 9.—Captieux.

After a most tremendously cold march, in frost and snow, over sixteen miles of sandy desert, a dead flat and straight road without a house, we are arrived thus far on our journey.

"I have, of course, always been tolerably well off for a quarter myself, but I have had the greatest possible difficulty in getting my brigade under cover, and then only by dispersing them over miles of country into the detached sheep-huts; but the weather is now so severe that it would kill both men and horses to bivouac them; and, as there is no enemy near, we may venture to be a little careless.

We expect at Bordeaux to meet with a quarter that will amply repay all our sufferings.

March 10.—From Captieux we marched through Bazas to the place from whence I now write this—Langon. The first part of our road was through sandy deserts and pine forests; our road made of pines laid across the road.

At Bazas we began to enter upon a better country, and between that and Langon it became delightful.

At Langon we just got a sight of that magnificent river, the Garonne; and here, in order to bring back some boats the enemy had taken to the other side, we fired three cannon shots across the Garonne—the first that have been fired by the English across that river, I apprehend.

Langon is a nice town, and we were admirably well received by the inhabitants—indeed, so we have been throughout.

★ ★ ★ ★ ★

Beresford, who reached Langon on the 10th, left Lord Dalhousie there with the bulk of the forces, and advanced with 800 cavalry.—*Life of Napoleon*, vol. 6 p. 549.

★ ★ ★ ★ ★

March 11.—From Langon we marched, on the 11th, to Castres, by a most delightful road on the banks of the Garonne, through the villages of Pignore, Sauterne, and Barsac.

Whoever would have believed that a British army would march through this country? Who would have thought that the British soldier would get drunk on their delicious wines, for which in England we pay 10s. a bottle, and which we purhase here for ten *sous*?

At Castres I was quartered at the house of a famous grower of Vin de Grave, who had in his cellar six hundred *barrigs* of wine that he could not sell. A *barrig* holds two hundred and sixty claret bottles; and he offered them all to me at less than £5 a *barrig*! I mean to purchase some as soon as I find I can get a conveyance for them to England.

March 12.—From Castres, on the morning of the 12th, we moved to this place—Bordeaux.

No words of mine can convey to you any idea of the events of this day.

We marched at daybreak. One regiment of my brigade (1st Germans) in front, two light guns, and one brigade of infantry. My other regiment had been left in the rear, dispersed through the different villages on the banks of the Garonne; and so also were the different brigades of the two divisions of infantry.

At about 8 o'clock my advanced patrol discovered that the enemy, about 600 infantry and 150 cavalry, had quitted the post they occupied the previous night, and we soon learnt that they had passed the Garonne about two o'clock that morning, and that no resistance would be offered to us.

I proceeded with my patrol into the suburbs, and at the gate I found about a hundred of the Guards of the city under arms. I rode quietly up to their commanding officer, and from him learnt that no opposition was intended.

I then also learnt that there was an intention of hoisting the white flag and declaring Louis XVIII., as soon as the mayor (Count Lynch) had made his speech to Marshal Beresford. It struck me that, at such a moment, such a declaration would appear as if dictated by the English; and, hereafter, should any reverse occur, and any dire misfortune befall the city (as I have no doubt would be the case should Buonaparte ever recover his power), that the English would be considered as the cause of it. I was most anxious that such a reflection should not attach to us, especially as, knowing we have an ambassador treating at this moment with Buonaparte the result of which may be peace with him, I felt that it would be actually base in us to allow it to be possible that, from want of explanation, it might ever be supposed we urged the hoisting of the white flag; and I directly rode back to Marshal Beresford and stated my opinion, and ventured to suggest to him the propriety of a message on the subject to the Mayor.

He immediately felt it, and desired me to go to the mayor and state that he had been sent by Lord Wellington with a corps to take possession of Bordeaux; that he was happy to enter it as a friend, and without bloodshed; that he understood there was an intention of hoisting the white flag and proclaiming Louis XVIII.; that he honoured the cause, and that, as long as the war against Napoleon existed, England would support it with their lives and fortunes; but that he was not authorised either to urge or disapprove such a step; and that whatever they did in this respect must be ever considered as an act of their own, and by no means as directed by the British.

This message I delivered verbatim in English, in the presence of Beresford's A.D.C.—Captain Sewell—and of Edward, to the Mayor, who spoke English himself, and who was also accompanied by a gentleman who spoke it perfectly. I was most particular in doing this, because, as I have said before, I felt that it might hereafter be said that we had caused any misfortune that might befall the Bordelais; and, moreover, because I was aware that there were those who would, even now, say that the English insisted on the white cockade being hoisted, in order to make those do so who might not otherwise be so disposed.

I am more particular in explaining this also to you, because you will see by the paper which I send herewith that, notwithstanding all the pains I took to explain myself on the subject, it (my message to the mayor) was interpreted as conveying an intimation that Marshal Beresford expected to find the *drapeau blanc* flying! This paper will probably get into the English papers; but, if ever it is necessary, I have witnesses as to the exact message I delivered being what I have given you. I made a memorandum of it immediately after; for hereafter it may be of consequence. The mayor replied simply that he was much obliged by the message, and that he would himself explain to Marshal Beresford his feelings on the subject.

Thus the parley ended, and we proceeded to meet the marshal; the mayor in his carriage, preceded by his *gendarmes* (twelve of them) and accompanied by an enormous mass of people, amongst them the most respectable of the city. I should have told you that the streets were crowded with people, who met us at a considerable distance from the town.

The procession of the mayor and the marshal having met, the former quitted his carriage and mounted on horseback to meet the marshal, who was also mounted.

The exclamations of the people were for some time so great that nothing could be heard. At length, silence having been obtained, the mayor commenced his speech, a copy of which I have not yet got, as it is not printed, or I would send it you—but it was almost an echo of his address, which I send; and it contained at almost the commencement a declaration in favour of Louis XVIII.

It was then I found the reason of the mayor having given me only the short answer of 'that he would himself explain to Marshal Beresford his feelings;' for the speech was a written one, and the determination to raise the white cockade was evidently their own act and deed, previously decided on; and never can it be said that the British dictated their conduct to them in this respect.

To proceed, however; as soon as the mayor had reached that part of his speech which declared in favour of Louis XVIII., the air was rent with acclamations. The mayor immediately took off the tricoloured sash, and substituted a white one; and white cockades were mounted in almost every hat.

Silence again obtained, the mayor proceeded in his speech, which was very loyal and very complimentary to the English; to which, after wonderful acclamations. Marshal Beresford, in a short reply, stated that he trusted the discipline of the British troops would prevent their ever regretting our arrival, and that, much as he honoured the steps the Bordelais had taken, he wished it fully to be understood that Lord Wellington had not directed him to urge them.

All this ended, the procession returned to the Hôtel de Mile. We all got into our quarters; and thus, thank God, without bloodshed, ended the counter revolution of Bordeaux.

I should tell you that immediately as the white cockade was hoisted a general cry of "*A bas le Tyran*" "*A bas les Aigles*" (the decoration of the caps of all the French soldiers) was heard, and, in one instant, the eagles of the *gendarmes* were flying in the air and the white cockade substituted!

Now, after all this, you will suppose the thing was finished and the Bourbons restored. Believe me, it is no such thing! There is in this city a very strong party still in favour of Buonaparte, and there are many thinking men who fear the Bordelais have been too hasty. But they have now committed themselves, and half measures will not do; they must now treat only with arms in their hands if peace should be made with the Allies and Bonev; and they must commence organising a force, or they will do nothing; and after all, I fear they want energy.

After the tumult of the day, with which I was most completely tired, I dined with Marshal Beresford and accompanied him to the theatre.

★ ★ ★ ★ ★

The mayor of Bordeaux, with the connivance of the Duke d'Angoulême, subsequently issued a proclamation stating that the Allies were united 'solely to destroy Napoleon and replace him by a Bourbon king, and that only by accepting that king could the French appease the resentment of the Spaniards;' and, when Beresford was withdrawn, they argued that Wellington, having allowed the Duke d'Angoulême to assume the civil government of Bordeaux, was bound to support him with soldiers and money!

Wellington was very indignant at these false statements, and wrote the Duke d'Angoulême that Count Lynch had not treated him with fairness or with truth; and that if his Royal Highness did not, within ten days, contradict the objectionable parts of the Mayor s proclamation, he would do so himself.—*Life of Napoleon*, vol. 6. p. 598.

★ ★ ★ ★ ★

March 13.— On the 13th I devoted part of the day to viewing this most magnificent town, much, very much, finer than anything I ever beheld, both from its situation and the arrangement of the streets and their width, the superb houses, and above all things, from the beautiful and prodigious length of the buildings on the banks of the magnificent river, the Garonne, having, in the front of the houses, a terrace on which ten carriages could pass abreast of each other,

It is impossible for me to attempt to describe every public building. The theatre is reckoned one of the most beautiful structures in the world. Of course I go to it every evening. The performance in the first place is a sort of farce, and that is followed by a ballet in which the dancing is admirable. Last night we had a most magnificent one. The Duke d'Angoulême was present, and the house crowded beyond conception. I dined with my host, a most delightful man—a Portuguese Jew, settled here for forty years as Consul, immensely rich—who gave me and my staff a most capital dinner and the most delicious wine I ever drank.

After this digression I must proceed in my account of Bordeaux. The cathedral is extremely fine, built by the English, and finer than any of ours I think. The bishop's palace, now inhabited by the Duke d'Angoulême, is a very fine building also. In fact, there are innumerable fine buildings.

Now to the living animals. The ladies promenade on the principal walks in crowds, about two o'clock. I was there, of course, to look at them! I did not much admire their faces generally; some were, however, excessively handsome. Their head-dresses were very lofty caps or bonnets, loaded with plumes of feathers. I did not like them, but, if the heads were bad, their heels repaid you; for such feet and legs, such shoes and stockings, I never saw—quite perfect, I assure you!

Now from the living animals I must proceed to the dead, and tell you that, of all things, nothing exceeds the market. The supply of fish or flesh, game of every sort, butter, &c., is the very best I ever met with; in short, the market out- markets every market I ever saw.

To be short, Bordeaux is a residence where you can have every luxury the world affords, and at about one-fourth of the price you can procure them elsewhere. I think it very fortunate that so few of the British pass here or we should lose half our population of England, for numbers would, I have no doubt, settle here.

Nothing, I assure you, that I can say can give you an adequate idea of the place, its luxuries, elegance, beauties, charms, enticements, &c. &c. &c. I do so wish you were here to see it. I declare, when we visit France, you shall visit Bordeaux; and, if there were any chance of our remaining here long, I would even now desire you to come out; but I expect we shall soon move on again.

Whilst writing this I was called to the window by Ned to see a fellow from the Landes who had come into the market walking on stilts. Anything so ridiculous you never saw! They are about four feet off the ground, and of course the man looks a monster. They say Buonaparte was frightened when first he saw them; and so also they say was a patrol of ours! They walk as quick as a horse can trot. They are obliged to use them, the roads are so covered with water.

March 15.—I dined yesterday with the marshal, to meet the Duke d'Angoulenie. He is really quite a good sort of man, but, I fear, by no means active or spirited enough for the business with which he is concerned.

I have just received a letter from poor old Thornhill, telling me that he was surprised in bed the other night by some *gendarmes*, and taken prisoner, but that after some time, when they were taking his horses out of his stable, he made his escape, losing his wardrobe, two horses, and one man!

He was sleeping in the very bed in which I had slept before. But I will send you the letter, as this is a large packet. He fancies they took him for me; but they would not have caught me so! It is a bad business; very disgraceful to the regiment, and not creditable to Thornhill. I fear it will cause a serious inquiry. There never was a post so easily guarded as Villeneuve. At a bridge, at the entrance of the place, which I barricaded, and where I had a picket, he had none. The old fool!

Lord W., with the rest of the army, is at or about Aire and Barcelone. I omitted to tell you this, and have only written about our corps.

Barsac, March 16, 1814.

My dearest Eli,—I had scarcely concluded my last sentence, which brought up my journal to yesterday, when I received an order to march this morning, at daybreak, to this place, and to join the army by forced marches.

The 4th Division also have the same order; and from all I can hear, Soult has been reinforced, so as to make it necessary for Lord Wellington to draw together as many troops as he possibly can. And now it appears that his movement upon Bordeaux with two divisions was by no means so well judged as might have been expected from his lordship. The cry it made in favour of the Bourbons has not added a man to the strength of the army; whilst the absolute necessity there is of leaving one division at Bordeaux and in the line of the Garonne to Langon, puts 5000 men *hors de combat* on our part.

It is now perfectly out of the question ever attempting to withdraw from Bordeaux; for it would compromise the safety of the town, and the entrance of one hundred French troops only would produce dreadful scenes. Even the march of my brigade caused a sensation greater than I could have supposed. The 4th Division was not in the city, so they did not see it depart. A good victory, however, would set all right very soon; but without that the affairs of the Bourbons are in a bad state in this part of the country, just now.

★ ★ ★ ★ ★

Beresford was recalled from Bordeaux with the 4th Division and Vivian's cavalry, and Lord Dalhousie remained there with only the 7th Division and three squadrons of cavalry.—*Life of Napoleon*, vol. 6 p. 595.

★ ★ ★ ★ ★

I expect there will be an action very shortly. All I fear is that we shall hardly reach the army before it is fought. We have, however, been at Bordeaux, and that repays us for retracing our steps over these horrid Landes.

The place from whence I now write is, you know, famous for its white wine, called after it. Depend on it we will not have the worst bottle in the place for our dinner this day.

I cannot tell you with what infinite regret I left the delightful Bordeaux, my most excellent quarters, and my still more excellent host. Whatever I may hereafter suffer as a soldier, the having had the good fortune to enter Bordeaux (the first British soldier) with the British army will ever reconcile me to my fate; and whenever I hear quarters talked of, I shall always say Bordeaux was the very best I ever was in.

Now for Toulouse. If I should happen to be the first British officer in there what a fortunate fellow I shall be!

More extraordinary things have happened. My brigade will generally have the good fortune to be employed on any flying expedition, I expect.

Now for a little military news, &c. I have already said that Soult is reinforced, they say to the extent of 10,000 conscripts, and 6000 from Suchet's army—the latter good troops, the former good for nothing—they will run away or desert. But, if he has the number I mention, he has about 43,000 men, besides about 4000 cavalry.

Now, we have five divisions of British, averaging about 4500 each, say 22,000; one Portuguese division, 2500; Morillo's and Frere's Spanish corps, about 10,000; altogether perhaps 35,000 infantry and 6000 cavalry. But I fear the ground where the two armies lie (between Girlan and Conchez, on the road from Pau to Auch) is bad for cavalry, so that the battle will be between the infantry; and, setting aside the Spaniards and Soult's conscripts, we shall have about 25,000 good soldiers against perhaps 33,000, or say 30,000; and we shall beat them even with this difference; but if Soult attacks before the 4th division reaches the army, he will have a still greater advantage.

Now, although I cannot too greatly admire, generally speaking, Lord Wellington's arrangements, still I think there have been great errors in many instances lately, both with our Ministers at home and our commander here.

In the first place, I think the lord was wrong to detach to Bordeaux before Soult was over the Garonne. It has taken 5000 men from him.

In the second place, the lord, it seems, has only lately, since the battle of Orthez, ordered our Anglo-Sicilian army to join; and they will not be with us for a month or six weeks; whereas part of Suchet's force has joined Soult.

In the third place, I think Ministers much to blame in not having long since sent the promised reinforcements of 9000 men to us.

And in the fourth place, I think Graham's army ought to have joined us as soon as affairs were settled in Holland.

On the lord's part also, I think there has been more delay in bringing our battery train up to Bayonne than necessary; but, however, of this I do not know much. This I do know, that the capture of Bayonne would give us 15,000 men, and also be of the utmost consequence.

Only conceive, if we had but our reinforcements, &c., as before enumerated, what an army we should have!

There are now in the field:

Infantry (British, Spanish, and Portuguese)	35,000
At Bordeaux	5000

Southern Army (British, Germans, &c.)	10,000
Before Bayonne (of these, 12,000 British and Portuguese)	15,000
Portuguese reinforcements expected	5000
British	9000
Spanish army of reserve coming up	8000
Graham's army	8000
British cavalry	7000
Portuguese and Spanish cavalry	2000
Total	104,000

I put them at the lowest figures. I have no doubt but that the Spanish could bring many more into the field. Indeed, I have omitted altogether Mina's troops at Pied-de-Port, about 11,000, which makes the total 115,000 men—a force fully sufficient to march to Paris if all together, be assured of it; and, as I have said before, there appears to me to be some little bad arrangement with such a force not to be able to be infinitely superior in the field to Soult. So much for military matters.

★ ★ ★ ★ ★

At this time Soult had not, as a fact, been reinforced by any men from Suchet's army, though Wellington believed he had been. Each general thought the other stronger than he in reality was.

★ ★ ★ ★ ★

Barsac, March 17, 1814.

We marched this morning from Barsac at six o'clock for this place, a very curious old town that has been regularly walled. It is now dilapidated. It was also a bishop's see, but it is now no longer so. It has a very magnificent cathedral, built by the English, but not so fine as that at Bordeaux.

In his last letter John said that they were, in Cornwall, getting some packages of hams, &c., ready for me; but France is a place of plenty, and, therefore, if they are sent to Plymouth, I wish my father to get them returned to him (he can do so by writing there), as they will probably never reach me; and if they were to do so, it would be when they were not wanted. The butter and ham at Bordeaux are delicious; the butter infinitely the best I ever tasted.

But why do I talk of Bordeaux? The remembrance of it only

brings regret at having left it! One good thing, however, I have done. I have made the acquaintance of some friends there who will send me any quantity of the best wine. At Sauterne, Barsac, Medoc (where the best claret is made), and at Beautiran, where is the best Grave, I know the proprietors of the properties where the best of each sort is grown; besides which, my dear old friend, M. Raba (*Consul Générale de Portugal* and *Chevalier de l'Ordre Royale Militaire de Santiago da Espada*, as his card tells me), has promised to send me whatever quantity I want of the very best quality whenever I write for it.

In addition to all these I have a friend—a German—who made me a present of a dozen, for immediate use, of the most exquisite claret that ever was tasted, and who has offered to supply me with any quantity; so that if my father or any friends wish to have any quantity of wine they have nothing to do but say what quantity and what sort.

I was very near speculating upon the opening of the river, and purchasing all Mr. Gravier's stock of *vin de Grave*, both red and white (the red is in fact claret of infinite flavour, but not so strong as the *vin de Medoc*). He offered me 600 *barrigs* at two guineas a *barrig*, holding 260 claret bottles. I think if I had turned wine merchant I should have made a good job of it had the port opened! I do think it must be a good trade, and if the war was over, and I had no other *métier*, I should be very apt to come to Bordeaux and set up as a *marchand de vins*.

Roquefort, March 18, 1814,
3 o'clock p.m.

After a most tremendous march of eight leagues which has pretty nearly knocked up all our baggage animals, &c, I arrived here about half an hour since.

I have already, in a former letter, described this place; to that description I have nothing to add.

* * * * *

Colonel Vivian was at this time making forced marches to rejoin Wellington, who was now moving on again against Soult.

* * * * *

Barcelone, March 19, 1814.

Another terrible march of seven leagues has brought us here;

nearly all horses, mules, &c., knocked up! We have now marched in four days considerably upwards of a hundred miles, and great part of it through sands up to the horses' fetlocks. One of my poor goats (Mayer's little one) has died from fatigue, and the others are rather sick; otherwise my establishment goes on very well. I have lightened my baggage by getting rid of my tents, and the mules get on very well with it.

This place has for fifteen days been full of British, Spaniards, &c, and consequently it is completely *abîméd*, as the French say.

I am sorry to say that though Soult has not been able to raise the country against us, he has nevertheless contrived to establish some partisan corps in our rear. One of these, the day before yesterday, took four officers and 30 men between Orthez and St. Sever; and a second destroyed a brigade of mules between Mont-Marsan and Villeneuve—the same fellows that took Thornhill out of bed!

The 7th, and a corps of Portuguese, are left in the rear to watch them.

★ ★ ★ ★ ★

Soult had retired to Lombez and Simacourbe, but his outposts still remained at Conchez; and Pierre Soult detached a hundred chosen troopers against the communications of the Allies with Orthez.

Captain Dania, commanding these men, making a forced march, reached Hagetmau at nightfall, surprised six officers, made a number of other prisoners, and returned on the night of the 18th.

This, owing to the distance from the army at which it took place, was attributed at the time to the insurgent bands.—*Life of Napoleon*, vol. 6. p. 611.

★ ★ ★ ★ ★

My brigade marches tomorrow to Plaisance. I shall then be able to tell you more about Soult.

People in general expect a battle. I do not, myself, until he passes Auch.

Rabastens, March 20, 1814.

Whatever might have been our marches before, that of this day has completely eclipsed them.

We have now arrived here—a full distance of 43 miles—and, thank God, have arrived at an end of our labours, so far as long marches go; for I have joined the 4th division with which my brigade is to act.

★ ★ ★ ★ ★

General Cole, still making forced marches with the 4th Division and Vivian's cavalry, followed the Allies' left wing, from Beaumarchez and La Devèze, sending detachments through Marciac, to watch P. Soult on the side of Trie.—*Life of Napoleon*, vol. 6 p. 616.

★ ★ ★ ★ ★

The principal front of the army is on our right; they have skirmished considerably with the enemy all this day, and so also they were yesterday, but nothing serious has taken place.

This town is at the very head of the River Adour.

Soult is retiring with his left flank to the mountains, but I do not expect he will go much further that way; indeed he must soon turn upon Toulouse.

Gondrin, March 21, 1814.

After a short march this day we have arrived here, in a wretched, dirty village.

The main army is on the great road to Toulouse, upon which Soult has retired. The 6th and 4th Divisions, and a heavy brigade of cavalry, and my brigade, form the left wing of our army.

The country in which we are is very beautiful; but the weather is bad.

Le Peña, near Trie, March 22, 1814.

After another short march we arrived here—another miserable village—with the brigade dispersed all over the face of the earth.

It rains in torrents, and I must put them up to save them from being drowned. If the enemy come on, we shall be, like Thornhill, surprised in our quarters!

★ ★ ★ ★ ★

Beresford had now taken command of the left column, with which Colonel Vivian's brigade was.

During the night Soult made a march of 30 miles to St. Gaudens, with a view of gaining Toulouse as rapidly as possible; for, having now seen nearly all Wellington's infantry and his 5000 horsemen, and hearing from his brother that the 4th Division and Vivian's cavalry were pointing towards Mielan, on his right, he feared that they would, by Trie and Castlenau, gain the plains of Muret and cut him off from Toulouse.

The Allies pursued in three columns, but their marches were short.—*Life of Napoleon*, vol. 6 p. 618.

★ ★ ★ ★ ★

Muigan, near Boulogne,
March 13, 1814.

A still more wretched village than that in which I was last quartered, and my brigade still more dispersed! The fine roads are all past and gone, and we are once more up to our necks in mud. We are, I see, evidently making a race of it to try and get to Toulouse before Soult, who is marching by the great road from St. Gaudens to Toulouse, followed by Hill; whilst we are endeavouring to cut him off—in which we shall not succeed.

Puylanzic, Near Lombez,
March 24, 1814.

Worse and worse, A still more wretched village, and my brigade still more dispersed in a completely open country, something like Salisbury Plain, cultivated without being enclosed. A fine cavalry country, if the ground was not too deep; but this wet weather has played the devil with it!

I am in a very tolerable *château*, with a very tolerable host, who has taken out several bottles of wine which he means to give us for dinner, but which, I fear, we shall not find so good as what we got at Bordeaux.

Sabonnères, near St. Foy,
March 25, 1814.

We marched in mud up to our horses' knees.

A wretched hovel—still worse than the others.

My poor brown goat has failed under the exertion and been left behind, I fear to die; and the little one that was so tame is obliged to be strapped on to a mule. I have, however, two long-legged country goats that travel like race horses, but, alas! they give no milk just now, and none is to be had, so we do without it.

In every other respect we do tolerably well, but the country, excepting for corn and bad wine, is not abundant in resources.

Leguevin, March 26, 1814.

A village on the high road from Auch to Toulouse, still worse, if possible, than any we have yet met with. I really did hope as we approached the banks of the Garonne that the country would have improved, but it appears to get worse and worse.

I am just returned from driving in the advanced posts of the French beyond the little river La Touch, which is about three miles from Toulouse. Soult's whole army is there, and ours is concentrating.

I suppose in a day or two the lord will show us what he means to do. I fear he will not find it an easy task to enter Toulouse. Soult has barricaded the entrances, and in many ways made it so strong as certainly to occasion us the loss of many men if we attempt to carry it; and then the bridge is blockaded in such a manner as to render it impossible it should be forced, and the heavy rains we have had have destroyed the fords, and will prevent our throwing a bridge over the river; so that I very much fear we shall be detained here for some time.

At all events, even when we do get to Toulouse, we cannot advance still further without being reinforced, nor without being re-rigged; for our men are in rags, and most of the infantry without shoes. Their sufferings are dreadful.

★ ★ ★ ★ ★

On the 26th, Beresford entered St. Lys, and marching in order of battle by his left, while his cavalry skirmished on the right, took post on the Auch road behind the Aussonelle stream, facing the French army, which was on the Touch covering Toulouse.

The Allies took seven days to march the distance Soult had covered in four.—*Life of Napoleon* vol. 6. p. 619.

★ ★ ★ ★ ★

Colomien, March 27, 1814.

My brigade marched to this place this morning, where I am quartered in the house of a *seigneur*—a very comfortable house.

The whole army is closing up, and we are in sight of Toulouse.

Colomien, March 28, 1814.

We all turned out this morning before daybreak. Sir Rowland Hill was to have thrown a bridge over the Garonne at Portet, but, unfortunately, he wanted two pontoons to have enough to make it so wide as to cross the river. No great proof of the superior abilities of our engineers!

There was no one to oppose the passage, and all the army had moved to the right, excepting my brigade and the Hussar brigade; and we were left to watch the two great roads leading from Toulouse to Auch and Boulogne.

About ten o'clock I observed the enemy in my front beginning to withdraw, and, not aware of the failure of the bridge, I concluded it was in consequence of the troops having crossed the river, and I determined therefore immediately to follow them up, and endeavour to enter the town with them.

I therefore moved on, and chased the 10th Chasseurs and some infantry along the high road up to the very suburbs; but there, however, I was brought up short by the discharge of five pieces of cannon, which they had placed in a battery enfilading the road.

I was obliged to put about; but the 18th, who were in front, were very steady, and did it very quietly; and I was fortunate enough to lose only four or five horses killed and wounded, and two or three men wounded, although they fired as fast as possible directly up the road on us; but they fired very badly indeed!

By this movement of mine, however, we gained an excellent position overlooking Toulouse, and Lord Wellington was very much pleased when he arrived and saw how we were posted, and directly ordered the 4th and 6th Divisions up to the ground.

★ ★ ★ ★ ★

Colonel Napier thus describes this operation:

Soult did not know of the attempt to cross at Portet till two days later.

Wellington, thus baffled, tried another scheme; he drove the enemy from the Touch stream on the 28th, and collected the infantry of his left and centre about Portet, masking the movement with his cavalry.

In the course of the operation a single squadron of the 18th Hussars, under Major Hughes, being inconsiderately pushed by Colonel Vivian across the bridge of St. Martyn-de-la-Touch, suddenly came upon a whole regiment of French cavalry.

The rashness of the act, as often happens in war, proved the safety of the British, for the enemy, thinking that a strong support must be at hand, discharged their carbines and retreated at a canter.

Hughes followed; the speed of both sides increased, and, as the nature of the road did not admit of any egress to the sides, this great body of horsemen was pushed headlong by a few men under the batteries of St. Cyprien.

Here again Colonel Napier attempts to disparage Colonel Vivian's action; and if the latter is correct in the account he gives of the affair, Napier is absolutely wrong.

It is noticeable that Major Hughes is mentioned in connection with this charge. Several years ago a correspondence took place between that officer and my father, the second Lord Vivian, on the subject of this charge and the one made later at Croix d'Orade, which correspondence I am unfortunately unable to obtain. I am informed, and have every reason to believe, that Major Hughes himself never attempted to detract from Colonel Viivian's abilities as a soldier, or to deny him the credit of these charges which Napier seems to attribute to Major Hughes alone. For his conduct in the affair with the French cavalry at the bridge of St. Martyn-de-la-Touch, Colonel Vivian was highly commended by Sir S. Cotton and Lord Wellington.

★ ★ ★ ★ ★

Colomien, March 29, 1814.

Here we still are, and with a day's rest, which we stood much in need of.

I conclude they are making preparations to pass the river, which we shall attempt again, I expect, tomorrow; but, I fear, not now without considerable loss, as the enemy are aware of our intention.

They say Soult has detached 8000 men to Bordeaux. I sincerely hope not; for if he has it will play the very deuce there, and hurt our cause very much.

The people of this country are excessively well disposed towards us, and they detest the French army. Nor am I surprised, for in my life I never saw such vile ravages as their soldiers have made in the beautiful country-houses of the citizens of Toulouse, near the ground on which we are encamped. Buonaparte may collect *procès verbaux*, and publish accounts of the atrocities of the *Cossacks*, but nothing can equal the 'Vandalism' of his own troops!

He is trying all and every means in his power, through the medium of the press, to stir up the people against the invaders; but I have not an expectation of his success. I send you two songs that are in a farce composed for the purpose. In a better cause they would be good, but the cause for which the present troops fight is not that of the conqueror of the oppressor of their country. After all, however, it must be admitted that Buonaparte has never shown himself greater than on the present occasion.

I send you also a proclamation of that worthy servant of his most unworthy master—Marshal Soult. Such an infamous production never escaped the hands of a man calling himself an officer and a gentleman. He is a vile wretch! I wish I was within sabre's length of him. The whole country exclaims against him.

Colomien, Near Toulouse,
March 30, 1814.

My dearest Eli,—I yesterday despatched my epistle to you, containing my journal up to that date, directed to the Quarter-Master-General.

Nothing new has occurred. The engineers are hard at work, making pontoons of casks, &c., to throw the bridge over the Garonne.

It rains tremendously, and the river is swelling much, so that I fear we shall still have some difficulty in crossing.

Colomien, March 31, 1814.

Still in our quarters. The day beautiful. The enemy, as before, posted in the town, and on the banks of the river, apparently intending to oppose our either penetrating by the town or crossing.

The river must fall today, and the result, I hope, will be our crossing tomorrow. This idleness begins to be stupid.

My landlord and his wife are very kind and civil; notwithstanding which I expect they must wish me away, for we are turning them out of their rooms, and eating up all their forage. Let me tell you, four officers (Keane, Campbell, my brigade-major, and myself), and about forty mules and horses, and a dozen servants and orderlies, are no joke in a country-house. I know I should, so circumstanced, wish them at the devil!

Colomien, April 1, 1814.

And proper April fools they have made of us!

We turned out this morning at daybreak, thinking to be in Toulouse, General Hill having crossed the water at Rochet, and marched to Cintegabelle, from whence he was to have marched upon Toulouse; but he has found the roads so bad that his artillery could not advance; so he is come back, and I expect the business will be done by the left wing. If so, my brigade will be in the thick of it.'

★ ★ ★ ★ ★

General Hill crossed the Ariege at Cintegabelle, and sent his scouts and cavalry towards Villefranche and Nailloux, but his artillery could not move owing to the bad state of the roads, and he returned during the night, and recrossed the Garonne.—*Life of Napoleon*, vol. 6 p. 631.

★ ★ ★ ★ ★

April 2.—Nothing settled.

The lord is now planning how to circumvent Mr. Soult, who is rather a serious playfellow.

April 3.—Half-past nine o'clock p.m.

It is just as I expected. I received an order this morning to accompany the lord and Marshal Beresford in a reconnaissance down the river, as my cavalry will be the first in case of a move this way. We had a long ride, and it was at last decided that the bridge was to be thrown over at a small village, near Grenade, at daybreak tomorrow morning.

Since this I have been dining with the lord; and tomorrow morning, at two o'clock, we move to the point of attack.

The ground is favourable for our artillery, as the heights on this side of the river are very commanding; but as the enemy's pickets are thick on the other side, I expect we shall very soon find their army in front. If so we shall have hot work of it.

My brigade of cavalry follow the 4th Division, which goes first; so the devil is in it if I do not get a hit at the gentleman tomorrow. I have always been in luck and got off well, and so, please God, I mean to do.

God bless you, dearest Eli. I will tell you all about it after it is over.

★ ★ ★ ★ ★

On the evening of April 3 the pontoons were carried to Grenade, where the bridge was at last thrown, and thirty guns placed on the left bank to protect it.

The 3rd, 4th, and 6th Divisions of infantry, and three brigades of cavalry, under Beresford, immediately passed over, and the cavalry being pushed out two leagues on the front and flanks, captured a large herd of bullocks destined for the French army. But now the river again swelled so fast that the Spaniards and Light Division were unable to follow, the bridge got damaged, and the pontoons were taken up.—*Life of Napoleon*, vol. 6 632.

★ ★ ★ ★ ★

April 4.—Yesterday (April 4) was so busy a day that I had not time to continue my journal.

Notwithstanding our expectation of opposition not a shot was fired.

The 3rd, 4th, 6th, and Light Divisions, with Lord E. Somerset's and my brigades of cavalry, marched at eleven o'clock at night on the 3rd to reach the bank of the river at daybreak in the morning, at which time the bridge was commenced. It was an operation of three hours and a half throwing it over; and at nine we commenced passing.

First the 4th Division, then my brigade, then the 6th Division, then half of Lord E. Somerset's brigade, then the 3rd Division, then the other half of Lord E. Somerset's brigade, then a Heavy brigade of Dragoons; and the operation was so long, the horses being obliged to be led one by one over, that only those I have mentioned could pass before night.

April 5.—Today (April 5) the Spaniards and Light Division and heavy Germans are crossing.

The weather during the preceding night had been tremendous. Such a flood of rain I never saw; and the river was much swollen, which made our operation a still more hazardous one; but either Soult was afraid, or deceived, for he never even attempted the slightest resistance. When first he heard we were coming he moved his army out of the town of Toulouse as if to oppose us, but he afterwards moved back again. I suspect he means to be off altogether; if not, he has missed a fine opportunity of fighting us. He never can mean to stay in Toulouse, for if he does, he and all his army will certainly be taken.

I conclude we shall move in the evening towards Toulouse, and I expect the bridge will be moved to Bluynau, which will connect our army. At present we are separated; General Hill being on the other side of the Garonne with his corps.

The passing of the Garonne was a beautiful sight. It would have been magnificent had the weather been fine; but it was cloudy, with showers; and the poor fellows, after a night march, drenched to the skin and up to their knees in mud, were looking rather miserable; still, however, the passing the river on a pontoon bridge, all the bands playing the 'British Grenadiers,' the trumpets sounding, and the banks lined with thousands of spectators, was, notwithstanding the weather, a beautiful sight.

As soon as I was over I had to send small parties into all quarters to chase away the detachments of the enemy's cavalry observing our movements, and at eight o'clock at night I reached this place with my brigade, more dead than alive from fatigue. I got a little warm soup and some hashed beef, and at half-past nine turned into bed, and at six this morning woke out of the soundest possible sleep, as well as ever I was in my life.

I expect as soon as the Spaniards and heavy guns are over we shall move on. I am just going to get on my horse to see what is to be seen, and hear what is to be heard.

Six o'clock p.m. I little thought when I wrote the last sentence, that I should have learnt we were in a most serious scrape.

Instead of passing the whole of the troops last night intended to be passed, Lord Wellington ordered the baggage of some of the divisions over. The consequence was that, owing to the immensity of rain that had fallen, the bridge, during the night, became impassable; and here we are—three brigades of cavalry, the 3rd, 4th, and 6th Divisions of infantry—completely cut off from the rest of the army, and liable to be attacked by double our numbers. We have just 10,700 bayonets, and 2200 swords. If Soult does not take advantage of this opportunity and attack us he is not worth his salt.

However, after all, if he does he will get thrashed; for my firm belief is that the three divisions here would beat his whole army; and nearly his whole army he can bring against us, for he is perfectly secure from any attack on the other side from the works he has thrown up in front of the bridge of Toulouse. We shall see tomorrow.

★ ★ ★ ★ ★

Alison, alluding to the position of affairs at this period, says:
On the 3rd, as the river had somewhat fallen, the pontoons were carried in the night to Grenade, fifteen miles below Toulouse, and the bridge having been quickly thrown over, a battery of thirty guns was established to protect it, and three divisions of infantry and three of cavalry immediately passed over, which captured a large herd of oxen intended for the French army.
But meanwhile a catastrophe, threatening the most terrible consequences, ensued.
The river rose again in raging torrents; the Light Divisions and Spaniards, intended to follow the leading divisions, could not be got across; the grappling irons and supports of the bridge were swept away; and, to avoid total destruction, it became necessary to take up the pontoons and dismantle the bridge; leaving Beresford with 15,000 foot, and 3000 horse, alone exposed to the whole weight of the French army, at least double their strength.

★ ★ ★ ★ ★

Castelnau, April 6, 1814.

The morrow has come and nearly passed without an attack. We had a flood of rain last night, and our difficulties increase. Soult might starve us in three days, if this weather lasts, by moving on against us in front and occupying the line of the little river Ers in our rear, and this without firing a shot. If he is not at us tomorrow he is indeed a cocktail of a fellow, and that I do not suspect him of being.
The weather is, however, holding up, and if it continues dry all night, tomorrow, I hope, will re-establish our bridge. If not, we will die hard—no surrendering, I promise you. If the worst comes to the worst I mean to start with my brigade and march upon Lyons to join the Austrians. I have no notion of capitulation; but, as I said before, if they dare attack us they will pay dear for it. I am more afraid of starving than of being beaten,
My baggage is on the other side of the water, and I have nothing but Higgins (who is very ill) with me, a clean shirt, and a toothbrush, but I can rough it as well as any man, so I care not a *sou*.

Castelnau, April 7, 1814.

Here we still are, and much to our surprise and disappointment still in peace. It is now four o'clock and Soult has not attacked us. I only wish he had! He would properly have caught it, for our position was such as could have been defended by the troops we have on this side of the water against the whole French army.

The weather is delightful. The river has fallen 3 feet since the morning, and at seven o'clock this evening we expect the bridge to be re-established, when the Spaniards and Light Division will cross to this side; and tomorrow we shall probably move on. But as Soult has not dared to attack our small force, cut off completely from the rest of the army, he will not, I expect, attempt to make a stand against us united, although, after all, we are miserably weak. Altogether we have not 32,000 bayonets, and Soult has as many, but we are stronger in cavalry.

Soult will retire, I expect, upon Carcassonne by-and-bye. He will perhaps be joined by Augereau and Suchet; but then we shall join Bianchi and Babna. Reinforcements from England we cannot expect, and as to Graham's army it is lost to us. What a pretty business!

We have French papers to the 29th from Paris. By them it appears that on or about the 30th Blucher must have been so near as to have been in a position to have attacked it; and Buonaparte, hastening from St. Dizier on the 27th, could not be in time to save it.

A private letter received here says the streets of Paris are strewed with dead and dying, but that King Joseph has induced the *Cohortes Urbaines* to fight under a promise of reinforcements and Boney's arrival. by this it appears as if Paris is not taken; but if the *Cohortes Urbaines* are like those we meet here, their resistance will be trifling.

★ ★ ★ ★ ★

On March 30th a battle was fought near Paris, when the French, under King Joseph, Marmont, and Mortier, were defeated, and Paris capitulated on the following day.

Napoleon abdicated on April 4th. All this, however, was unknown to Wellington and Soult.

★ ★ ★ ★ ★

I expect the white cockade will be hoisted in Toulouse on our entrance. In short, I hope *l'affaire est finie*, and the tyrant will soon cease to reign. After all, he has made a grand resistance; he never showed himself so great.

Why do we not proclaim Louis XVIII.? Everyone here wishes it. Everyone complains of our not doing so. This once done, and the game is over, and our own; not that the people care a *sou* for the Bourbons, but that they hate Buonaparte; and, if we once pledged ourselves to support the Bourbons, they would join us to put down Buonaparte.

Castelnau, April 8, 1814.

The bridge was not re-established until four o'clock this morning. The baggage has been until now (eleven o'clock) passing over, and at twelve o'clock we expect to advance towards Toulouse, but not so far as to bring us into action today.

Tomorrow we shall probably have a gentle brush with them, but I do not expect that Soult will fight much,

We have just heard a report that Paris is taken and the white flag hoisted. If true, this accounts for Soult's inactivity.

The post goes tomorrow, and I am so busy I have not a moment to add anything more, so God bless you!

★ ★ ★ ★ ★

The above is the last letter written by Colonel Vivian during this campaign, which is accounted for by the fact that he was mistaken in thinking that nothing would take place on the 8th; for Wellington advanced upon Toulouse, and in the course of the day Colonel Vivian was himself seriously wounded.

From Napier's *History* I extract the following account of the events of the day:

> On the 8th the waters subsided, the bridge was again laid down, Frere's Spaniards and the Portuguese crossed, and Wellington advanced to Fenoulhiet, within five miles of Toulouse.
>
> Marching up the two banks of the Ers his columns were separated by that river, which was impassable without pontoons; and it was essential to secure as soon as possible one of the stone bridges.
>
> Hence, when his left approached the heights of Kyrie Eleison, on the great road of Alby, Vivian's horsemen drove Berton's cavalry up the right of the Ers towards Bordes, and the 18th Hus-

sars descended towards that of Croix d'Orade.

The latter was defended by Vial's Dragoons, and after some skirmishing, the 18th was suddenly menaced by a regiment in front of the bridge, the opposite bank of the river being lined with dismounted *carbineers*.

The two parties stood facing each other, hesitating to begin, until the approach of some British infantry, when both sides sounded the charge at the same moment; but the English horses were so quick that the French in an instant were jammed up on the bridge. Their front ranks were sabred, and the mass, breaking away to the rear, went off in disorder, leaving many killed and wounded, and above a hundred prisoners, in the hands of the victors.

They were pursued through the village of Croix d'Orade, but beyond it they rallied and advanced again.

The Hussars then recrossed the bridge which was now defended by the British infantry, whose fire stopped the French cavalry.

Colonel Napier then goes on to volunteer the remark that:

...the credit of this brilliant action was given in the despatch, inaccurately, to Colonel Vivian, for that officer was wounded by a carbine shot previous to the charge at the bridge. The attack was conceived and conducted by Major Hughes of the 18th.

This is another occasion when Colonel Napier detracts from Colonel Vivian's performances; and it is again noticeable that Major Hughes is the officer he names as deserving of all the credit of the action.

In 1871 my father, writing to the editor of *Historical Records of the 18th Hussars*, who had quoted this passage from Napier, said:

I can only contradict this assertion on the authenticity of the statement which has often been made me by my father, the late Lord Vivian.

He stated that he ordered the advance on the bridge which was made by the 18th, and whilst with the squadron was shot in the arm by a dismounted carbineer. Colonel Hughes only carried out the order given by my father.

Wellington in his despatch most undoubtedly gives the credit of the performance to Colonel Vivian, and Sir S. Cotton thanked him in Cavalry Orders.

Wellington's despatch is as follows:

The continued fall of rain and the state of the roads prevented me from laying the bridge across till the morning of the 8th, when the Spanish corps and the Portuguese artillery, under the immediate orders of General Frere, and the Headquarters, crossed the Garonne.

We immediately moved forward to the neighbourhood of the town; and the 18th Hussars under the immediate command of Colonel Vivian had an opportunity of making a most gallant attack upon a superior body of the enemy's cavalry, which they drove through the village of Croix d'Orade and took about 100 prisoners and gave us possession of an important bridge over the Ers, by which it was necessary to pass to attack the enemy's position. Colonel Vivian was unfortunately wounded upon this occasion and I am afraid I shall lose his services for some time.

When Chaplain-General Gleig disputed a statement of Napier s relating to the battle of Vimiera, the latter writer fell back on the authority of the Duke of Wellington, which of course Napier preferred to that of Gleig, adding tartly that "the two authorities may be weighed by those who are fastidious." A similar process may be recommended as to Wellington's and Napier's authority touching Vivian's share in the affair of Croix d'Orade.

I may also add the significant fact that the officers of the 18th Hussars sent the following letter to Vivian on the day after the action:

Dear Sir,—In proportion to the gratitude we entertain for the occasion you obtained for us yesterday of meriting your approbation, is the regret we feel that it should have deprived us, we trust but for a short time, of your continued protection. Although so much above any consequence our compliments and congratulations would give you, yet with our condolence permit us to say we feel and justly appreciate the vigilance, activity, and great gallantry with which on all occasions, and on this occasion particularly, you have sought our honour. As a memorial and tribute of our gratitude we request that you do us the honour to accept a sword which, God grant, you may be enabled to wield at the head of your brigade.

The sword, which was presented when the regiment returned to England a few months later, bore on one side the inscription "Croix d'Orade, 8th April 1814," and on the reverse, "The officers of the

18th Hussars express by this token their regard for, and confidence in, Major-General R. H. Vivian, who was wounded at the head of their regiment."

Further than this, amongst the heraldic allusions to his distinguished career granted to Vivian later in life, is a soldier of the 18th Hussars bearing a pennon with the words "Croix d'Orade" on it. As this was in 1827—fourteen years after the event and when the truth of the action would have been thoroughly thrashed out—it is scarcely probable that Vivian would have accepted, or have been allowed to bear without challenge, a device which he had not justly merited.

A perusal of the correspondence which took place on the subject in 1840 and 1841 will convince most people that Colonel Vivian did conceive and direct the attack, and that only his wound prevented him personally conducting it. Major Hughes did what hundreds of others did during the war, he gallantly carried out an order conceived and directed by a superior officer.—*United Service Magazine*, October 1896.

Colonel Vivian's wound was of so serious a nature that he was unable to take any further part in the operations against Toulouse, and his brigade was afterwards commanded by Colonel Arentschild, and took part in the battle of Toulouse on April 10, which town Wellington entered on the 12th. On the 13th information of Napoleon's abdication reached the armies, and on the 17th hostilities ceased.

The British cavalry marched through France and embarked at Boulogne on July 12, 1814. Colonel Vivian returned to England in June, and on the 4th of that month he was, at the age of thirty-eight, promoted to the rank of Major-General, and in January 1815 nominated a Knight Commander of the Bath.

Shortly afterwards he was appointed to the command of the Sussex district. His promotion necessitated his relinquishing the command of the 7th Hussars, when the officers, to show their respect, affection, and high appreciation of his bravery and efficient services, presented him with a handsome piece of plate valued at three hundred guineas.

CHAPTER 4

Quatre-Bras and the Retreat of June 17

In February of 1815 Napoleon Buonaparte, in Elba, came to the conclusion that with the assistance of the army he could overthrow the Bourbons. On March 1, he landed near Cannes, and on March 20 entered the Tuileries, Louis XVIII. having driven out of it only a few hours before.

When Buonaparte left Elba for France, Wellington was in Vienna, attending the Congress, where the Ministers of various European Powers were wrangling over the division of the lands that had been ceded by France on Napoleon"s retirement to Elba. The news at once stopped all their dissensions, and on March 12 the Allied Powers joined hands, and declared Napoleon to be beyond the pale of civil and social relations, and that, as a common enemy and disturber of the peace of the world, he had delivered himself over to public justice.

There was not a nation in Europe that felt the slightest particle of trust in Napoleon. Great Britain, Russia, Austria, and Prussia, bound themselves each to provide 150,000 men to work together for the common end "until Buonaparte shall have been rendered absolutely unable to create disturbance, and to renew attempts for possessing himself of supreme power in France."

On March 29 Wellington left Vienna and arrived in Brussels on April 4, where he took command of the Dutch-Belge, as well as of the British and Hanoverian troops which were there assembled and assembling. It was not, however, till April 16 that Sir Hussey Vivian embarked to join the brigade to which he had been appointed. He was now a K.C.B. and was the first Major-General sent in command of a brigade to join the army at Brussels.

His diary, which he kept with care, and in which he jotted down the chief events in which he took part, commences:

* * * * *

April 16.—Sailed from Ramsgate, on board of the *Lord Liverpool* packet.
The 10th Hussars sailed at the same time.
Wretchedly seasick.

April 17.—Landed at 10 o'clock a.m. on the beach near Ostend, and walked up to the place with Lieut.-Col. Sir A. Fraser, Royal Artillery, and Brig.-Major Harris.

At Ostend I found the Duke of Wellington inspecting the troops and works. He left it about half an hour after I landed, for Ypres. He appeared most anxious to know what infantry were coming from England.

Ostend is very large, and tolerably well fortified; by Buonaparte, in a great measure. The works are very extensive and would require a very large garrison; and, excepting for the facility of inundating the country about it, I consider it as a place of no great strength. It might, I apprehend, be taken by *a coup de main,* especially from the seaside.

On the hills beyond the river is a work of considerable strength, erected by Buonaparte after the defeat of Sir E. Coote's expedition, which landed near the sandhills, near where the works stand. Guns from it can reach the town, but not so as to drive troops out, I imagine.

At Ostend I occupied the house that Buonaparte had inhabited, and afterwards the Emperor Alexander.

* * * * *

Lieut.-Col. Sir Augustus Fraser commanded the whole of the Horse Artillery during the campaign. One of the three who walked together up to the town on this day was not destined to return to England. Brig.-Major Harris was killed at Waterloo. He was Brig.-Major to Sir Hussey Vivian's brigade.

* * * * *

April 18, 19, 20, and 21.—Remained at Ostend, my horses not having arrived till the 19th.

April 22.—Left Ostend in the gig, in the most tremendous rain imaginable, and blowing so hard that I could not hold an umbrella to it.

Dined with Major-Gen. Sir J. Lyon K.C.B., at Bruges, a very large town, but apparently at present a place of little traffic and much deserted, to judge from the number of houses that are shut up.

There are some monuments in the churches of this town.

★ ★ ★ ★ ★

Sir J. Lyon commanded a Hanoverian brigade at Waterloo.

★ ★ ★ ★ ★

April 23.—Went on the barge by the canal to Ghent. A most admirable conveyance, in which your passage and a good dinner costs you 7s., with wines of all sorts. The distance is about 25 miles.

Ghent is a very considerable town; stands on an immense space, and contains 50,000 inhabitants. It is famous for its linen and lace manufactories.

At Ghent I expected to have found my brigade assembled, as they had been marching by detachments as they landed; but I found an order for the different regiments to march at once into quarters at Harlebeke, Avelghem, and Berchem; villages upon, and between, the Scheldt and the Lys rivers.

I must here notice the very curous circumstance of part of one of the regiments of my brigade, the 18th Hussars (the other two were the 7th and 10th), having marched from Canterbury on the morning of the 17th and into Bruges on the evening of the 18th.

At Ghent there are many curiosities worth seeing, especially the church of St. Bavon, in which there is some beautiful sculpture; and under which is what is called another church, and is, in fact, used as such; but it is really nothing more than a cavern or vault in which there are windows. Its age, however, makes it a curiosity, having been built by Charlemagne. In the church of St. Michael also there are some good paintings. Ghent is a very fine city, and very clean.

★ ★ ★ ★ ★

At this point it will be well to state what was the disposition of Wellington's army at this time.

As early as the 11th of April he had divided his troops into two *corps d'armée* and a reserve; the two former commanded respectively by the Prince of Orange and Lord Hill, the last by himself.

The whole of the cavalry was under the orders of Lord Uxbridge (afterwards Lord Anglesey) and the British portion was kept united in cantonments.

Hooper says:

Wellington was occupying an immense front. Commencing from the right at Ostend, the line followed the frontier. Nieuport, Ypres, Courtrai, Tournai and Mons, had been strengthened so far as to be able to embarrass the march of an army attempting to break into Belgium between the Scheldt and the Lys, or between the Scheldt and the Sambre. From Courtrai to Mons ran a chain of cavalry posts in observation, and in rear of these stood the divisions of the army.

The great mass of the troops was cantoned in the wide plains between the Scheldt and the great road from Charleroi through Brussels to Antwerp.

Lord Hill's headquarters were at Ath, and the brigades of his corps extended to the right as far as the Lys, and to the left in the direction of Mons. The first corps formed the left of the army; the headquarters were at Braine-le-Comte, and the divisions were on each side of the high road from Mons to Brussels. The most forward post was at Binche, and the furthest to the left at Frasnes.

In the rear of Lord Hill lay the great body of the cavalry, in the valley of the Dendre, the headquarters being at Grammont; and in rear of the Prince of Orange was the Reserve, at Brussels, and one brigade of Cole's division at Ghent.—*Hooper*, p. 41.

★ ★ ★ ★ ★

April 24.—Went with Keane, in a *curricle* of the country, to Brussels.

We were invited to dine with the Duke of Wellington, but the invitation arrived after the hour named for dinner. Dined with Sir E. Barnes.

April 25.—Visited my friends in Brussels; amongst others, Greathead, the Duke of Richmond, Lady E. Somerset, &c. Dined with the Duke of Richmond.

April 26.—Walked about the city.

Lord Uxbridge arrived from England to take command of the cavalry.

There is nothing that I could discover particularly worth seeing in Brussels, excepting the park, which is really a very magnificent appendage to the city; and the upper part of the town also, about it, contains some fine buildings; the lower part is dirty and bad. There are a few good pictures in the Museum.

Dined this day with the Quartermaster-General, Sir Hudson Lowe, and met Pozzo di Borgo, and the Prussian general, Ryder.

*****

Sir Hudson Lowe was afterwards the Governor of St. Helena, when Napoleon was sent there.

Pozzo di Borgo was with Wellington's staff at the battle of Waterloo.

*****

April 27.— Brussels.
Dined with Lord Uxbridge at the Hôtel d'Angleterre

April 28.—The Knights Commander of the Bath not invested by the Prince Regent were this morning invested by the Duke of Wellington, and he gave afterwards, to about seventy or eighty of the principal officers of the army, a dinner at the Hôtel Bellevue, and afterwards at the room called the 'Concert Noble,' a very brilliant company assembled to dance. Never did I witness a more beautiful sight. The French head-dresses, and the different national uniforms, formed a splendid sight.

April 29.—Attended the levée of the King of the Netherlands, and dined afterwards with the Paymaster-General, Mr. Smith. Sir C. Alten, Sir J. Lyon, and Mr. and Mrs. Small, were of the party; Mrs. Small very handsome indeed—very like Mrs. George Wyndham of Norfolk.

April 30.—Left Brussels in a hired carriage for Ghent. Arrived there late at night. A carriage I had bought was out of repair, and delayed my journey.

May 1.—At Ghent.
Rode out with Lord Uxbridge, and dined with the Comte with whom he was quartered. Had an excellent dinner, and a very pleasant party. Two very delightful women, his daughters-in-law, were there; one very pretty and very interesting.

At night I received a letter to say that the brigade marched the next day from its cantonments to Ninove and the villages on the left bank of the Dendre. Thinking this move might arise from some movements in the French army. Lord Uxbridge and myself gave up a plan of going to see Antwerp; and he started in the morning of the second for Oudenarde.

I did the same for Ninove, where I arrived as soon as the 7th, and dined with my host, a most kind and excellent man.

* * * * *

With regard to this movement of Sir H. Vivian's brigade to Ninove, Hooper, in his history, says:

> The first of May arrived, and with it false reports of the march of the Imperial Guard, and of the intention of Buonaparte to visit the frontier.
>
> Yet uncertain of their value Wellington issued the first orders directing a concentration of the cantonments of the troops.
>
> Informing the Earl of Uxbridge of this order, he said, 'All dispositions are so made that the whole army can be collected in one short movement with the Prussians on my left.'
>
> The line of operations which he deemed it probable that the French would select was either between the Lys and the Scheldt, or between the Scheldt and the Sambre, or by both; and for each contingency he was prepared.

* * * * *

May 3.—Ninove.

A very nice, pleasant little town, situated on the Dendre, which divides it.

Lord Uxbridge and his staff dined with me.

A large portion of the army appears to have collected about Enghien, Nivelles, and Grammont, as if something was expected. I have no idea of Buonaparte making any attempt whatever.

The force is at present about 13,000 British, 7000 German Legion, 25,000 Hanoverians, and as many Dutch; of them about 10,000 are in garrisons, and the others are, many of them, but badly composed. The proportion of cavalry is about 8000 or 9000; of them 3500 are British. More are expected. The Duke of Wellington must be much stronger before he can attempt a forward movement.

* * * * *

Although no forward movement was as a fact made, Wellington was at this time urging offensive, instead of defensive, steps being taken.—*Hooper*, p. 51.

* * * * *

May 4.—Ninove.

Inspected my brigade in watering order, and found a dreadful number of sore backs; especially in the 7th and 18th.

Oh that the age of reason would but come, and that those who have influence enough in these matters would discern that it would be money well spent to provide every British Dragoon with one of the best old English saddles that can possibly be made, and not with such ridiculous things as the Hussar saddles, which require a day s labour to put on, from the numerous straps and trappings, and which, after all, cut the horses' backs to atoms! The day must and will come when the folly of these things is discovered. I never have had but one opinion on the subject, and I never can have but one. Every day's experience but confirms me in the belief that nothing can be so truly ridiculous as mounting English Dragoons on German saddles.

The very principle of the saddle is false. It contains in it that which must inevitably do mischief. No tree of a Hussar saddle will bear the test of mathematical trial as to its being true in all its bearings. It cannot. Wood will bend and warp with heat and damp, and consequently, if the bearings are not even, some part of the horse's back must be pressed more than the other; hence sores arise. Not so with the English saddle. An iron tree may be made exactly true to rule; and where the injury was formerly done from the English saddle it arose from their being badly and clumsily made. I would have every Dragoon ride on as good a saddle as can be put out of hand.

To this might be added a peak behind and before, the first of which would carry the baggage off the horse's back—the sole advantage of the Hussar saddle. Oh, ye rulers of these like matters, when will you learn from experience to adopt that which is useful, and feel persuaded that a good appearance is not only to be considered (not that the appearance even, to my mind, is good), and that *that* only can be beautiful which is in reality useful? The very subject makes me wretched. I feel persuaded that a service campaign will destroy every horse's back in the brigade. These opinions, here recorded, have been ten thousand times expressed.

May 5.—Ninove.

Rode with Lord Uxbridge to the quarters of the Heavy Dragoons, at Denderhautem, St. Lieven, Estre, &c.

Nothing can be more beautiful than the cultivation of this country—not a weed to be seen anywhere; and the inhabitants are, without exception, the civilest, and appear to be the happiest, people possible.

May 6.—Lord Uxbridge inspected my brigade in mounting order. The 7th had twenty-nine, the 18th thirteen horses dismounted on account of sore backs.

He afterwards inspected the King's Dragoon Guards and the Greys. In the former regiment was not one instance of a sore back; and in the latter, one only. How much does this prove in favour of the Hussars' saddles? The whole of the regiments were in perfect order.

May 7.—Lord Uxbridge, Captain Wildman, and Shenewitz and myself left Ninove, in Lord Uxbridge's carriage, to visit the advance of the army. We went by Grammont and Lessines to Ath; and from thence rode to Tournai, where we dined, and walked round the fortifications in the evening. Slept at Tournai. The inn—the 'Singe d'Or'—a very tolerable one.

Tournai is a very considerable town, and has been very strong, but Joseph H. dismantled it. they are now at work repairing the citadel, which is a very neat little work.

★ ★ ★ ★ ★

After Wellington arrived at Brussels a large number of sappers were engaged throughout the country in repairing the chief fortifications on the frontier.

★ ★ ★ ★ ★

May 8.—Lord Uxbridge inspected the 1st Hussars, K.G.L., and found them in very high order. My old friends did me the honour to express themselves very anxious again to return to my brigade.

From Tournai we rode to the field of Fontenoy, a position strong beyond measure from the beautiful glacis that was in front of it, and from its flanks having been so well protected. Nothing could be more daring than to attack it.

From Fontenoy we rode to the field of Genappe, a position totally indefensible by 20,000 men, which was about the force of the Austrians when the French attacked it. In short, a position, to my mind, very bad under almost any circumstances; but under those in which the action was fought, the only thing that surprises me is that Dumourier allowed a man of the Austrian right wing to escape.

At Mons we dined with General Domberg, and slept at the 'Hôtel de la Couronne Impériale'—an excellent house.

★ ★ ★ ★ ★

The battle of Genappe was fought between the French and Austrians on November 6, 1792, and resulted in a victory for the French. It was the first pitched battle that was gained by the Republican army, and led to the immediate conquest of the whole of the Netherlands.

At Waterloo the 1st Hussars were in Sir H. Vivian's brigade. The 7th Hussars were in that of Sir C. Grant.

★ ★ ★ ★ ★

May 9.—Rode to Grandglise to inspect the 3rd Hussars, K.G.L., and a squadron of the Regent's Hussars, having first seen two squadrons of the Bremen and Verdin regiments, beautifully mounted and altogether very good. The 3rd Hussars in excellent order; the horses not so good as those of the Bremen and Verdin regiments.

From Grandlise to Ath, by Belleisle, the magnificent seat of the Prince de Ligne; and from Ath to Ninove, in Lord Uxbridge's carriage.

May 10.—Received an order to move that part of my brigade in Ninove into other quarters. Sent my baggage, &c., to the Château de Murat, near Grammont, and rode over to Brussels and dined with Greathead.

May 11.—Returned from Brussels to the *château* near Grammont. Found my host, the count, by no means disposed to form an acquaintance, and altogether possessing all the love for money of the people of this country, and all the pride of an old German nobleman.

As a proof of this, I asked him where I could purchase some Rhine wine, and he told me he would send a friend who would get me some from a *wine merchant*. His friend was not long in arriving for it was his own steward: and he sold me wine at 3.9. a bottle, out of the count's cellar, that I could have bought at Grammont for 2s.!

May 12.—Rode to the quarters of the 18th Hussars.

Fuller, Hodge, Lord R. Manners, and Captain King dined with me.

May 13.—Still no appearance of a move.

Reports from the front state that the National Guards will neither march nor give up their arms, and that the conscripts will not obey the orders to appear at particular depots. In short, things certainly wear the appearance of uneasiness, and there are those who fancy that the march to Paris will be an affair of pleasure, and without opposition. I confess I am not one of them,

Dined with Lord Hill.

May 14.—Still at my *château* in a morass—as famous a place for ague as ever was seen. I shall be surprised if all my household escape it.

One admirable thing I have observed here, and well worthy of imitation. It is that the mangers in the stables are of stone, and the front of glazed tiles; much cleaner and less liable to infection than wooden ones, evidently.

Dined at Ninove with Lord Uxbridge.

May 15.—Exercised my brigade in a meadow near Schendelbeke; I fear somewhat to the injury of the crops; but when thousands of acres are inundated for the protection of fortresses that probably will never be attacked, surely it may be permitted to do some little mischief to a few, for the purpose of perfecting in their manoeuvres a brigade, which, if there is a war, is sure to be engaged, and the very success of which may perhaps, in a very great measure, depend on the state of their discipline in the field.

Dined at home—a large party of the 7th with me.

May 16.—Rode to Ninove, and afterwards with Lord Uxbridge to Denderhautem, to see some scrambling races made up by the 10th.

Dined at home; a party of the 10th with me.

May 17.—Rode to Enghien to see the cricket match. Met the Duke and Duchess of Richmond, and the Ladies Lennox there. Rode round the superb park of the Duke d'Arenberg, in whom is an instance as strong as (or even more so than) that of the Cavendish family, of the little happiness riches alone can afford—or rather how truly unfortunate and unhappy a man overwhelmed with riches may be. The Duke d'Arenberg himself had his eye shot out by a friend whilst out shooting. (The friend, Sir W. Gordon, died of grief in consequence.) He lost his wife, of whom he was fond beyond measure, in the prime of life. His daughter, the Princess Schwartzenberg, was burnt at Paris. His third son was killed by the fall of a horse at Vienna. Another lost his feet in the French service in the Russian campaign. Another was, in the French service also, wounded and taken prisoner in Spain: and all of them are considered but bad subjects, and great Buonapartists.

Dined at home with Fitzroy.

May 18.— Neder Boulner. At home alone.

May 19.—Neder Boulner. Went in the morning to see the review of Prince Frederick of Orange's corps of 9000 men—some very young men. One fine brigade—Indian troops.

Breakfasted with Prince F.

May 20.—Went in the carriage to Brussels. The spring broke. Dined with Major-General Sir C. Grant. Major Hodge there.

May 21.—Brussels. Dined with Hodge and Keane at the 'Hôtel d'Angleterre.'

Rode in the evening to the Allée Vert, where, at about six o'clock, all the royal family, and all the inhabitants of Brussels, assemble on horseback, or carnages, or on foot; and a very gay and lovely scene it is.

May 22.—Went to a review of the corps of the Duke of Brunswick, and a very neat and complete corps it is—about 5500 infantry, 800 cavalry, and sixteen guns; all perfectly equipped and dressed in a most convenient and soldierlike manner in black. It rained very hard; but it had no other effect on their dress than to make it look brighter. Not so had they been decked out with pipe-clay and feathers.

Dined afterwards with the Duke of Wellington, and met the Duke of Brunswick and staff, and a Saxon *Chef de Brigade* of Cavalry, from whom I learnt that there was much dissatisfaction in the corps of Saxons against the Prussians, and a great wish on their part to serve with the British. To explain this was the object of his visit to Brussels.

May 23.—Returned to Neder Boulner, and went to the races at Grammont. Very good.

The Prince of Orange came and dined with me, with part of his staff. If I am not much mistaken. Colonel Knaife, his A.D.C., is more attached to his late master than to his present one, in spite of all the attentions he receives. Colonel Knaife served with Buonaparte in the Russian campaign.

May 24.—Went to the inspection of the Household brigade, and Sir W. Ponsonby's brigade, and dined afterwards with Lord Uxbridge; a very large party. The Prince of Orange, and Prince Frederick, a most delightful young man and a good soldier, dined there.

I have before remarked on the very beautiful manner in which the ground in this country is cultivated. The more I see of it the more I like it; not a weed anywhere to be seen. In no country is dressing more sought after, or better applied. The cattle are never turned out, and everything that can be converted into manure is collected into a general sink. From this liquid manure is carried on to the potato ground, and every plant is *blessed* with a ladle full of the highest perfume that one can imagine. The air, for an immense distance, is tainted when this is going on, and one can only wonder that the potato itself is not tainted.

The cattle are all kept in the houses. This surely must be an admirable plan. Nothing is wasted, neither manure nor fodder; and the little extra labour must be amply repaid, I should imagine, in the saving of these articles.

They do not, in this country, cut the potato into eyes to plant them, but put a whole one into each hole. Query: Does it answer to cut them? Does not a whole potato, with four eyes, produce more fruit than one of the eyes would? And supposing this to be the case, suppose a whole potato with four eyes produces ten fruit, and one of the eyes produces eight only, then it would be wise to plant whole ones; for by cutting the potatoes into four you have thirty-two fruit, whilst by planting four whole ones you have forty fruit. This gives a balance of eight in favour of planting whole potatoes. From this balance you must deduct three potatoes saved out of four by the cutting, and then five still remain in favour of planting whole ones. I cannot, for my part, think but that a whole potato must produce more fruit than one eye of one. However, I suppose it has been tried, for it is a very simple proposition.

May 25.—Lords Uxbridge, Bradford, and Hill dined with me at Neder Boulner.

May 26.—Dined with Lord Hill to meet Lord Bradford. They went afterwards to the Duke's ball at Brussels.

In the morning Vandeleur's and my brigades were out to mark the ground for a review of cavalry. Lord Uxbridge did not take it up as I thought best. He looked more to effect than to showing the brigades as they ought to be, under their respective commanders; and consequently divided Grant's brigade, because two regiments were Light Dragoons and one regiment Hussars. In my opinion a general inspecting a corps ought to see every man at the head of his proper division, brigade, and regiment. Then he is responsible for them.

★ ★ ★ ★ ★

The 7th Hussars at Waterloo were in Sir C. Grant's brigade, which then consisted of two Hussar and one Dragoon regiment; whereas at the time the above entry in the diary was made, it consisted of two Dragoon and one Hussar regiments.

The 7th Hussars, which at the commencement of the campaign were in Sir H. Vivian's brigade, were replaced by the 1st Hussars, K.G.L., who thereby obtained the wish they had expressed to him, as previously mentioned in the diary.

★ ★ ★ ★ ★

May 27.—Officers commanding regiments, and adjutants, &c., in the field for taking up the ground. Lord Uxbridge made a total change of the direction of the line; but still not quite what I could have wished.

Robbins, ——— (*illegible*), and Hozier, dined with me.

May 28.—General Fagel, Count Goltz (the Prussian Minister *auprès* Louis XVIII.), and Sir Sidney Smith dined with me. The three former slept at my house, having come to see the review the following day.

May 29.—The Duke of Wellington, Marshal Blucher, two Princes of Orange, General Gneisenau,[1] Duke de Berry, and a multitude of the general officers of all nations, came to see the review of the British cavalry and Horse Artillery.

There were present in the field the 1st and 2nd Life Guards (two squadrons each), Blues (two squadrons), King's Dragoon Guards (four squadrons), Lord E. Somerset's brigade; Royal Dragoons, Greys, and Inniskillings, Sir W. Ponsonbys brigade; 11th, 12th, and 16th Light Dragoons, Sir J. Vandeleur's brigade; 13th, 15th Hussars, and 23rd Light Dragoons, Sir C. Grant's brigade; 7th, 10th, and 18th, Sir H. Vivian's brigade; and six troops of Horse Artillery and thirty-six guns; and a force in more perfect order never was seen. The Duke merely passed down the line and saw them march past.

We afterwards dined, a party of 120 persons, the Duke, Blucher, &c., with Lord Uxbridge at Ninove; and never was anything better managed than the whole was, and I was happily disappointed in my fears as to the manner in which Lord Uxbridge proposed drawing up the cavalry not answering. Still, however, I think it was not done as it ought to have been. The day was beautiful, and the ground beautiful.

May 30.—Races at Grammont, of which I was one of the stewards; Lord H. Manners and Sir R. Hill my coadjutors. The races tolerably well attended, and very good, considering it rained.

Dined afterwards with Lord Hill, the two Princes of Orange, Sir S. Smith, Lord Bradford, &c.

May 31.—Neder Boulner.

June 1.—Do.

Lord Bradford and a large party dined with me. Lord and Lady Waldegrave, &c.

June 2.—Dined at Kerrison's.

* * * * *

Sir C. Kerrison was Colonel of the 7th Hussars, and, it will be remembered, took command of that regiment when Colonel Vivian (as he then was) was appointed to the command of a brigade during the campaign of 1813-14.

* * * * *

June 3.—Went into Brussels with Lord Uxbridge, after an inspection of the necessaries of cavalry, in which Lord Uxbridge got rid of some light articles of baggage, such as two shoe-brushes, a shirt, &c., per man; but he kept the *shabraques*. When a man keeps a *shabraque* of seven pounds weight, and gets rid of a shirt of one, it is no use attempting to talk reason on a subject where such folly exists and leads. The cavalry might easily be lightened, if all ridiculous articles were got rid of, and useful only retained.

In the evening went to a ball at Sir C. Stewart's.

June 4.—Returned from Brussels to Neder Boulner.

June 5.—Field day with the 10th, in a flood of rain.

Dined at home quietly.

June 6.—Races at Grammont, in a flood of rain. Lord and Lady Waldegrave came to see the races.

Dined at home *en famille* with them.

June 7.—Lord and Lady W. still with me,

Sir H. Ellis, Beauchamp, Croker, &c., met them at dinner.

June 8.—Rheumatism very bad. The Waldegraves left me. Shakespeare dined with me.

June 9.—At home with rheumatism.

June 10.—At home with rheumatism. Collins, Taylor, and two of the 18th dined with me.

June 11.—Dined Lord Uxbridge.

---

1. Gen. Gneisenau was second in command of the Prussian army under Blucher. During the retreat from Ligny, after Blucher had been knocked over and disabled, Gneisenau took sole command, and arranged the retreat which was so excellently and skilfully carried out. Blucher was greatly attached to Gneisenau, and used to say that it was Gneisenau who made up the pills which he (Blucher) administered. On one occasion at a party, when charades and riddles were going on, Blucher said that he could do what no one else could—*viz.*, kiss his own head; and on being asked to explain the riddle, he walked in the most affectionate and touching manner up to Gneisenau—who was one of the party—and embraced him, saying, "This is my head."

June 12.—Went to Tournai to inspect the 1st Hussars.

June 13.—At Tournai. Dined with the 1st Hussars. Nothing could be more gratifying and flattering than the reception this regiment gave me.

Heard that Buonaparte meant to advance on the 15th.

★ ★ ★ ★ ★

The 1st Hussars had now been placed in Sir H. Vivian's brigade, in lieu of the 7th Hussars, who had gone to Sir C. Grant's brigade.

Wellington at this time was in Brussels. Napoleon's army had been rapidly and secretly concentrating between the Sambre and the Meuse: but the frontier was so well guarded by outposts that but little information could be gained as to the movements of the French. Hooper states that:

> Wellington learnt from Sir Hussey Vivian that some movement of concentration was in progress; Napoleon, as he himself states, having arranged his outposts on the line of the Scheldt and Lys, to create expressly an impression that he was concentrating to his left.
>
> Napoleon intended to surprise the Allies. He quitted Paris on June 12, arrived at Leon that night, where he slept; went on the next day to Avesnes, and gave all directions for an advance on the 15th on Sombref and Quatre-Bras.
>
> This fact, however, was on the 13th, and up to a late hour on the June 15, unknown to Wellington.

Siborne, in his *Waterloo Campaign*, says:

> On June 12 Lieut.-Col. Wissell, whose regiment, the 1st Hussars, K.G.L., formed an extensive line of outposts in front of Tournay, reported to Major-Gen. Sir Hussey Vivian, to whose brigade the regiment belonged, that he had ascertained, from information on which he could rely, that the French army had assembled on the frontier, and was prepared to attack.
>
> Vivian desired him to report upon the subject to Lord Hill, to whose corps the regiment was attached while employed on that particular service.
>
> The next morning Vivian repaired in person to the outposts, and found that the French cavalry picket, which had been previously posted opposite Tournay, had a short time before marched to join the main army, and had been relieved by Douaniers.
>
> These, upon being spoken to by Vivian, did not hesitate to say

that their army was concentrating, and that if the Allies did not advance their troops would attack.

On returning to his quarters, Vivian communicated what he had seen and heard both to Lord Hill and the Earl of Uxbridge, by whom the circumstances were made known to the Duke of Wellington.

Sir H. Vivian's letter on this point is quoted later. It corroborates both Hooper and Siborne.

★ ★ ★ ★ ★

June 14.—Returned to Neder Boulner.

★ ★ ★ ★ ★

On this day Wellington was all day at his headquarters in Brussels. Blucher was at Namur, and early on the 14th had heard of Napoleon being at Avesnes. But neither he nor Wellington knew, nor could they know, that Napoleon's object was Sombreffe and Quatre-Bras. Blucher, however, being nearer the French, had more information than Wellington, and began to concentrate his forces at Fleurus.

Wellington, who would make no move except on accurate and ample information, did not alter the disposition of any of his troops, except to give orders for their assembly at the several alarm posts, till he should hear of a decided movement of the French army, and the real line of their attack became evident.

★ ★ ★ ★ ★

June 15.—Went to Brussels, to a ball at the Duchess of Richmond's, At the ball we heard that the French had advanced and driven the Prussians from Binche.

We all immediately left the ball and returned to our quarters, to march the next morning upon Enghien. From thence we proceeded by Braine-le-Comte to Nivelles; and from thence, as fast as we could go, to Quatre-Bras, where we arrived, after a march of forty miles, in dreadful roads, just too late to assist in defeating an attack of the French on the British force, which had lasted several hours, and in which, although a very small part of the army was up and no cavalry, Lord Wellington had completely defeated the enemy's plans; and this with a very great loss on their part, especially of *Cuirassiers* and *Lanciers*, who made a desperate attack on our infantry in squares, but completely without success.

The brunt of this action fell upon the division of Sir T. Picton (the

5th) of British, composed of the Highland brigade under General Pack, and another under General Kempt; and on the Guards, commanded by General Cooke and Generals Maitland and Byng; and some Dutch troops. The Duke of Brunswick was killed this day.

The French on the same day made an attack on the Prussians under Marshal Blucher, and, after some severe fighting, broke through his line of infantry at 9 o'clock at night with his cavalry, and took 14 pieces of cannon, and created great confusion. This occasioned the Marshal's retreating from the position he held on the road between Namur and Quatre-Bras to Gembloux and Wavre.

★ ★ ★ ★ ★

It was not till 3 o'clock in the afternoon of the 15th, when the Prince of Orange arrived to dine with him, that the Duke of Wellington heard that the French had attacked Thuin and Lobbes, and that the enemy appeared to be threatening Charleroi. That was all the information as to the movements that had taken place on the part of the French that the Duke then had.

★ ★ ★ ★ ★

In a letter to his wife, written on June 23, 1815 (the first halt after the battle of Waterloo), Sir H. Vivian writes:

> I take an opportunity of the first day's halt to give you a detailed account of our proceedings during the last eight days.
> On the 13th, you know, I went to Tournai, to inspect the 1st Hussars. I there heard that the whole French army had concentrated at Maubeuge, and that the persuasion in France was that Buonaparte would arrive from Paris and advance on the 15th. We treated this with contempt, supposing that he would hardly dare such a thing, although well aware that he had collected on the frontier the elite of the whole army.
> On the 14th I returned to my quarters at Neder Boulner, and on the 15th I went to Brussels, to attend the Duchess of Richmond's ball; and I should here notice that so little did the Duke of Wellington expect an advance of the enemy that he was to have given a ball on June 21, the anniversary of the battle of Vitoria.
> At dinner on the 15th, however, he heard that the enemy had advanced and driven the Prussians, who were at Binche, out of that place.
> At the ball reports came which proved the enemy were advanc-

ing in great force. Things became serious, and most of the officers about 12 or 1 o'clock left Brussels to join their respective corps.

We received orders to march at daybreak upon Enghien, 12 miles from Grammont.

From Enghien we moved, by Braine-le-Comte—12 miles more—to Nivelles, 12 more—the roads dreadful. Before arriving at Nivelles we heard a very considerable firing of artillery and musketry, and of course pressed on with all speed we possibly could, but unfortunately arrived too late at Quatre-Bras, six miles from Nivelles, to participate in an action which had been going on from early morning, but which had been very serious towards the end of the day, and ended, on the part of the British, with the complete defeat of every attempt upon their line, although made with desperation by the French, and in which they had a vast advantage owing to their having a great body of cavalry in the field, whereas the British had only a few Beige and Brunswick Light cavalry.

The roads through which we had to pass all day were dreadful; through forests knee-deep in mud. In fact it was almost impossible to get on.

The Prussians also were engaged within a league of us. The exact result of their battle we did not that night ascertain; but having stood our ground, and concluding they had stood theirs, we threw out our pickets and bivouacked on the field of battle.

★ ★ ★ ★ ★

In a letter to Mr. E. Vivian, Sir Hussey says:
★ ★ ★ ★ ★

We heard prior to the 15th that Buonaparte had been collecting his men near Maubeuge, and was himself about to leave Paris to attack us. Lord Wellington had felt persuaded he would do so; but what reason he had to form his opinion I know not, but certain it is that on the 15th, at a ball at the Duchess of Richmond's, we were all surprised to find that the French were pressing on with great force upon Binche and Nivelles.

We all left the ball and returned to our quarters, and on the following morning, about 5 o'clock, marched upon Enghien, Braine-le-Comte, and Nivelles; from thence to Quatre-Bras, where we came too late to join in a very severe affair, in which a small part only of our army had been engaged; for, to tell you the truth, our great general had committed a sad blunder in not having collected his forces before.

★ ★ ★ ★ ★

Writing in June 1839, Sir Hussey says:

★ ★ ★ ★ ★

In respect to the Duke being taken by surprise. That he must have been aware that the enemy was concentrating there can be no doubt.

I myself, on the 12th and 13th, visited Tournai and Mons. I found that in front of Tournai, where there had been a picket of French cavalry, they were replaced by *Douaniers*. I spoke to them, and they did not hesitate to say that their army was concentrating, and that if they did not attack us they expected we should attack them; and this I communicated on my return to my quarters, both to Lord Anglesey and to Lord Hill.

On the 15th I went to Brussels, and dined with Lord Anglesey. After dinner Sir Pulteney Malcombe came to us from the Duke, where he had dined, and said that the French had advanced, and, I think he said, had taken Charleroi.

At night we all went to the Duchess of Richmond's ball.

It was only during the ball that the Duke called several of those who commanded divisions or brigades together, and told us to be prepared to move in the morning; and it was during the night only that orders were issued for the actual march of the British army from the right towards Nivelles; and it was on the march that we received orders to continue our march on Quatre-Bras.

That the Duke must have been aware, therefore, that the French were concentrating, there can be no doubt.

That the uncertainty of the front on which they would make their attack prevented his concentrating his force sooner, I think is equally clear; and that he did not expect the attack quite so soon, I am very much disposed to believe; and he was probably led to this from the fact of information having only about the 14th, I think, reached him of the Imperial Guard having left Paris, and from his not calculating that they could so soon have arrived with the army, and been in a state of readiness to advance. (See *Waterloo Letters*. Published by Leonaur)

★ ★ ★ ★ ★

Major-Gen. Napier, writing in 1842 (see *Waterloo Letters*), gives the following interesting account as to when and how the Duke of Wellington first heard of the advance of the French; which account. General Napier says, he had from the Duke's own mouth.

He (the Duke) found the Prince of Orange at the Duchess of Richmond's ball on the evening of the 15th.

He was surprised to see him, because he had placed him at Binche, an important outpost, for the purpose of observing and giving notice of the enemy's movements.

He went up to him, and asked if there was any news. 'No; nothing but that the French had crossed the Sambre, and had a brush with the Prussians. Have you heard of it?'

This *was news*! So the Duke told him quietly that he had better go back to his post, and then, by degrees, he got the principal officers away from the ball, and sent them to their troops. This was done, I think he said, about eleven o'clock.

He then went to his quarters, and found Müffling there, coming from Blucher with the news. He ought to have arrived long before, 'but,' said the Duke, 'I cannot tell the world that Blucher picked the fattest man in his army to ride with an express to me, and that he took thirty hours to go thirty miles."

According to other historians, however, the Prince of Orange lunched with the Duke as early as 3 p.m.

Within twenty-four hours from the time he had received decisive information, the Duke of Wellington had collected upwards of 30,000 men at Quatre-Bras.

As Sir Hussey Vivian's brigade arrived too late at Quatre-Bras to take any active part in the action, he gives only a short account of that battle in his diary, which requires slightly augmenting in order to explain the state of affairs, both with regard to the British and Prussian positions and movements.

The French army had concentrated near Maubeuge, and on the 15th, about noon, had crossed the Sambre—one of the points of attack that Wellington had anticipated, but not thought most probable. Ney (who had only received orders to join the army on the 11th) came up with Napoleon about 4.30 on the 15th, and was at once placed in command of a large portion of the French army, and simply instructed to drive ahead, and push back the enemy on the left of the

French advance.

The Prussians were gradually drawing their troops together, and whilst opposing, or rather making a show of resistance so as to impede the French advance, were at the same time gradually, and in good order, falling back on Fleurus. On the Allies' left. Prince Bernhardt of Saxe Weimar had also retired and united his brigade at Quatre-Bras, to which place Ney followed him.

On the morning of the 16th Napoleon was extraordinarily late before making any movement; and Ney also, apparently, had received no orders as to occupying Quatre-Bras.

It was not till between 7 and 8 in the morning of the 16th that Napoleon seems to have made up a plan, when he divided his army into two wings. The left wing of 33,520 infantry, 8800 cavalry, and 96 guns, was under Ney; the right wing consisted of 42,869 infantry, 15,023 cavalry, and 144 guns, and was under Grouchy. In addition to these the reserve was composed of the Imperial Guard, 13,206 infantry, 1718 horse, and 96 guns, under Napoleon himself.

The right wing was to march upon Sombreffe, and there take up a position. Napoleon, before noon, was to be in Fleurus, and if he met an enemy was to push on to Gembloux; and the left wing was to march on Brussels, occupying Quatre-Bras, Genappe, and Marbais, *en route*.

Napoleon thought the Prussians would concentrate at Namur, and that Wellington would do so at Nivelles. Napoleon's object was to impede the junction of the British and the Prussians, to vanquish them in detail, establish himself in Brussels, and arouse the people.

Ney received his orders to push on about 11 o'clock, and Grouchy his about 9.30, in the morning of the 16th. But, as the Prussians were now in force near Fleurus, the latter could not move further forward, and was still there when Napoleon drove up about 1 o'clock, unwilling to believe that Blucher had dared to court an encounter so soon. He could not bring himself to realise that three-quarters of the Prussian army were there drawn up in battle array.

Wellington during this time had ridden over from Quatre-Bras, to which place he had gone early on the morning of the 16th, to communicate with Blucher; and whilst on his way, learning that the Prussians were forming their troops in columns and not in line, because Blucher was of opinion that the Prussian soldier would not stand in line, said: "Then the artillery will play upon them, and they will be beaten damnably." He afterwards saw Blucher, and it was then agreed that Blucher should fight, and that Wellington should, as soon as possible, move up troops from Quatre-Bras against the French left, and support Blucher by an attack on the French flank.

Wellington rode back to Quatre-Bras to find that he himself was being so vigorously attacked by the enemy that there was no possibility of his carrying out the arrangement he had made with Blucher. But for this it might have been possible that the English at Ligny might have played the part that the Prussians afterwards did at Waterloo.

With regard to Ligny, the battle fought by the Prussians, all that it is necessary to say for the present purpose is that it was most gallantly contested by the Prussians, and was a most bloody battle because of the hatred that existed between the two nations. None demanded, none gave, quarter; and there were no survivors but the victors. Eventually Napoleon turned the Prussian flank, and gained the battle, but he had not routed the Prussian army. There was no flight.

During the night the Prussians, without the slightest interference from the French, and apparently even without their knowledge, quietly and secretly withdrew the whole of their army towards Wavre, leaving their camp fires burning.

Whilst the battle of Ligny was being fought Ney, about 9, o'clock in the afternoon, began to attack the British and Dutch-Belge forces at Quatre-Bras. When the action first commenced there were but few English soldiers present, but all through the afternoon they kept hurrying up from their various quarters at their utmost speed.

One of the chief characteristics of the battle of Quatre-Bras was that Wellington had practically no cavalry there, and had consequently to fight the enemy's cavalry and artillery with artillery only and with squares of infantry.

Picton's brigade, which arrived at the scene of action about 2.30 in the afternoon, behaved with extraordinary gallantry, and, in squares, resisted successfully most furious charges made by Ney's cavalry. The 42nd, even when in the act of forming square and when only half formed, successfully resisted a charge of *Lanciers*. And the 44th did even more; they actually resisted a charge when *in line*; for when the cavalry unexpectedly rushed on them the rear rank of the 44th faced about and delivered so steady a fire that the *Lanciers* were driven off, and they thus defeated the cavalry charge when standing only two deep and with one line only opposed to the charge.

In one charge of the French made during this battle Wellington himself, having been carried away by a somewhat precipitate retreat made by some foreign troops, was nearly captured, and only saved himself by leaping his horse over the 92nd Highlanders, who lined a ditch and stopped the enemy.

The 69th lost a large number of men in one charge of the French *Cuirassier's*. They had been warned by Sir C. Halkett to form square, and were in the act of doing so when they were heedlessly stopped in the movement by the Prince of Orange. A moment afterwards a body of *Cuirassiers* charged and took them in flank, rode over and sabred the men, and captured one of the colours. The 30th just managed to form square in time, having disregarded the Prince's commands, and successfully repulsed the vanquishers of the 69th.

Wellington grew stronger, and Ney weaker, every moment; and in the evening, about 6.30, the Guards arrived under Major-Gen. Cooke, and their gallantry and marvellous discipline and training enabled the British to retake all the ground they had previously been obliged to partially cede.

Both armies eventually took up for the night the positions they had originally occupied, Ney having lost one-quarter and Wellington one-seventh of the forces actually engaged.

★ ★ ★ ★ ★

June 17.—The British, Hanoverians, and Belgians remained during the night on the same ground where the battle had been fought.

This morning we learnt that the Prussians had retreated (as before stated), and it became necessary for us to do the same. It was commenced about 8 o'clock by the infantry, the cavalry being left to cover them. The French army remained quietly looking on, opposite to us, until about 2 o'clock.

We then perceived an immense column of cavalry making their appearance on our left, and we commenced our retreat at the instant that the most tremendous storm came on I ever witnessed.

The enemy pressed us very severely in the centre, and in one instance did very considerable mischief to the 7th Hussars, and by a cannonade killed several of the Blues.

The army occupied a position in front of Waterloo, having its right at Braine l'Alleud and its left in front of Verd Cocu, its centre at Mont St. Jean.

★ ★ ★ ★ ★

The above is all that is contained in Sir Hussey's *Diary* as to the retreat from Quatre-Bras to the position where the battle of Waterloo was fought. He could have had but little time for writing, because, as a matter of fact, his brigade had some severe fighting and hard work whilst assisting to cover the retreat of the army.

After the battle of Ligny the Prussians had retreated, but, owing to the negligence of Napoleon and his officers in not sending out scouts, no Frenchman knew exactly whither they had gone, or indeed that they had gone at all, so quietly and with such regularity had their retreat during the night and early morning been conducted.

Ney had not been informed of the battle of Ligny, and Napoleon did not know the result of the contest at Quatre-Bras until eleven hours after the last gun had been fired. Wellington's patrols, on the other hand, had brought him early intelligence of the retreat of the Prussians and of the inactivity of Napoleon, and he wondered at Ney not moving to attack him. Hooper says:

> Within an hour of daybreak Captain Wood, who had patrolled long the Namur road, reported to the Duke the retreat of the Prussians; and Colonel Gordon, with Grey's troop of the 10th Hussars [one of the regiments in Sir Hussey's brigade] communicated with General Ziethen, then on his way to Wavre.
> An officer from Blucher himself confirmed the information acquired by Colonel Gordon, and Wellington determined to retreat.
> He sent word to Blucher that he should fall back on the position of Mont St. Jean, and there, if the Marshal would support him with two corps, fight the enemy.
> Blucher's reply did not reach Wellington till the evening of the 17th, when he had arrived at Waterloo. It said:' I will join you, not only with two corps, but with the whole army; and if the enemy does not attack you on the 18th, we will attack him together on the 19th.'
> Fuller details of the movements of the patrol sent out on the morning after Quatre-Bras are given in Siborne's *History*.

It was not long before Wellington, who had slept at Genappe, arrived at Quatre-Bras, where he found Major-Gen. Sir Hussey Vivian, whose brigade of Light Cavalry, consisting of the 10th British Hussars under Colonel Quentin, of the 18th British Hussars under Lieut.-Col. the Hon. Henry Murray, and of the 1st Hussars of the King's German Legion under Lieut.-Col. Wissell, was posted on the left of that point, with two strong picquets thrown out—one of the 18th Hussars, under Captain Croker, on the Namur road, and the other of the 10th Hussars, under the Hon. F. Howard, in front, with a picquet from the latter, under Lieutenant Arnold, on the right of the Namur road.

Vivian, on being asked what account he could give of the enemy, communicated to the Duke the results of his observations, which were necessarily very limited, as, with the exception of the firing that had taken place at early dawn between some outposts along the line of picquets, the French had continued perfectly quiet, and had as yet given no indication of any offensive movement.

The Duke then took a general survey of the field, and while sweeping the horizon with his telescope he discovered a French *vedette* on some rising ground in the direction of Fleurus and a little to the right of the high road leading to Namur, apparently belonging to some picquet thrown out from Ney's extreme right on the previous night after the battle had ceased, or to some detached corps placed in that quarter for the purpose of observation and for the maintenance of the communication between Ney and Napoleon.

The Duke had received no intelligence of Blucher. Probably judging from the advanced position of the *vedette* in question that, whatever might have been the result of the battle of Ligny, the Prussians could not have made any forward movement likely to endanger Ney's right, he came to the conclusion that it was quite possible that on the other hand Napoleon might have crossed the Namur road and cut off his communication with Blucher.

The Duke, therefore, desired Vivian to send a strong patrol along the Namur road to gain intelligence respecting the Prussian army.

A troop of the 10th Hussars, under Captain Grey, was accordingly despatched on this duty, accompanied by Lieut.-Colonel the Hon. Sir Alexander Gordon, one of the Duke's A.D.Cs.

As the patrol advanced along the road the *vedette* before mentioned began to circle, evidently to give notice of the approach of an enemy, and then retired.

This induced the patrol to move forward with great caution so as to guard against the possibility of being cut off. Nevertheless it continued, but with all due precaution, advancing along the road, until, after passing a few scattered cottages comprising a hamlet called Petit Marbais, it reached, about a mile and a half further on, some rising ground about five miles from Quatre-Bras and beyond which was another height.

A *vedette* was observed posted upon the latter, but who had evidently not yet discovered the approach of Captain Grey's troop; down in the intervening hollow was an isolated house, at the door of which stood a dismounted sentry, and some horses were standing in an adjoining yard.

Captain Grey directed Lieutenant Bacon to patrol towards the house, whilst he remained with the remainder of the troops concealed from the enemy's view; a disposition favoured by the nature of the ground and the trees and hedges on both sides of the road.

When Lieutenant Bacon's party moved forward it was discovered by the *vedette* who began circling and fired his carbine. The French picquet posted in the house instantly rushed out; several of the men had their jackets and accoutrements off, and the post could have been easily captured, had the special duty on which the British patrol was engaged admitted of an attack.

The French turned out very quickly and galloped to the rear along the high road, while Bacon's party was recalled. A few French cavalry galloped up to the *vedette* on the heights, but evinced no disposition to advance.

It had now become sufficiently evident that, commencing from this point, the French were in possession of the Namur road; but the principal object which Sir A. Gordon had in view was yet to be obtained.

The patrol now retired a little until it reached a cross road, which a peasant pointed out as the Prussian line of retreat.

Pursuing the track, the patrol, within an hour, reached Tilly, where General Ziethen, who had been placed in temporary command of the cavalry, was covering the retreat of the Prussian army.

After remaining here about a quarter of an hour, during which Sir A. Gordon obtained from General Ziethen the most ample information respecting the movements of the Prussians, the patrol commenced its return at a quick pace, striking into a cross road which joined the high road at a point nearer to Quatre-Bras than the one whence it had quitted it.

The patrol reached Quatre-Bras about 7.30, and Sir A. Gordon immediately reported to the Duke that the Prussians had retreated towards Wavre; that the French occupied the ground on which the battle had been fought; but that they had not crossed the high road, along which the patrol had proceeded almost into the immediate vicinity of their advanced outposts.

In a footnote Captain Siborne mentions that Lieut.-Col. Wood of the 10th Hussars, in the *Naval and Military Magazine* for July 1841, and March 1847, published a statement to the effect that he was sent forward to patrol previous to Captain Grey being sent; that he fell in with the Prussian stragglers, who agreed that Blucher had retired; that at a village on the high road he had found the French *vedettes*; that he had met Sir A. Gordon's patrol and suggested their bearing to the left, and that he then told the Duke what he had seen, who sent directions to the brigades on the march to turn on Waterloo.

Hooper continues his account of the retreat thus:

About 8 o'clock on the 17th Wellington began his retreat, sending off the infantry first, and leaving the cavalry in masses to cover the retreat.

Vivian's and Vandeleur's Light cavalry were on the left, and the Duke himself was with the 10th Hussars, who stood in echelon of squadrons on the scene of Picton's exploits.

In the centre were the Heavy cavalry and the Union brigades, and on the right Grant and Dornberg.

Ney's horsemen were gradually pressing forward. On the British left Subervie's Lancers, coming from Marbais, were in action with the outposts of Vivian's Hussars; and behind them came Milhaud's *Cuirassiers*, whose mail gleamed in the noonday sun. Vivian threw back his left to face the force bearing down upon their flank, and soon the skirmishers were engaged from the Namur road to the eastern fringe of the wood of Bossu.

Wellington did not intend to resist; so the three columns of cavalry went about and retired: Vivian and Vandeleur by a byroad that led to Thuy, a few miles below Wais la Hutte; but this left column had no sooner gone about than the French guns opened upon them, and their horse seemed intent upon outflanking the rear regiment and coming to close quarters.

Vivian halted and prepared to charge, but no sooner had his artillery begun to fire than a violent and drenching thunderstorm broke over them and made rapid cavalry movement impossible.

The ardour of the pursuit relaxed, and no further incident occurred until the brigade reached the river by Genappe.

Vandeleur, who had left to Vivian the glory of guarding the rear, was still crossing by the bridge. The French were pressing on. Vivian, to check, them, immediately brought up the 10th to support the 1st K.G.L., and kept the French at bay until Vandeleur had crossed. Then he sent back the 10th with orders to dismount and line the banks on the other side of the bridge.

The situation was critical. One squadron of the 1st, retiring, was cut off and compelled to seek a ford lower down. The French coming up in great force seemed to be sure of overthrowing the Germans, when Vivian gave the word and his Hussars galloped down the road and over the bridge.

The French dashed after them with loud shouts, but they were too late. The 10th Hussars on the opposite bank saluted them with a brisk fire; and a regiment and a half were ready to charge if they ventured to cross. They refrained, and the brigade proceeded to Verd Cocu on the east of Mont St. Jean.

★ ★ ★ ★ ★

Sir H. Vivian, in the account he wrote to his wife, alluding to this affair, says:

> It then became necessary for us to retreat, for it was obvious that Buonaparte would bring all his forces against us. Orders were given accordingly, and the cavalry left to cover the retreat; the Hussars in front, Grant's brigade on the right, mine on the left.
>
> We remained quietly on the ground till about 2 o'clock, when immediately on my left I observed a great dust, and by looking a little nearer, I discovered an enormous column of *Cuirassiers, Lanciers*, Hussars, &c., moving over a hill into the high road, which was on my flank.
>
> My pickets were soon engaged and driven in. A brigade of the enemy trotted up the road and formed opposite to me, a little ravine separating us. I opened upon them with my horse artillery, and they very soon returned the compliment with theirs, and knocked over a man of the 10th and a few horses. A large body also moved up the road to attack our centre, where Gen-

eral Dornberg was posted with the 7th Hussars and 23rd.

The line of Heavy Cavalry and Light Dragoons in our rear had by this time received orders to fall back, and we in advance were to do the same. This I did very *contre gré*; for at this moment a brigade of *Lanciers* and *Chasseurs-à-cheval* were about to attempt crossing the ravine in my front, and my fingers were itching to have a hit at them.

However we retired quietly enough. They cannonaded my rear, and pressed my rear squadron, until we crossed a little river (the Dyle) which runs by Genappe, and there I formed the 10th to support my rear guard, and they molested me no more.

Not so the poor 7th, who were in the high road parallel to me on my right. The principal body of cavalry pressed down the road with horse artillery, &c., and some very severe work they had. Poor Hodge, Mayer, and Elphinstone, gallantly leading a charge of the regiment, were wounded and made prisoners. The report was that both Hodge and Mayer were killed. The regiment suffered very severely, and I believe things were not exactly what they ought to have been, owing to some mistake; the officers were all broken-hearted about it. After this the Blues and Lifeguards were brought up to cover the retreat, and behaved admirably and suffered severely.

We reached our position extending from Braine-le-Comte to Mont St. Jean, in front of Waterloo, in the centre, to a small village in front of Verd Cocu on the left. The Prussians at Wavre and Gembloux were on our left, but at a considerable distance. In the retreat of the previous day a most tremendous storm had soaked us all to the skin.

In his letter to Mr. E. Vivian, Sir Hussey says:

On the 17th, owing to the Prussians having been beaten on our left and retreated, we were obliged to do the same to Mont St. Jean, near Waterloo, where we occupied a position, and no very strong one either.

On our retreat we were considerably pressed by the enemy's cavalry, who gave us a pretty good specimen of their boldness. They played the d——l with my old regiment, the 7th, which is not in my brigade. They did not press me much. I covered the retreat of the left column,

We had the most tremendous rain I ever beheld, and were

soaked to the skin without anything to change, and the canopy of heaven for our covering—no very comfortable commencement of a campaign which was to take us, almost without a blow, to Paris.

In a letter to Captain Siborne, written in 1839 and published in *Waterloo Letters* p. 150, Sir Hussey gives more details as to what occurred on this retreat of June 17.

On the morning of the 17th at daybreak, or soon after, the Duke came to Quatre-Bras. I believe he had slept at Genappe. I was on horseback, near the house at Quatre- Bras, looking about. Some few of the enemy's *vedettes* only were to be seen, and, my brigade being on the left, I had two strong picquets out; one of the 18th, on the Namur road, and one of the 10th Hussars in front. The 1st Hussars had only joined me from Tournai in the night, after an immense march.

The Duke asked me what account I could give of the enemy. I told him all I knew, which was not in fact much, for they had been very quiet. He then desired that I should send half a squadron with an A.D.C. of his (Colonel Gordon) on the Namur road. I did so, and in about an hour, or rather more, they returned, reporting that the enemy were to be seen on the right of the road, about two miles distant, where they had been engaged with the Prussians the preceding day; but that they could not learn that they had crossed the road. This patrol, however, seeing the enemy on the right, had not ventured to push on very far, from a fear of being cut off.

Soon after the patrol was sent off the Duke received some despatches from England; and shortly after that, I think, he gave orders for the retreat, having satisfied himself that, although the enemy were not in motion, still they were preparing to move.

He then laid himself down on the ground, covered his head with one of the newspapers he had been reading, and appeared to fall asleep; and in this way he remained some time, when he again rose and mounted his horse and rode down the field in front of Quatre-Bras a little distance, and looked about with his glass; and I perfectly well remember his expressing his astonishment at the perfect quiet of the enemy, and his saying that it was not at all impossible that they also might be retreating.

He remained for some time longer anxiously looking out, when on a sudden, on the road to Namur, at a considerable distance, I should say about three miles, we saw something glittering in the sun, which was rising brilliantly. The Duke at first said they were the French bayonets, but on looking through my glass I saw they were *Cuirassiers*, moving on the road and forming in the field by the side of it. Very shortly after, the picket of the 18th Hussars began skirmishing, as did that of the 10th in our front, and also that of the 7th (I believe) on our right.

My brigade, with their guns, formed on the left of the house at Quatre-Bras; Vandeleur's in their rear and on their right somewhat. Presently the 18th picket came galloping in, followed by two or three squadrons of French cavalry, on which my guns opened a fire; and, if I am not mistaken, some guns of another brigade on the right did the same. This checked the advance of the French, but we presently saw them very active in bringing up guns, and soon a fire was opened upon us.

The Duke had by this time left us to go more to the right. Lord Anglesey, who remained, told me we were to retire, and that Vandeleur's brigade would support mine, and he then left me.

I saw the enemy pressing on in vast numbers, not only in my front, but on my left flank. I therefore ordered off the guns at once. Fortunately, I had early in the morning sent an officer of the artillery, Lieutenant Swabey, to reconnoitre the passages of the little River Dyle, and he had discovered a bridge to which a road, parallel to the high road, led from the rear of Quatre-Bras, and which was a little higher up the river than Genappe. To this bridge, then, he at once moved, at a trot, with his guns, and passed without interruption from the enemy.

I put my brigade about and retreated in line, covered by skirmishers.

Across a small dip in the ground, and standing rather in a commanding position, Vandeleur's brigade was drawn up, distant from me about 600 or 700 yards. I fully calculated on his allowing me to pass through, and his taking the rear. The enemy had brought some guns to bear on us, and I recollect a soldier of the 18th being killed by a shot immediately before me, in the ranks of that regiment, as we were retiring.

On my retiring within about 50 or 60 yards of Sir J. Vandeleur, he put his brigade about and retired; upon which I moved to the ground he had occupied, and directed the 1st Hussars to cover the left flank and left front.

In this manner we stood some time skirmishing with the enemy, and during which Lieut.-Col. Thornhill, A.D.C., came from Lord Uxbridge to me to see what we were about. I told him I had enough upon my hands, but that I hoped to get my people all well off, and I sent an A.D.C. to Sir J. Vandeleur to desire he would, as fast as possible, get his brigade over the river in order that I might have no interruption in my retreat in case I was hard pressed.

About this time the most tremendous storm I almost ever witnessed came on, in a very short time rendering the ground so deep that the horses had some difficulty in moving- quick through it. To this I am persuaded I am in a very great degree indebted for the little loss I experienced in the retreat over the bridge.

The enemy began to relax in their preparations for enveloping me, which considerable bodies assembling on my left appeared preparing to do. Those in my front were content with simply skirmishing.

I sent off the 18th and the 10th, ordering both regiments to form on the other side of the bridge and the 10th to dismount some of their men, who were armed with rifles, to defend it, and prevent the French from pursuing our rearguard over it should they press us hard; and I remained with the 1st Hussars K.G.L. This regiment had now taken the whole of the rearguard of our left and skirmished with the enemy, but no charge took place. On the high road to our right skirmishing was also going on, and I observed the greater portion of the enemy's cavalry were directed to that road.

After some time I sent off a squadron of the 1st Hussars towards the bridge, and when we began to do this the French again pressed on so much as to interpose between the left squadron and the body of the regiment, and obliged that squadron to pass the little River Dyle higher up than the bridge over which we passed.

When I found all was ready, I galloped off down the road to the bridge with the remaining troops of the Hussars. The French followed us, cheering, and took a sergeant, whose horse was wounded. On our passing the bridge, and the enemy's arriving at it, some of the dismounted men fired, and from that moment no attempt was made to molest us.

I halted my brigade some little time on the ground beyond the bridge, and then moved quietly on the narrow lane which runs parallel to the high road by an old abbey—I think called the Abbey of Ayanors—to the hamlet of Verd Cocu, where I bivouacked, the officers occupying three small houses.

★ ★ ★ ★ ★

Captain Tomkinson, an officer in the 16th Dragoons, which regiment was in Vandeleur's brigade, confirms Sir Hussey's main statement as to the above affair and Vandeleur's brigade; for in a letter he wrote to Captain Siborne, sending an extract from a diary he had kept (and which has since been published under the title of *Diary of a Cavalry Officer*, [published by Leonaur as *With Wellington's Light Cavalry*]) and which is hereafter referred to in connection with another matter), he says:

> I have no doubt Sir Hussey Vivian expected us to cover him, and *so we were ordered to do*; but the events I have mentioned changed that purpose, and made it impossible.

The words underlined by me appear conclusive as to Sir J. Vandeleur having been told to support Sir H. Vivian.

The extract from Captain Tomkinson's diary contains these words:

> The two brigades of Hussars were in the first line, General Vandeleur's brigade in the second line, and the Heavy cavalry in support some distance to the rear.
>
> The intention of Lord Uxbridge was to keep the Hussars to take advantage of any favourable opportunity, and on the enemy advancing in such force as to oblige us to retire, they were to *pass through the second line* (our brigade), *and it to cover the retreat.*
>
> I saw the French cavalry when turning out of their bivouack, and I thought from their numbers that we must either bring all our force to oppose them, and keep our ground, or that if a retreat were determined on the sooner we marched the more prudent.
>
> They came out column after column, and in greater force than I ever recollect seeing together at one point.
>
> They advanced in very great bodies, and Lord Uxbridge soon saw that so far from having any chance of charging, he had

nothing left but to get his troops away with the least possible delay.

We, the second line, were ordered away immediately, and retired, leaving Genappe on our left on retiring.

The first line got away without much loss, retiring with the Heavy brigade on Genappe, but had not time allowed it to retire through the second line as at first intended. There was not time for the Hussars to pass through our brigade, the enemy was so close upon them; and had we not got off with the least possible delay, the Hussars and our brigade would have been in one confused heap. We had learnt the necessity of making way for those in front when we and they were retiring.

The infantry being all clear and the enemy showing so large a force of cavalry, we ought not to have waited so long.

Colonel Childers sent to Captain Siborne the following account of the matter, as given by Lieut.-Gen. Sleigh in 1845:

Previous to the brigades retiring, the 4th (Vandeleur's) was formed in rear of the 6th (Vivian's) some short distance.

We received instructions to send an officer to ascertain where we could cross the Genappe River, and to commence our retreat as soon as this had been found.

Before the officers returned who had been sent from the two brigades, that tremendous rain commenced.

We moved off, and gradually proceeded to the bridge, Vivian's brigade and the guns following.

We took up no new or commanding position until the brigade had crossed.

The 11th Dragoons was the leading regiment when they broke into column to pass the bridge, and I fully remember Sir J. Vandeleur desiring me to form as soon as I could find an open space, leaving the road clear for the guns and rear brigade.

This was done, and the 4th Brigade remained until Lord Vivian's and the guns had passed; and this is shown, I believe, if I recollect rightly, in Siborne's statement; as it will be found we were the last brigade that got to the final position; then, if Sir J. Vandeleur had received instructions to allow the rear brigade to pass and relieve them, he did so the moment he could and at the most material point.

Colonel Childers, in commenting on the above, says:

It only shows how hopeless it is to expect (after such a lapse of time) an account from those who were actors in what then took place in which all should agree. For my part, I do not even recollect the bridge to which the Lieut.-General refers.

The account given in Siborne's *History* (3rd edition) of the affair at the bridge of Genappe runs thus:

> These skilful dispositions had scarcely been arranged when the picquet of the 18th Hussars on the left came in at a good round trot, upon which Vivian's battery of horse artillery opened fire, whereby the enemy's advance was checked.
>
> The enemy, however, was observed to be very active in bringing up his artillery, which soon opened upon the Hussars.
>
> Vivian having received the Earl of Uxbridge's instructions to retire, *accompanied by an intimation that he would be supported by Vandeleur's brigade*, then in his rear, and observing that the French cavalry was pressing forward in great numbers, not only in his front but also on his flank, put his brigade about and retired in line, covered by the skirmishers.
>
> The French followed with loud shouts of '*Vive l'Empereur*,' and just as the brigade reached a sort of hollow, their guns again opened, throwing shells which mostly flew over the heads of the 18th Hussars, against which regiment they appeared to be principally directed.
>
> In the meantime, Vandeleur's brigade had been drawn up in support on rather a commanding position, and Vivian *approached it in the full expectation that it would open out for the passing of his own men and take the rearguard in its turn*; but on the Hussars arriving within fifty or sixty yards of the 4th Brigade, Vandeleur put it about and retired; *Vivian not being aware that Vandeleur had previously received orders to retire and leave the road clear for the retreat of the cavalry in his front*.
>
> Vivian immediately occupied the ground thus vacated, and with a view to check the enemy's advance more effectually ordered the 18th to charge as soon as the French appeared within favourable distance.

Captain Siborne then gives an account of how Sir Hussey got his men over the bridge and checked the enemy by the dismounted men of the 10th and the remainder of his brigade drawn up on the other side of the river.

The earlier editions of Siborne did not contain the words: "Vivian not being aware that Vandaleur had previously received orders to retire and leave the road clear for the cavalry in his front;" and the statement originally published led to considerable discussion and correspondence.

Sir Hussey appears to have stuck to the main facts as being absolutely correctly stated, but he never intended in any way to insinuate (as seems to have been inferred) that Sir J. Vandeleur had acted in anything like a cowardly manner; for in one of Sir Hussey's letters he speaks of Sir J. Vandeleur as being "as gallant an old fellow as ever breathed."

It would seem that Sir J. Vandeleur received orders to retire, but that this fact was not brought to Sir Hussey's knowledge, who on the contrary had been informed by Lord Uxbridge that Vandeleur would support him; and there can be no doubt that Sir Hussey fully expected that this would be done, and that he was thrown into an awkward and critical position through his expectation not being realised.

Sir Hussey, however, was willing to admit as a fact that Vandeleur might not have been instructed to support him; and did not therefore contest the assertion afterwards made by Sir J. Vandeleur to the effect that he, Vandeleur, had absolute orders to retire.

A letter showing that this was so appears in *Waterloo Letters*, (published by Leonaur) where Sir J. Vandeleur writes to Captain Siborne:

> I am perfectly satisfied with your proposal, *viz*., that the last declared opinion of the late Lord Vivian was that Sir J. Vandeleur had received no instructions to support his. Sir H. Vivian's, brigade on the 17th June; and with the alterations you propose to insert and which Colonel Childers approves of, namely adding the following sentence 'Vivian not being aware that Vandeleur had previously received orders to retire and leave the road clear for the retreat of the cavalry in his front.

The third edition of Siborne, therefore, contains these words; but, as already pointed out, whether Sir J. Vandeleur received instructions (as Captain Tomkinson says he did) which were subsequently altered; or whether he received no instructions at all to support Sir Hussey; the main fact remains the same—Vandeleur did not support Sir Hussey when the latter expected him to do so, and the consequence was that Sir Hussey was placed in a critical and anxious position with his brigade.

Colonel Taylor gives a full and interesting account of the part played by his regiment, the 10th Hussars (and part of Vivian's brigade) during the march to Quatre-Bras, and the retreat of the 17th; which account he, at the request of Sir H. Vivian, put into writing in 1829.

He says:

On the 15th June I rode home from Brussels to Vivorde, by myself, in the evening, and found that there were orders for a field-day the next morning.

On the 16th, about half-past 4 a.m., my servant called me and said the regiment was to turn out in full marching order to change quarters.

The brigade assembled on the road from Vivorde to Grammont. We waited some time for the 18th Hussars,

When assembled we commenced our march about seven. We proceeded through Grammont and Enghien, falling in with other corps of cavalry on the march.

At Enghien lieutenant Parsons, of my troop, joined, having come across from Brussels, where I had left him the day before; he informed me of the advance of the French; that the troops had turned out of Brussels, and that there would probably be an action in the course of the day.

After some hours' march we turned off the road to the right, dismounted and fed, and the men and officers dined on what they had in their haversacks or could procure.

Continued the march to Braine-le-Comte. In passing through a deep wood beyond that town we began to hear firing; on our issuing from the wood it became quite distinct, and soon we were enabled to see the line of fire of the action of Quatre-Bras from the right bank of the road.

An order arrived from Lord Uxbridge to throw away our hay and to trot at nine miles per hour towards Nivelles, which we did accordingly.

We passed through Nivelles, in which we saw several wagons with wounded.

We had then an order to proceed two miles on the Namur road, and the brigade, with its horse artillery, trotting up the road made no small clatter.

We met several wounded coming out of action. When we got near the left of the wood at Quatre-Bras the firing was still going on and some cannon shot passed us; a horse of the 18th, I heard, was killed.

We formed half squadrons, and were then ordered to canter, and in this way advanced to the field and halted.

Our horses, in spite of the long march—between thirty and forty miles, I should think, for some of the corps—were very fresh. One horse of ours broke his neck by falling into a hollow road we passed, in consequence of his pulling and throwing up his head.

The action was now over; only a gun firing now and then, and a few occasional shots of *tirailleurs*.

We heard of the Duke of Brunswick's death, and of the battle of Ligny and that the Prussians had retired. [*This as a fact could not have been so till later in the day.*]

We retired and dismounted, and bivouacked in a wheat field behind the left of the wood in which the Guards had been engaged.

June 17.—About 2 a.m. a troop was ordered to patrol with Sir A. Gordon, the Duke of Wellington's A.D.C. Captain Grey's troop went, they had twelve miles out and as many back [*Sir H. Vivian has here noted in the margin 'Not five,' which seems to be more probable*] but were, I believe, unsuccessful in communicating with the Prussians.

Firing commenced at daybreak between the pickets of infantry and lasted with little intermission till near 12.

Major Howard's squadron had been on picket during the night at a farm in front and to the left of Quatre-Bras, whither we all went in the morning, by squadrons, to water, and then returned to the brow of the hill and dismounted and breakfasted, having a good view of the infantry skirmishing.

The infantry, guns, and baggage commenced retiring, the pickets were withdrawn, and the firing ceased.

At about 12 o'clock the French infantry began to cook, as we saw by their fires.

Our regiment mounted, and was moved down to the low ground, where it stood in *echelons* of squadrons—a picket of the 18th, where the road came through the enclosures, in advance of us.

About this time we saw the French cavalry filing over the rising ground in front, beyond the pickets, and forming their columns of assembly.

The Duke of Wellington and staff, with Lord Uxbridge, came down to look at them, and stood near the front of my (the centre) squadron.

I heard the Duke say, 'Well, I suppose we shall fight them here,' and I understood Lord Uxbridge to answer that he did not think it a favourable situation as there were defiles in our rear, &c.

The Duke then said, stretching himself and yawning, 'Then I suppose we must retreat.'

Just after, the cavalry forming two lines along the brow of the rising ground to the left of the road (to Namur, I believe)—the heavy cavalry in second line—we were ordered to retire and form in our place in brigade.

The French cavalry then commenced its advance, the 18th picket falling back, not by the road but in line across the field under us, a squadron of *Lanciers*, advancing upon them, both having skirmishers out.

When the enemy's cavalry was pretty thick in the opening between the fences, our brigade of horse artillery gave them a few rounds, apparently with effect, knocking men and horses off the road.

Both lines of cavalry were then ordered threes about, and retired in line over the cornfields. On our getting rather into a hollow the enemy's guns opened upon us, throwing shells, which fell over us. I saw one burst near the 18th.

Just then commenced a thunderstorm worthy of the tropics for the abundance of the thunder and violence of the rain. This, with the sort of ballet of war of the retiring and advancing cavalry, and the French guns firing, altogether made a picturesque and grand scene.

Our brigade then filed off into narrow roads and through a village, the 18th leading (I think), the 10th in the centre, and the 1st German Hussars following. I heard that their rear was attacked by the enemy just as we entered the narrow roads, but the French soon left us for the main road.

On issuing from the village there was a hollow way, with an ascent, commanded by high banks. Here Sir H. Vivian formed a division of the 10th on the bank, in rank entire, with carbines advanced and ready to fire into the hollow way and check pursuit had the enemy come on; but as they did not, the division resumed its place, and the brigade marched quietly and unmolested through narrow roads, hearing occasional cannonade on the main road and the shouts of the attacks that took place. Lieutenant Smith, of the 10th, was sent across to the main road, and was present at the affair between the 7th Hussars and the French *Lanciers;* during which, at considerable risk to himself, he saved Lieutenant Gordon of the 7th, who was wounded, from capture or death by dismounting and lending him his horse to carry him to the rear till he could meet his own led horses. Lieutenant Smith escaped being taken by leaping over the ditch off the *chaussée* till, the *Lanciers* being driven back, he got his horse again.

It will be seen that there are a few discrepancies between this account and the one given by Sir Hussey Vivian, though they in the main agree.

With regard to the time Sir A. Gordon went off to patrol, it could scarcely have been as early as two in the morning. Sir H. Vivian says it was soon after daybreak that the Duke came up to him, and it was after that event that the patrol was sent off; and Colonel Gordon did, as a fact, communicate with the Prussians,

Again, the pickets of infantry could scarcely have been exchanging shots with the enemy quite so late as twelve o'clock in the daytime, for their retreat began, so far as the infantry were concerned, at eight in the morning.

Nor do I think Colonel Taylor could have heard quite correctly, at the time he mentions, the conversation that he says took place between the Duke and Lord Uxbridge; for from the moment that the Duke knew the Prussians had retreated, which he did early in the morning, he could have had, and had, no other plan than that of retiring, so as to co-operate with the Prussians and avoid having the whole French army on him. At 12 o'clock in the day, the time apparently alluded to, the retreat had, as a fact, actually commenced. Such a conversation might have taken place quite early in the morning, *before* the Duke knew for certain of the line of retreat of the Prussians or of their intentions, and possibly took place when Colonel Gordon was being sent off to find out about them; or it might have taken place with reference to the resistance to be offered by the cavalry.

Colonel Taylor, having been with his regiment in advance, and having passed over the bridge before the time when Sir Hussey was placed in the critical position which has been alluded to, naturally cannot give any particulars as to what took place with the 1st K.G.L. Hussars, who were then alone guarding the rear of that part of the retreat, and were on the other side of the bridge at Genappe.

Captain Ingilby, who was in the Artillery attached to Sir H. Vivian's brigade, in his account of the retreat, says (*Waterloo Letters*):

> The cavalry formed in three lines; the Hussars in the first line, the Light Cavalry in the second line, and the Heavy cavalry in the third line.
>
> It suddenly became insufferably hot and close, and the sun became absolutely darkened by a black cloud, while at the same time a heavy cloud of dust rising showed the advance of a very large body coming on to reinforce the enemy. They came from a direction on the right of the enemy.
>
> I had heard Lord A. Hill say that Lord Uxbridge had positive orders not to have an affair of cavalry.
>
> The French cavalry I have before adverted to now advanced boldly in great force, and for some time partially under cover of a wood, until their *vedettes* tired on our front line.
>
> We commenced a cannonade, which was promptly returned; and as the enemy continued to advance, and I think had commenced a deployment, an affair seemed inevitable.
>
> The interest, and even silence, until the guns and skirmishers opened, up to this moment, was intense; for it was not generally known that the cavalry general was to avoid an affair.
>
> At the last moment the order was given, and the whole commenced a rapid retreat in three columns and by different roads.
>
> At this instant the heavy black cloud broke with a tremendous clap of thunder and torrents of rain.
>
> We formed the left column in retreat. The road and ground became so quickly deluged with the heavy rain that was falling that it became impracticable for the French cavalry to press our columns in any force. In fact, out of the road in the track of our own cavalry the ground was poached into a complete puddle. Seeing this, and having lost a shoe from a gun horse, I halted, and had it put on in spite of some skirmishers who began to press on us, but were kept at bay by our own skirmishers forming as if to charge them. This will show how impracticable it was for them to press us on this cross road. But at this moment I could see the centre column on the main road on my right, and

they apparently charging and accompanied with much cheering.

In our column not a man was lost. The retreat for the guns the whole way, with the exception of the gun mentioned, was at a hand gallop for six or seven miles until we came upon the infantry in, and getting into, position.'

In Sir H. Vivian's letter some words are erased having reference to the affair of the 7th Hussars at Genappe, which would no doubt have thrown some light upon that subject, and coming from a general officer who had been for years in that regiment, who was extremely fond of it, and in whose brigade the 7th had been up to a very short time previously, would have been of considerable interest.

The words were evidently scratched through at a date later than when the words were written, for the ink is of a much darker and of a different character.

It would be wrong to attempt to make out what was originally written; but there appears to have been something not altogether right about the charge then made by the 7th, and it would seem, by looking at the various accounts given by officers who were present, that the charge was made at a time and in a place where the 7th was not by any means the best regiment suited to the occasion, or the charge itself, from the position of affairs, likely to be successful.

As the regiment was one in which Sir Hussey had for so long served and been intimately acquainted, an account of what took place will be of interest to those for whom this collection of his writings is put together.

In the retreat of the 17th, the 7th Hussars, with the Heavy cavalry, were in the centre, and had to pass through the village of Genappe.

There being only one street by which the army could pass through that village, and that a narrow one, the progress of the troops at this point was considerably retarded; the French pressed close upon the English rear, planted guns at the left of Genappe, and opened a heavy fire. As the English artillery were considerably further in front, the latter were without a gun to return the fire.

The British troops having at last got through the village some of the cavalry, among others the 7th Hussars, were formed on the other side of the village in order to check the French in their advance.

Major Banner (*Waterloo Letters,*) describes what took place thus:

The enemy's cavalry, having entered Genappe, began to press

upon our rearguard, the last division of which had scarcely quitted the rear when Lord Uxbridge came to the rear to reconnoitre, and . . . . perceiving the boldness of the French, directed the 7th Hussars to charge in order to check their advance.

The 7th, being animated by the presence of their Colonel, rushed on the enemy with the greatest spirit and intrepidity, and drove the French advanced squadrons back into the street of Genappe upon the main body of their cavalry which occupied the town, where a most obstinate conflict commenced, each party fighting with the utmost desperation.

The French, being backed by a long, dense column of cavalry, flanked by the houses on each side of the street, were enabled to make a most formidable resistance. Notwithstanding their numerical inferiority, it was only when menaced by such a heavy force that the 7th were obliged to retire; but, although they fell back, the fault did not lie with them, nor was it in consequence of the lightness of their horses, as has been insinuated.

The conduct of this corps on this occasion was heroic in the extreme; their spirit and ardour was universally admired and acknowledged by all who witnessed the gallant affair.

The French became exceedingly elated in thus having repulsed the 7th Hussars in this, the first, attack made by the British cavalry.

The French, jubilant in their temporary success, debouched from Genappe, and when their leading squadrons had ascended about halfway up a hill beyond the village the Life Guards were ordered to charge, and although the French sustained the attack with firmness they were eventually "overthrown with great slaughter, and ridden down in such a manner that the road was covered with men and horses scattered and sprawling in all directions down to the main body of the enemy's advanced guard."

Colonel O'Grady, an officer of the 7th Hussars, who was in the charge, says that the French were so jammed up in the narrow street of Genappe, and so pressed forward by the mass of cavalry following them, that they could not go about. The charge of the 7th, under these circumstances, "could make no impression, but we continued cutting at them, and we did not give ground, nor did they move. Their commanding officer was cut down, and so was ours (Major Hodge)."

Colonel O'Grady afterwards says: "As we never could find Major Hodge or Adjutant Mayer, I only say they were killed because I hope so." By which I presume he meant that he hoped they had been killed fighting.

Lord Anglesey (*Waterloo Letters*) writes that the charge of the 7th was made most—

> ... gallantly, but they could not penetrate the Lancers. In their turn these now advanced and drove the 7th upon their reserve. Here the 7th rallied, and again drove the Lancers to the town. Again the Lancers, being reinforced, rallied and drove the 7th; and again the 7th rallied; and thus a determined seesaw was kept up for a considerable time. At length, after the 7th had lost several excellent officers and men, I withdrew them.

And he subsequently ordered the Life Guards to charge, which was done with the result already described. The French, however, were then through the village, and no longer "jammed up in its narrow street where they could not possibly go about," even had they felt so inclined.

Vivian's brigade, passing through Glabais, Maransart, Aywiers, Frischermont, Smohain, and Verd Cocu, arrived in the evening of the 17th in the vicinity of the Forest of Soigne, and bivouacked there; while Vandeleur passed the night somewhat nearer to the ground which had been selected as the position to be taken up by the Anglo-allied army, and on which, on the following day, the great battle was fought.

In the course of the evening the Duke of Wellington received Blucher's reply to his reqest for "two corps," which has already been alluded to. The Prussian officer conveying this communication was brought to headquarters by an escort from a squadron of the 1st Hussars K.G.L., which Vivian had detached to the left with orders to patrol as far as Ohain.

★ ★ ★ ★ ★

That the brigade, together with the rest of the army, spent a wretchedly uncomfortable night is beyond doubt. Sir Hussey, in one of his letters, states that on the 17th:

> .... one of the most tremendous storms I have ever witnessed had soaked us all to the skin, and it had continued to rain all night. The poor fellows in bivouack were dreadfully off, and the officers, although some got shelter, but little better; for, wet to the skin, we had no baggage or anything to change, nor had we seen a servant or baggage since we first marched from our

quarters on the morning of the 16th. We ate such eggs, &c., as we could pick up.

It was in this state that the English army passed the night previous to that battle which was to hurl Buonaparte from his ascendency, and put an end for ever to his ambitious schemes.

CHAPTER 5

Waterloo 1815

By eight o'clock on the morning of the 18th June 1815, the allied forces had taken up the position they were destined to occupy during the ever-memorable battle of Waterloo. After the fatigue and anxiety of the previous day's retreat they had spent a night of the utmost discomfort, soaked to the skin with rain, and without any adequate food or shelter. They consoled themselves, however, by reflecting that the French had been in no better plight than they; they realised the enormous responsibility that rested upon them; and they were actuated with the greatest determination to do their duty, and show that courage which has always been one of the characteristics of an Englishman when placed in dire emergency.

The French were somewhat later in taking up their ground, but they were now deploying with the greatest precision, and with all the pomp and display of a grand review. Napoleon was exulting in having been successful in separating the Prussians from the rest of the Allies by the battles of Ligny and Quatre-Bras, and he was congratulating himself on having got Wellington and those "accursed English" into his power and to himself.

Whilst the French were getting into position for attack, the Duke of Wellington occupied his time by taking a survey of his own lines.

Sir Hussey Vivian was in command of the 6th Light Cavalry brigade, composed of the 10th (Prince of Wales') Hussars, the 18th Hussars, and the 1st Hussars of the King's German Legion.

> The 10th and 18th were drawn up in line in rear of the Wavre road, withdrawn a little from the crest of the ridge; the right of the 10th resting upon the lane which, leading up from Smohain, crossing over the position and ascending along its reverse

259

slope, proceeds in a direction for Verd Cocu. The 1st Hussars were also in line and formed in reserve.

The left of the brigade was completely *en l'air*, upon high, flat ground, the main ridge widening considerably in that direction.

A picket, consisting of a squadron of the 10th Hussars, under Captain Taylor, occupied the village of Smohain down in the valley, which, having its source a little to the westward of La Haye Sainte, takes an easterly, and therefore parallel, course with that part of the ridge which formed the left of the British position.

The advanced posts of this picket were on the further side of the village, and its *vedettes* formed a chain on the rising ground beyond, within half carbine shot of some French cavalry standing dismounted in close column. A party was detached from the picket as a patrol on the road to Ohain.

During Wellington's progress along the left of his lines he heard from Vivian that a Prussian officer had reached Smohain and had informed Captain Taylor that Bulow was on the march with his whole corps, and that the advanced guard was then only about two miles distant. The officer, however, who brought this cheering intelligence, did not of course know that a fire, which had accidentally broken out in Wavre, was destined to seriously impede the march of the main body of the corps, and cause the hour of the arrival of the Prussians on the scene of battle to be much later than anticipated.—Siborne.

★ ★ ★ ★ ★

The entry made in Sir Hussey Vivian's diary, as to the initial stage of the battle is—

This most memorable, most glorious day is beyond my power to describe.

Commanding a brigade on the left, it is impossible that I can tell every movement, or position of the divisions.

Lord Hill's corps was on the right; the Prince of Orange in the centre; Sir J. Vandeleur's and my brigades on the left.

About eleven o'clock the pickets reported the advance of the enemy, and very shortly a most serious attack on a wood on the right of our centre, in which were posted the Guards, commenced.

The whole line stood to arms. All the cavalry moved up into their places in position.

We soon saw the French forming in enormous masses on the side of the hill opposite to us. We heard the repeated cheers of '*Vive l'Empereur,*' and we waited with anxiety, but with perfect steadiness, those tremendous attacks for which Buonaparte is so famous, when, caring not for the loss of men, he sacrifices whole bodies for the sake of carrying a particular point of the enemy's line.

In this instance the high road, which was about the centre of the position, was the principal object of his attack.

Three several times did he, with the whole French army, rush with desperation against this part of our position. Three several times, under cover of near one hundred pieces of cannon, did the *Cuirassiers* endeavour to break through our squares of infantry, and in one instance they got possession of our guns; but the steady determination of our glorious infantry, and the handsome conduct of our cavalry, who instantly charged on the enemy reaching the position, defeated all these attempts.

The way in which these attacks were met was by our infantry forming squares, and our cavalry immediately charging those of the enemy as they appeared on the flank of them.

It is impossible to imagine anything more desperate than this sort of combat. The dreadful loss sustained by both sides speaks plainly as to this. Of two Heavy brigades of cavalry, of 1000 men each, scarcely 200 remained in line at the end of the day! Whilst these attacks were going on on the right and centre, a similar effort was being made on the left of the centre.

On the extreme left nothing very serious took place. It was *appuyéd* on a village which was immensely strong, and defensible by a very small number of men.

★ ★ ★ ★ ★

It was at or about one o'clock that the first of Napoleon's great attacks on the left and centre of the Allies was made; and it was in charges made at the end of this attack that a considerable number of English cavalry, belonging to Sir W. Ponsonby's brigade, in the exultation of having successfully repelled a charge of the enemy, and of momentary victory, pursued their flying foes too far, and recklessly crossed over the road to the south of

La Haye Sainte, with disastrous result.

Jacquinot's Lancers, in open order, taking advantage of the disordered pursuit of the British, fell diagonally upon their left; while Milhaud's two regiments of *Cuirassiers*, sent by Napoleon himself, took them full in front.

"With wearied arms and blown horses the English Dragoons strove to regain the British position; but most of them were overthrown and killed." Help, however, was, although somewhat late, at hand; for Vandeleur, who was nearest to, and therefore best able to act as a support to the fleeing English, retarded by a hollow road which prevented him acting as speedily as needed, at length brought up his brigade, and with the 16th and 12th Dragoons charged the pursuing French and drove them up their side of the valley again.

Vivian, who had come forward in person from the extreme left and proceeded some way down the slope for the purpose of making his observations, upon perceiving Ponsonby's brigade pursuing recklessly and in disorder up to the French heights, had immediately sent back word for the 10th and 18th Hussars to move at once through the hollow way to their right, and to leave the remaining regiment of his brigade, the 1st Hussars K.G.L., to keep a look-out to the left. The execution of these orders was immediately commenced, but the brigade being further to the left of the line, and even more impeded by the formation of the ground near it than that of Vandeleur's, was necessarily some time before it could reach the desired position.

Two guns, detached in advance from Vivian's Horse artillery, drew up on the brow of the main ridge, but they had scarcely opened fire when a well-directed shot from one of the French batteries passed through the ammunition boxes of one of the limbers, causing an explosion which drew forth a shout of triumph from the French artillery men.

In the meantime the charge of Vandeleur's brigade having succeeded without the aid of even its own support (the 11th Dragoons), the further advance of the 10th and 18th was not needed, but they remained in the new position they had taken up on the right of the lane leading to Verd Cocu, and the two guns rejoined their battery.—*Conf.* Siborne and Hooper.

In *Cavalry at Waterloo*, Sir E. Wood, (published by Leonaur) commenting on the lack of support given to Sir W. Ponsonby's Union brigade at this period of the day, says that—

Lord Uxbridge, who had accompanied the charge made by Sir W. Ponsonby, looked round anxiously for the support of one of the Light brigades from the left of the position (Vandeleur's and Vivian's).

It does not appear that he had warned them of the attack he was about to make, and the brigade nearest at hand (Vandeleur's) was commanded by an officer who, however brave, was more accustomed to wait for orders than to act on his own initiative. He had served for a long time under the Duke of Wellington, and knew how heavily he could vent his wrath on officers who moved without orders.

When the Prussian Military Attaché, seeing what was about to occur, urged Vandeleur and Vivian to move to the support of the Union brigade, they both declined, saying, 'Alas! we dare not move without orders,' and Müffling, eventually having left them before Vandeleur moved, remained for years under the impression that neither had advanced.

The Brigadiers do not seem to have been aware that the Duke had put the cavalry entirely in Uxbridge's hands.

There was, however, some ground for their apprehension of the Duke's displeasure, as is shown by his observation to Müffling, when discussing the question years afterwards, that he would have tried either of them by court-martial had they moved, even if they were successful.

I do not know where Sir E. Wood derives his authority for the above statement, but I cannot think that the statement is well founded; for Sir J. Vandeleur has placed it on record that the only orders received by himself and Sir H. Vivian previous to the charge made by Vandeleur's brigade was that they were "to engage the enemy whenever they could do so to advantage."

As a fact Sir J. Vandeleur did move his brigade to the support of Ponsonby as soon as he could, looking to the difficulties of the ground; and Sir H. Vivian sent orders to his brigade to move up in support also; but, as has been seen, his assistance was not required.

After the French had been checked in their pursuit of the remains of Ponsonby's brigade no further attack of any importance was made on the extreme left of the Allied line during the day; and as it was in that part of the position that Sir H. Vivian's brigade was posted, and it is with the doings of his brigade alone that I am concerned, I refrain from attempting to give any account of the various acts of valour which were being performed in other portions of the battlefield.

★ ★ ★ ★ ★

Sir H. Vivian writes:

My brigade did not suffer much till towards the close of the last attack. The ground on the left did not admit of the cavalry advancing, and I, being on the left of all, consequently suffered only from the cannonade.

About six o'clock I learnt that the cavalry in the centre had suffered terribly, and the Prussians having by that time formed to my left, I took upon myself to move off from our left, and moved directly to the centre of our line, where I arrived most opportunely, at the instant that Buonaparte was making his last and most desperate effort; and never did I witness anything so terrific; the ground actually covered with dead and dying, cannon shots and shells flying thicker than I ever heard even musketry before, and our troops—some of them—giving way.

In this state of affairs I wheeled my brigade into line close (within ten yards) in the rear of our infantry, prepared to charge the instant they had retreated through my intervals. (The three squadron officers of the 10th were wounded at this instant.) My doing this, however, gave them confidence, and the brigade, which was literally running away, halted on our cheering them, and again began firing.

Lord Edward Somerset, with the mutilated remains of the two Heavy brigades, not 200 men and horses, retired through me; and I then remained for about half an hour exposed to the most dreadful fire of shot, shell, and musketry that it is possible to imagine. How a man escaped is to me a miracle.

We every instant expected through the smoke to see the enemy appearing under our noses; for the smoke was literally so thick that we could not see ten yards off; but we, at last, began to find that the shot did not come so thick, and I discovered that the enemy were, instead of endeavouring to gain our position, retrograding on theirs.

The first Prussians that came into action, I should say, were the advanced guard of a corps not exceeding two regiments, and were supported by another. They passed the hedge of Pappelotte and drew up across the valley in line, almost at right angles with us. They were directly under where I stood, and I saw the operation as plainly as if at a field day.

The French at once advanced against them (their left flank rather) and drove them back; they then occupied the village of Smohain or Pappelotte (I forget exactly the name). This must have been somewhere between five and six o'clock. I should say nearer five.

It was a considerable time after this that the Prussians appeared in force. We remained long enough for me to see the French reserve and right form line, *en potence,* in order to meet the attack on Planchenoit; and I was surprised to see the tremendous fire the French were able to direct against the Prussians. It was just as this took place that I moved to the right.

★ ★ ★ ★ ★

Siborne, in his account of this part of the battle, says:

Vivian was informed by patrols that the Prussians were advancing. Having satisfied himself of the fact, and perceiving their advanced cavalry coming on, Vivian felt that there could be no longer any apprehension of the left of the army being turned; and having previously understood from Sir W. Delancy and other staff officers that fresh cavalry was much needed in the centre, he proposed to Vandeleur, who was on his right, and who was his superior officer, that the two brigades should move towards the centre, where they might be of service.

Vandeleur, however, declined to act without orders; whereupon Vivian put his own brigade in motion, passing along the rear of Vandeleur's; and soon after having commenced his march he met Lord Uxbridge, who was much pleased to find the Duke's wishes had thus been anticipated, and sent orders to Vandeleur to follow, accompanying the former brigade himself towards the centre.

When Vivian took upon himself to move his brigade from the extreme left to the centre of the Allied position. Napoleon was at length being attacked on his right rear by the Prussians, near Pappelotte and Planchenoit.

For a time the Young Guard, under Lobau, sufficed to stop the progress of the Prussians; but the latter renewing the contest again and again drove the French out of Planchenoit. Napoleon, however, retook the village with some of the Old Guard, and the Prussians were, for the time, driven up the heights to the eastward.

Seeing the Prussians thus recoil, Napoleon thought that Bulow had exhausted his strength, and that he had still the time and the means at his disposal to crush Wellington. He determined to assail the British right with the Guard, and to support the onset with every available bayonet and sabre from the ravines of Pappelotte to the Nivelles road.

Hooper says:

Napoleon himself directed the attack, which it was Ney's business to see executed; he exhorted alike officers and men; he urged them forward; he accompanied them on their way; he pointed out their enemies with a commanding gesture; he told his 'children' that he 'desired to sup at Brussels,' and they knew that he expected them to hew out a path for him; he spread the report that Grouchy had arrived, in order to encourage his men, though it was not Grouchy, but Ziethen's Prussian cavalry that had shown themselves, as he well knew. The delusive statement was, however, believed by the French soldiers, and it was, for the moment, confirmed by the fact that the Prussians, deceived by the Nassau uniforms, at first opened fire upon these defenders of Smohain and La Haye.

The whole French line advanced, Donzelot and Quiot forcing their troops forward with a fury that seemed irresistible. At one moment the Brunswickers, the Nassauers, and the Hanoverians receded from the front. Some of them fell back to the very heads of Vivian's leading horsemen. But Vivian, and the Duke himself, once more roused their spirits with homely words; and Kilmansegge and the Prince of Orange led them back into the fight and pushed the French from their forward position.

The smoke hung in clouds, darkening the light of the declining sun. The rattle of musketry, the booming of guns, wore incessant. At no period of the day had these troops been exposed to so murderous a fire.

To the troops comprising Vivian's and Vandeleur's brigades, as they arrived quite fresh from the extreme left, the air of ruin and destruction which met their view in rear of the centre of the line; the desperate struggle which appeared to be carried on upon the crest of the main ridge by a single line of infantry, evidently exhausted by the continuous fight; the almost total absence of British cavalry in support of that line; the numbers of wounded retiring both singly and in groups; the whole scene was calculated to inspire thoughts by no means akin to anticipation of victory. They quickly partook of the feelings of extreme uncertainty which pervaded the rest of the army as to the result of the contest, and many imbibed the idea that they had been brought from the left for the purpose of covering a contemplated retreat.

'Where is your brigade?' said Sir Hussey Vivian to Lord Edward Somerset.

'Here,' replied his lordship, as, pointing firstly to a small band of horsemen, and then to the ground, covered with dead and dying, clad in red, and with mutilated horses wandering or turning in circles, he displayed to him the wreck of what had been the Household and Union brigade combined—a force amounting at the commencement of the action to upwards of 2000 Dragoons!

The French skirmishers crowded close up to the Allied line, maintaining a most rapid and destructive fire. Vivian's brigade, by its proximity to the wavering infantry, against whom so close and unremitting a fire of musketry was maintained, was placed in a very trying situation for cavalry, and suffered much in consequence.

As soon, however as the infantry, which Vivian and others had cheered on, had rallied and resumed their former position in the line, he withdrew his brigade under the crest of the hill, a distance of not more than thirty yards, to place his men a little out of fire; and when thus posted he was better prepared to make an attack, if required.

The French were making this, their last great attack, in two huge columns. The first column bore directly on that point of the ridge behind which lay the British Guards.

When the Imperialists appeared above and upon the level of the ridge, the Allied guns opened a terrific and rapid fire upon them, and, at the command of the Duke, Maitland's men, four deep, sprang suddenly to their feet, within fifty yards of the advancing and astonished Frenchmen, and poured in a volley which struck the column like an iron bolt, and crushed it into a shapeless, confused, and retreating-mass.

The defeat of the right column, however, in no way arrested the advance of the second (left) one, which steadily pursued its way across the field; and once more the fortunes of the day seemed to hang upon a single thread.

Partly to avoid the artillery fire, but mainly in order to bring its front parallel with that of Maitland's brigade, now visible upon the ridge, this left column diverged into a hollow on its right and rapidly ascended the slope.

The Allied guns again opened fire, and the British Guards renewed their destructive volleys; yet the daring Frenchmen kept on their way.

At this critical moment Sir J. Colborne wheeled the 52nd upon its left company and brought it nearly parallel to the left flank of the attacking column. 'What was he going to do?' was the inquiry of his superior officer.

'To make that column feel our fire,' was the prompt reply. The Duke and Lord Hill had seen and approved of the movement, and the next moment the 52nd was over the brow and its whole fire, full and close, was brought to bear upon the heavy masses before it.

Napier's guns, double shotted; the muskets of the British Guards; the rifles of the 95th; and the rapid fire of the 52nd, shook the column from front to rear. Reduced to an unsteady crowd, it yielded and fled, when, at Colborne's command, the 52nd brought down their bayonets to the charge, cheered, and dashed on.

This splendid regiment, supported on the right by the 71st, and on the left by the 95th, did not halt in its victorious career until it had swept from right to left along the front of the British centre. When it halted, its left flank was in advance of La Have Sainte, 800 yards from the ground at which its charge had commenced. Before its steady march the broken Imperialists withdrew without a halt; but not without looking back, fiercely and grimly, upon their pursuers.

The British leader, watchful of the course of the fight, had been patient and persevering for over nine hours. It was now his turn to attack.

★ ★ ★ ★ ★

Sir Hussey Vivian describes this portion of the battle thus:

The moment to attack them was arrived. I received orders to advance, and wheeling my brigade by half squadrons to the right, trotted in column round the right flank of the infantry in my front, to attack the French squares and cavalry during their retreat.

Having cleared the smoke, I observed the French retiring up the hill and along the high road, covered by their guns—two large bodies of cavalry and two squares of infantry—whilst our infantry was gallantly moving on after them.

I led the head of my brigade diagonally across the ground for the left body of cavalry. The enemy, seeing this, opened a fire upon me from the squares and with grape from their guns, and I suffered some loss; but every man was at his post. We gave them a cheer in reply, and I instantly ordered the regiment to form line on their front half squadrons. They did this with as much accuracy as if manoeuvring at a field day in England.

I led the 10th against a body of *Cuirassiers* and *Lanciers*, much superior to them in force, on the French left, and, having seen them fairly in—the enemy flying and falling under their swords—I rushed to the 18th, and with them attacked the *Cuirassiers*, who were formed on the French right in support of the squares and guns.

They were routed by the intrepidity and gallantry of this regiment, and the artillery men cut down at their guns.

I ordered the advance at a trot, and that the leading squadron moved off at a trot there cannot be the slightest doubt. Captain Taylor, who commanded the centre squadron, may have had to gallop in order to preserve his distance, perhaps from not having moved off the position at the same moment. There is one circumstance which proves that the advance was at a trot and not a hurried one.

The leading half squadron, as we were moving off the position, on approaching some of our guns, wheeled to the right instead of to the left, and was consequently moving to the rear.

I was on the flank of the squadron. I immediately (I recollect perfectly well) with a *considerable degree of emphasis, &c.*, and *a good hearty damn*, galloped to the flank of the second half squadron, and said that it was towards the enemy and not from them that they were to wheel.

I then took the flank officer's place and I led the column down the hill in the direction I wished it to move, until the leading half squadron was brought back into its place, when I went to the front of that half squadron and in this way conducted the column some little distance.

Had our advance been at a very rapid pace the half squadron which had wheeled from us and been left behind, somewhat perhaps confused and entangled with the guns, would never have returned to its place in so short a time.

When we arrived in the plain at the bottom of the hill there was a pause, and I may say a halt, in the front. The very circumstance of Sir Colin Campbell coming to me from the Duke, and desiring me to halt, and the conversation which took place (the affair of a minute, or perhaps, moment only, I admit) proves it.

When I moved on again and ordered the formation on the leading half squadron, and the advance and attack, the order was to form line on the front half squadron; but that the formation was rather *en echelon* of squadrons than in line I think was much more than probable; and if any halt occurred in the next squadron it was rectified at once; for I well recollect the instant it was in line giving the order to charge, and the others, no doubt, took it up in succession.

I sent orders to the 18th to remain steady in reserve.

I charged with the 10th, and as soon as we were well into the enemy and mixed up, the French making off, I gave the word 'Halt,' and galloped off to the 18th.

En route I was attacked by one of the *Cuirassiers* whom we had passed. I was fortunate enough to give him a thrust in the neck with my left hand (for my right was in a sling and I was just capable of holding the reins with it only) [*in consequence of the wound he had received at Croix d'Orade,. near Toulouse in 1814*], and at that moment I was joined by my little German orderly, who cut the fellow off his horse. I then went to the 18th. A circumstance which occurred at this time made a great impression on me, *viz.*, a man of that squadron having had his horse wounded was struggling to get from under it, when a French Lancer, immediately before me, blew out his brains.

To the 18th I said, 'Eighteenth, my lads, you will, I know, follow me.'

On which Sergeant-Major Jeffs, afterwards adjutant of the 7th, who was near me, answered, 'Yes, General; to hell, if you will lead us.'

With the 18th I charged the second body of *Cuirassiers* and *Chasseurs* that were supporting a square of Imperial Guards; and the 18th not only defeated them, but took fourteen pieces of cannon that had been firing grape at us during our movement.

By this time the remains of the 10th had again formed—the 1st Hussars being still in reserve—and I determined that the glory of ending the day should rest with the regiment of my royal master.

I ordered the 10th to charge a square of infantry still steady and close to us. This they did most gallantly, and as gallantly was the attack received.

Here fell poor Howard, as amiable a young man and as gallant a soldier as ever breathed. Here we took prisoner Count Lobau, who commanded one of the *corps d'armée*; and here was fired the last shot for the night. The 10th cut down the French in their ranks; some few then escaped under cover of a hedge, but from this time every man was in retreat, and eventually every man was taken during a pursuit which lasted as long as we were able to see—so long indeed that, until actually having cut some Prussians down, we were obliged to desist, and give to them the pursuit, they having suffered much less than we had in fact, they having scarcely suffered at all.

I was by the side of Major Howard at the time of his charge, and myself advanced with the squadron.

Such is the short account given by Sir Hussey (mostly in his diary, written two days after the battle) of the doings of his brigade in the closing charge made at the battle of Waterloo.

★ ★ ★ ★ ★

Siborne (whose history of the campaign was one of the first of the many books that have been published, and which was founded on the accounts given by officers who were present at the battle, and collected by him at great trouble) gives a full and similar description of the charges made by Sir H. Vivian's brigade.

He states that Wellington, as soon as he saw that the success of Adam's brigade was so decisive, requested Lord Uxbridge to immediately launch forward some fresh cavalry to check the probable advance of that of the enemy, and to second the efforts of the infantry in front by boldly attacking the French reserve, which appeared collected in front of La Belle Alliance—the critical point of Napoleon's line.

Lieut.-Col. Lord Greenock, assistant quarter-master-general of the cavalry, was despatched to Vivian with orders for him to move his Hussar brigade to the right, from its position in the rear of Alten's division, so as to get clear of the infantry, and then to advance directly in front by the right of Maitland's Brigade of Guards.

Vivian, the moment he received the order to advance, wheeled his brigade half squadron to the right. Thus the 10th became the leading regiment, the 18th Hussars followed, and the 1st Hussars K.G.L., which had stood in second line, moved off as soon as its front was clear, in rear of the latter corps.

The brigade proceeded at a trot, a short distance in rear of the infantry and parallel to the crest of the position; and as it approached the right of Maitland's Brigade of Guards, Vivian, ordering the leading half squadron to wheel to the left through Napier's battery, led it perpendicularly to the front.

As the column thus advanced across the ridge in left front of Vandeleur's Light Cavalry brigade it was saluted by the latter with cheers of encouragement; and in a similar manner by Maitland's Brigade of Guards as it passed their flank.

The smoke lay heavily along the entire position, and especially at this moment over that part of the exterior slope of the ridge on which the struggle with the French Imperial Guard had taken place, and across which Vivian was now leading his brigade.

On advancing further and getting clear of the smoke he obtained a more distinct view of the disposition of the enemy's forces in his direct front.

A very considerable portion appeared in great confusion; disordered columns of infantry were hurrying back to their main position up the slope, on which were numerous stragglers of all arms, and in various uniforms, mixed together, and retiring in crowds.

Guns were firing from various points to cover the retreat, and the discharge of musketry in and about Hougoumont continued very brisk.

On arriving about midway towards the enemy's position, well

formed bodies of troops were observed on the French left of La Belle Alliance, posted as if fully prepared to resist the threatened attack. They consisted of two squares of infantry, with cavalry and guns formed on the flanks and between them.

The cavalry on their left was somewhat advanced, comprising several bodies partially covering one another, but presenting a general front and posted on some rising ground about 200 yards on the Allied left of the south-eastern angle of the Hougoumont enclosures.

The two squares here alluded to were the two battalions of the Grenadiers of the Old Guard which had been placed as a reserve of the main attack of that force.

The cavalry on the left was thus disposed. First, on the slope of the little eminence a portion of the Lancers of the Imperial Guard; then in left rear of the latter, on lower ground, were two squadrons of Dragoons of the Guard; and in their right rear, two more squadrons of the same corps; and in right rear of these again, and on the summit of the eminence, stood the Brigade of *Carbineers*.

In rear of these and of the squares themselves, as also on the right of the latter, were collected the remainder of that portion of the French cavalry which had made such repeated attacks upon the Duke's line during the day.

All these different bodies of cavalry were but mere wrecks of their former selves—regiments, and in many instances entire brigades, were diminished to less than squadrons.

Vivian, as soon as he perceived the disposition of the enemy's forces in his immediate front, decided upon forming a front line with the 10th and 18th Hussars, and upon holding the 1st Hussars K.G.L. in second line in support.

For this purpose, and also with a view to oppose, and if possible to turn, the left of the enemy's cavalry, he made the leading; regiment—the 10th Hussars—incline to its right.

Shortly afterwards Vivian was joined by Colonel Sir Colin Campbell, of the Staff, who brought him an order from the Duke that he was not to attack before the infantry came up, unless he felt confident of success.

Vivian remarked that as the Allied infantry, in its anxiety to get on, was probably not in compact order, its safety might be seriously endangered should it be exposed to a cavalry attack; and that in his opinion it would be better that not a moment should be lost on his part in driving off the cavalry which appeared in front.

Sir Colin Campbell coincided in this opinion and returned to the Duke.

After a very short pause at the head of the column, consequent upon this little discussion, Vivian, continuing his advance, ordered the 10th Hussars to form line on the front half squadron, and at the same time sent orders to his other two regiments also to form line on their leading half squadrons respectively, but then to remain in support.

The rapid pace which had been maintained by the head of the column, and the incline to the right which had been given it, required great activity on the part of the left half squadron to get up into line; and as Vivian ordered the charge as soon as the first squadron was formed, it was executed, not in line, but rather *en echelon* of squadrons, which, under the circumstances of the moment, as will presently be seen, was the preferable and more desirable formation.

Just as the charge was ordered the Second Light Dragoons K.G.L., in a column of squadrons, which had been detached from the main position almost simultaneously with the advance of Vivian's brigade, came up on the right of the 10th Hussars, and in a direction rather crossing the front of the latter regiment which had its left thrown rather forward, whilst the Germans were moving straight to their front and directly upon the French Dragoons of the Guard before mentioned as posted in the hollow on the Allied right of the eminence on which stood the French cavalry about to be charged by Vivian's brigade.

The Dragoons at first appeared disposed to resist the Germans, and received them with a tolerably effective carbine fire; but the former charged home, cut down several of the enemy's horsemen, and made some prisoners. In following up the charge, however, the regiment exposed its left to a body of *Cuirassiers*; by which it was thrown into disorder. It afterwards rallied, and made another charge, which put the enemy's cavalry to flight. The regiment then continued moving forward with proper precaution along the base of the higher ground on the left, over which the 10th Hussars were also charging and advancing.

In the meantime the latter regiment made its charge; the right, centre, and left squadrons, in rapid succession, dashed in amongst the French cavalry posted as before mentioned.

The left squadron of the 10th had scarcely closed with the enemy before the whole of the cavalry on the French left of the squares of the Guard were in full flight.

Vivian, perceiving the complete success of this brilliant charge, ordered a halt; and then returned as quickly as possible to the 18th Hussars.

On his way to the 18th Vivian was attacked by a *Cuirassier*. His right arm was in a sling, in consequence of a wound received at Croix d'Orade, near Toulouse. Taking the reins in this hand, which was barely capable of holding them, he contrived to give the *Cuirassier* a thrust in the neck with his left hand, whilst at the same moment he was joined by his German orderly, who cut the Frenchman off his horse.

After the 10th Hussars had pursued the enemy about 200 yards a body of *Cuirassiers* charged their right flank, and forced it about a hundred yards away on the left; whilst the centre and left squadrons, not being aware of Vivian's order to halt, continued their pursuit, inclining to their right under Lt.-Col. Lord Robert Manners, then commanding the 10th.

Previous to describing the subsequent proceedings of the brigade, it is necessary to advert to other matters in order to connect them with the general disposition of the main army.

Wellington, perceiving the confusion of the French Imperial Guard, remarking also the beautiful advance of Vivian's Hussars brigade against the French reserves posted close to La Belle Alliance, in the very heart of Napoleon's position; the steady and triumphant march of Adam's brigade; and that the movement of Bulow had begun to take effect; ordered a general advance of the whole line, and he himself galloped off to Adam's brigade.

Sir Colin Campbell now rejoined the Duke and explained the grounds upon which Vivian had decided upon attacking the French reserves; on learning which Lord Uxbridge, who was present, determined upon personally leading the attack with the Hussars and participating in the final and decisive triumph of the British cavalry, and was darting off to that part of the field when his intentions were frustrated by a grape shot striking and severely wounding his right leg.

Having watched Adam's brigade for some time, the Duke rode up the valley and came upon the plain upon which Vivian was successfully attacking the French reserves.

The gallant charge made by the 10th Hussars upon the French cavalry in its front has already been described.

After ordering the halt and rally, Vivian galloped towards the 18th Hussars, which regiment he found well formed in line, and in perfect order.

In its front stood two squares of the Grenadiers of the Old Guard; in its left front, and much nearer to it, were posted artillery and cavalry in advance of the proper right of the squares. This cavalry consisted principally of *Cuirassiers*, the wrecks of entire brigades.

Nearer to, and partly in rear of the squares, stood the *Chasseurs* and *Grenadiers-à-cheval* of the Imperial Guard, greatly diminished in numbers.

It was immediately evident to Vivian that the attack must, in the first instance, be directed against the advanced cavalry and artillery; and having put his line in motion, he placed himself in the centre beside the Hon. Henry Murray, the commanding officer, for the purpose of putting the regiment into the required direction.

This having been effected he ordered the charge, when the Hussars dashed forward with the greatest impetuosity and at the same time with as much steadiness as if they had been at a field day exercise on Hounslow Heath.

Thus the direction of the charge of the 18th diverged as much to the left as that of the 10th had inclined to the right.

Just as the charge commenced some French artillery, coming from their right and slanting across the right of the 18th, made a bold push to cross the front of the latter at a gallop. But the attempt failed, and the Hussars were instantly among them, cutting down the artillery men and drivers, and securing the guns.

In the next moment they fell upon the advanced cavalry, which they completely dispersed; and then, bringing forward their right shoulders, they attacked the cavalry and guns which stood to the right front and near to the right square, which was now retiring.

This cavalry appeared at first determined upon making a stand,

and an officer in its front dashed forward and fired at Lt.-Col. Murray; but in another moment the 18th were fiercely and dexterously plying their swords amongst them. They were forced to give way; the artillerymen were driven from their guns; and the whole fled in disorder.

The charge then ceased to be compact, for the assailants and the flying were intermingled pell-mell, all riding as fast as the confusion of the *mêlée* would permit; a part of them along the high road, but the principal portion on the Allied right of the latter; the whole, however, passing by La Belle Alliance and leaving the two squares of the Guard on their right.

Vivian, satisfied with the complete success of the charge, ordered the regiment to halt and re-form; whilst he proceeded himself to bring up the 1st Hussars, K.G.L., which he had left in reserve.

On his way he found Major the Hon. Fredk. Howard, with the right squadron of the 10th Hussars, which, as before stated, had been driven to the left by a charge of *Cuirassiers*.

This squadron stood formed within a short distance of the left square of the Grenadiers of the Guard, from the fire of which it was losing men fast.

Vivian doubted for a moment how far it might be advisable to attack the square; but perceiving an infantry regiment in red advancing on his left, and calculating on its immediately charging the face and angle of the square next to it, he ordered Major Howard to charge the face and angle to which he was opposed.

This was executed with the greatest gallantry and determination. Vivian himself joined in the charge on the right of the squadron. The Hussars charged home to the bayonets of the French Guard, and a fierce conflict ensued. Major Howard was killed at the head of his men. He was shot in the mouth and fell senseless to the ground, when one of the Imperial Guard stepped out of the ranks and brutally beat his head in with the butt end of his musket. Two other officers, Lieuts. Arnold and Bacon, were wounded. Lieut. Gunning was killed immediately previous to the attack.

The regiment of infantry, however, did not charge as Vivian had expected, but continued pursuing a separate column in its own immediate front on the high road.

Although the square—a very strong one—cannot be said to have been broken by the shock (for the veteran soldiers of whom it was composed knew too well their power of resistance against such a handful of horsemen), still the manner in which the latter, notwithstanding the rapid diminution of their numbers, continued cutting at their ranks, parrying the bayonet thrusts, and pertinaciously pressing on, reflects the highest credit on the 10th Hussars.

The men fought with desperation, maddened, probably, by the fall of their officers. The square, yielding to the pressure, continued to fall back until it reached the hollow way formed by the narrow road that leads from the *chaussée* in rear of La Belle Alliance towards the left of the French position. Into this the Guards hastily descended in confusion, and escaping by either outlet, mingled with the host of fugitives hurrying along the general line of retreat of the French army.

In the meantime the remainder of the 10th Hussars, consisting of the left and centre squadrons, that had in the first charge crossed over to the right of the rise of ground on which the French reserve cavalry had been posted, continued its course, under Lord R. Manners, down into the valley south-east of the Hougoumont enclosures.

The routed cavalry spread out in the utmost confusion—*Cuirassiers* of an almost gigantic size galloped as hard as they could, and numbers tumbled off their horses to save themselves.

The Hussars now came upon retiring infantry that appeared seized with a panic as their routed cavalry dashed past them. The large bearskin caps worn by several of them betokened a portion of the Imperial Guard; they commenced throwing down their arms, numbers of them loudly calling out 'Pardon.' Then, crossing the same road, already mentioned as leading from La Belle Alliance to the left of the French position (but on the Allied right of the hollow road by which the square of the Guard effected its escape), the Hussars brought up their right shoulders and ascended the height in rear of the hollow road.

Upon the slope of the hill about half a battalion of the French Guard had rallied and formed, with some cavalry close behind them, and opened a sharp fire upon the 10th. Part of the 18th Hussars at this time reached the hollow way, an obstacle, however, which rendered their attacking wholly impracticable.

Lord R. Manners halted for a minute within about forty paces of them to allow his men to form up. He then gave a cheer and charged, when the Imperial Guard and the cavalry instantly fled, the greater portion of them throwing themselves down and many of the latter tumbling off their horses.

The Hussars pursued up to the brow of the hill, on the further or south side of which was a deep hollow and beyond this a knoll (on the Allied side of the Charleroi road and nearly opposite De Coster's house) upon which another square of infantry had formed and appeared very steady.

At this time a party of the 18th Hussars—not more than thirty to thirty-five men—continuing the charge before mentioned close along the right of La Belle Alliance and Trimotion, and crossing the narrow road near its junction with the Charleroi road, dashed down the hollow and, ascending the height above mentioned, charged the square in the most gallant style; but, as might have been expected, was checked and turned by the latter.

Lord R. Manners and Captain Taylor had rallied a party of the 10th Hussars, with a view to support the 18th, should these be charged in their turn, which however did not occur.

The two last-mentioned regiments had by this time been thrown so much in confusion by their charges that it became necessary to check their further advance in order to give time for collecting and re-forming their ranks.

Although this measure was supported by the coming up of the 1st Hussars, King's German Legion, to take post in front of the brigade, and was also rendered secure by the advance on the right of Vandeleur's brigade (which had come up on Vivian's right, and between him and the enclosures of Hougoumont, in column of squadrons, at the moment he was preparing to charge the square of the Imperial Guard with the party of the 10th Hussars under Major Howard), still the rallying and re-forming of these two regiments was attended with considerable difficulty, inasmuch as they had been completely intermingled with the fugitives.

The very forward movement of Vivian's brigade, and the vigorous attack which it had made against the centre of the French position, having rendered obvious the necessity of an immediate support, Vandeleur's brigade was despatched across the ridge; and it was by this time in advance, and rather in right front of Vivian's.

In this manner Vivian's brigade, which had not only broken but completely pierced the centre of the French position, had its right effectually protected; and due advantage was promptly taken of the disorder into which its bold and successful advance had thrown the French troops that had been moving in that quarter. At the same time Vivian's left was secured by the advance of Adam's brigade, which continued to drive before it, along the left side of the Charleroi load, the square of the Guard as well as the *Cuirassiers* by whom the former were supported.

★ ★ ★ ★ ★

Sir H. Vivian writes:

The time between the attack of my brigade (the 6th) and the advance of that of Sir J. Vandeleur must have been at least twenty minutes, if not thirty.

It may be judged of from the following facts: the 10th had charged and rallied; the 18th had charged after the order to halt had been given to the 10th; the order to halt had been given to the 18th; the rallied body of the 10th had charged; and it was after this that Capt. Keane was sent by Sir H. Vivian to beg Sir J. Vandeleur to move on in his support; and Sir H. Vivian was in the act of moving on with two squadrons of the 1st Hussars when Sir J. Vandeleur, with his brigade, passed his right flank, and a conversation took place between them.

I have been thus particular in stating these facts, because the confusion occasioned by the attack of cavalry from the left has been attributed to an attack of both these brigades; whereas in fact it was one only that made the most important impression. In saying this, it is not my object to take from the merit of the conduct of Sir J. Vandeleur's brigade. That brigade had been much exposed and suffered severely, and had behaved gallantly, early in the day; whilst mine was in comparative security. It was fair and right therefore that the brunt of the battle should at last fall upon me; and having so fallen it is equally fair and right that we should have credit for it.

Truth is history, and history without truth does not deserve the name; and I am anxious, for the sake of the gallant men that I commanded, that, one day at least, the truth may be known.

I assert positively that when I advanced I left Vandeleur's brigade standing on the position, and they cheered me as I passed.

The 10th charged; the 18th charged; the squadron, or more, of the 10th, under Howard, formed, and charged again; and I had myself ordered the 10th and 18th to be re-formed and to follow me.

Having placed myself at the head of two squadrons of the 1st Hussars, two other squadrons being in support, I was advancing in pursuit of the broken enemy when I found on my right and front the 11th Regiment, part of Vandeleur's brigade.

So completely had I found myself alone with my brigade prior to this that I had actually, some time before, sent my A.D.C., Capt. Keane, to Sir J. Vandeleur to request he would come on and support me; and the gallant old soldier (for he was as brave an old fellow as ever lived) was very angry with me for so doing, saying 'I had no business to send orders' (which I did not) 'to my senior officer.'

After having made the charges that have been described, Vivian's brigade, which, with that of Vandeleur, was the most advanced of the British forces, found their progress most seriously obstructed and retarded by the vast crowd of fugitives of all arms, mingled in the wildest confusion.

* * * * *

Siborne says:

In fact, the cavalry thus situated in the van of the Duke's victorious army had now become almost helpless; it seemed as if carried aloft on the billows of the agitated sea, yielding rather to its impulse than controlling the angry element.

As might have been expected, there were innumerable instances in which the rage and disappointment of the conquered foe gave rise to covert assaults.

The 10th and 18th Hussars, of Vivian's brigade, whilst attempting to re-form between La Haye Sainte and Rossomme, found themselves in the midst of an enormous mass, composed partly of defeated soldiers of the Imperial Guard, who could ill conceal their mortification, and who seized every opportunity that afforded to gratify their hatred and revenge.

Lieut.-Col. the Hon. H. Murray, commanding the 18th, was nearly bayoneted by one of them, and his orderly was compelled, for the safety of his master, to cut down five or six of them in succession.

About half-past eight—perhaps somewhat later—the darkness, which had been rapidly setting in, had become so great as to render it difficult to distinguish one particular body of troops from another.

Some little time before this one of the Prussian advanced regiments of cavalry, suddenly entering the highroad between La Belle Alliance and Rossomme, came into partial collision with the 18th Hussars, who, not anticipating the presence of any other foreign troops in that vicinity than those of the French army, commenced an attack on them; cuts were exchanged and some few lives lost before the error was corrected.

The 1st Hussars, K.G.L., while advancing along the right of the road, came upon the rear of Vandeleur's brigade, and were all but in collision with the 11th and 16th Light Dragoons, which regiments having pireviously ascertained that a brigade of French artillery (Fire's) was on their right, and perceiving, though but dimly in the dark, the approach of a strong body of horsemen towards their rear, concluded that an attempt was being made to intercept their retreat. They immediately went threes about and struck into a charge.

On the other hand, the 1st K.G.L., not being aware that any British cavalry was in their front, and misled in great measure by the sudden clamour of French voices proceeding from the various fugitives who, taking alarm, were endeavouring to get out of their way, prepared to charge, and gave a loud cheer.

This cheer fortunately was recognised by the British Dragoons, when in the act of charging, as being that of the 1st German Hussars, and was thus the means of preventing a *rencontre* that might have been productive of the most fatal consequences to the parties concerned.

Napoleon had taken part in the last encounter; during the attack of the Imperial Guard he had ridden as far as the orchard of La Haye Sainte; when the 52nd had pursued so promptly he had fallen back, surrounded by the veterans of the Guard.

When Vivian and Vandeleur had tried to cut in upon his line of retreat a majestic body of Horse Grenadiers, resolute and compact, barred the way, and walked superbly from the field in unassailable order.—Hooper.

As to the effect that the charges made by Sir H. Vivian's brigade had on the result of the battle, the following extracts speak.

Siborne's *History*, says:

There is not perhaps an instance in modern history in which the threatening tide of battle has, through the lightning-like promptitude of decision, and the energetic application of yet remaining resources, been so suddenly and so powerfully controlled, and so majestically and irresistibly hurled back, overthrowing all and everything that, in the previous plenitude of its force, it had borne aloft with buoyant hopes, and carried along with exultation in its course, as it was by the immortal Wellington in this, his last, his crowning victory.

Never did a battlefield present so complete, so magical, a transition of scene as that which succeeded the defeat of the Imperial Guard of France by the Guards of the Sovereign of England and the British Light Cavalry brigade.

Wellington's perfect knowledge of the character and composition of the French army told him that a signal defeat of the Imperial Guard would be certain to exercise a powerful influence on the *morale* of the enemy's troops; but it also told him that unless instant advantage were taken of that defeat, unless it were followed up in such a manner as to render the incipient panic which it had created, general and incontrollable, that same army might recover the shock. D'Erlon's and Reille's columns, although faltering for a moment, might pursue their advance with determined efforts to regain the footing which the Guards had lost. The veterans of the latter force might speedily rally.

This view had scarcely crossed the mind of the Duke when his decision was fully made up. With those critically slender means to which allusion has been made, and which in the hands of many a commander would have been deemed totally inadequate for even the maintenance of the position at such fearful odds, Wellington determined to compensate for the awfully reduced and exhausted state of the fighting portion of his troops and the utter want of confidence in the remainder, by one of those bold and daring acts which, when hazarded at the right moment, carry with them the prestige of conscious superiority, and allow an enemy no time to discover deficiencies or to calculate mischances.

No sooner was the second attacking column of the Guard defeated and dispersed than he ordered it to be vigorously pursued and the rallied forces of the first column to be attacked by Adam's brigade; whilst at the same time he launched forth Vivian's Hussar brigade against the cavalry reserves near La Belle Alliance before these had made their disposition for attack, and even before they had recovered from the surprise and hesitation which prevailed among them on witnessing the discomfiture of the Guard.

In eulogising the gallantry and services of Lord Uxbridge, Captain Siborne attributes special praise to him for having so judiciously economised the strength of the cavalry as to have been able—

.... when at the critical moment its services were required, to bring forward two fresh brigades which fulfilled those services in a style the most brilliant that can be conceived, and with a success which commanded the admiration of all who witnessed it.

In a footnote Siborne further says that the French historians "invariably attribute the final rout of their army to the charges made by the Light Cavalry launched against it immediately after the attack by the Imperial Guard."

★ ★ ★ ★ ★

In a letter to Mr. E. Vivian, written on June 23, 1815, Sir Hussey says:

Whether the Duke will do my brigade justice or not, I know not; but Buonaparte has given them their due in his account. We are the cavalry that he alludes to when, at the end, he says: 'At eight o'clock,' &c,; and the Colonel of the 3rd Chasseurs, who lodged the night before last in the house I occupied last night, told the proprietor that two regiments of British Hussars decided the affair. The third regiment I kept in reserve.

The words in Napoleon's account referred to by Sir Hussey are doubtless those contained in the official bulletin of the battle, which appeared in the *Moniteur* on June 21, as follows:

At 8.30 the four battalions of the middle Guard, who had been sent to the ridge on the other side of Mont St. Jean in order to support the *Cuirassiers*; being greatly annoyed by the grape shot, endeavoured to carry the batteries with the bayonet.

At the end of the day a charge directed against their flank by several English squadrons put them in disorder.

The fugitives recrossed the ravine. Several regiments near at hand seeing some troops belonging to the Guard in confusion believed it was the Old Guard, and in consequence were thrown into disorder.

Cries of 'All is lost, the Guard is driven back!' were heard on all sides. The soldiers pretend even that on many points evil-disposed persons cried *Sauve qui peut*. However this may be, a complete panic at once spread itself through the whole battlefield, and they threw themselves in the greatest disorder on the line of communications; soldiers, cannoniers, caissons, all pressed to this point; the Old Guard, which was in reserve, was infected, and was itself hurried along.

In an instant the whole army was nothing but a mass of confusion; all the soldiers of all arms were mixed pell-mell, and it was utterly impossible to rally a single corps.

The enemy, who perceived this astonishing confusion, immediately attacked with their cavalry and increased the disorder; and such was the confusion owing to night coming on, that it was impossible to rally the troops and point out to them their error.

Writing in 1830, with reference to criticisms which had appeared in the *Quarterly Review* on the conduct of the cavalry at Waterloo, Sir H. Vivian, after pointing out the important results of the charge made by Sir W. Ponsonby's brigade, and stating that the only effective cavalry left at the end of the day were the brigades commanded by Vandeleur and himself, says:

These brigades then were moved to the right, and arrived at a most opportune moment. The effect of their formation immediately in the rear of the line of infantry on the position was to give confidence to the troops, almost worn out with the protracted and murderous combat; and to the effect of their charges the quotations from French authors (for they, at least, have done them justice; and those who feel the blow may be supposed to know, under such circumstances, from whence it came) will bear testimony.

The details of the proceedings of Sir H. Vivian's brigade will show that the cavalry referred to is this brigade, and this only. That Sir J. Vandeleur's brigade did not attack any of the French cavalry, nor indeed until they all had been driven from the field, is proved by their having taken no horses; whilst a very large number, nearly 200, were captured by Sir H. Vivian's brigade.

The principal loss sustained by Sir J. Vandeleur's brigade occurred whilst formed on the left of the road and in support of Sir W. Ponsonby's brigade. There indeed its loss had been great, especially in the 12th Light Dragoons.

The attack that was made at night upon the body of French infantry that had collected, was made by the 11th and part of the 16th Light Dragoons.

★ ★ ★ ★ ★

Sir Evelyn Wood, in *Cavalry at Waterloo*, writes:

No one who has perused the vast library of English literature on Waterloo can have failed to notice how comparatively little credit is given to the British cavalry for its work on June 18.

No one, indeed, can read the account of how our cavalry charged home, and later, with the gunners and infantry, stood up for hours, never flinching when their ranks were being decimated, without feeling the deepest admiration for them and their gallant chief.

It is strange that the conduct of our regimental officers and men, especially of the cavalry, has been generally more appreciated by our foes than by our countrymen.

★ ★ ★ ★ ★

The comments on the battle made by Sir H. Vivian in his diary are these:

Thus ended this most triumphant day, and thus our dreadful fatigues of the preceding forty-eight hours were crowned with the most brilliant victory perhaps ever gained.

On the part of the British, Lieut.-General Sir T. Picton and Major-General Sir W. Ponsonby were killed, and eight others wounded; and of inferior officers the killed and wounded were innumerable; in fact, the question was, not who was killed, but who was not killed.

The Prussians, having had very little of the severe fighting of the battle, followed up night and day, and the results were more glorious than ever could be imagined; 170 pieces of cannon remained in their possession. In short, the enemy appears to be totally destroyed.

I bivouacked this night at Hilaincourt.

In the first letter he wrote after the battle Sir Hussey says:

Never was battle so contested, never was contest so gained.

Nothing that I can say can add to the laurels of the Duke of Wellington; but it is to his example as well as to his abilities that we are indebted. Never was courage so conspicuous; never was it so necessary.

Our dear Lord Uxbridge, too, most worthily imitated this great hero, would to God he had been equally fortunate; but, alas! he received the dreadful wound which deprived him of his leg almost from one of the last guns fired with grape at my brigade, when we were charging the enemy. I did not see it, but soon heard the sad news. He bore his sufferings and the amputation like a hero.

No action that ever was fought was certainly so contested. The dreadful list of those who have fallen will prove this. Never did I see such a battlefield. I have no certainty of our loss, but on the field, within the space of a square mile, I think 10,000 men of both sides must lie, and horses innumerable.

The question in the army is not who is killed, but who is alive: and the cavalry have suffered dreadfully. We are not 3000 men who were near 10,000. Most of those returned missing are killed. 170 pieces of cannon and about 8000 prisoners are, I hear, already in our possession. To night only they owe the escape of a man.

I know not what will be done for Lord Wellington, or what will be done for the army; but some mark of distinction will, I trust, be bestowed on every man present that day. I know if it is a mere piece of brass with Mont St. Jean (for that I think ought to be the name of the battle, as it was at that village the centre rested) on it, I should wear it with more pride than the most brilliant star that could be given me for any other occasion.

My poor Brigade-Major—Harris—an admirable and gallant soldier, is severely wounded; lost his right arm and shot through the body.

Fitzroy was hit in the thigh slightly, and I myself received a graze with a grape shot, or shell, in my leg, of which I thought nothing, but which has since prevented me wearing a boot and obliged me to ride in a cart; but the inflammation has abated and I shall soon be all right.

In a letter to Capt. Siborne, dated June 3, 1839, Sir Hussey says: That the Prussians were seen advancing to our support long before their arrival on the field cannot be doubted. The French at first took them for Grouchy's corps,

That its being an understood thing between the Duke and Blucher that they were to support us, and that such an understanding was a necessary part of our remaining in our position and risking a battle, is equally certain. Any attempt therefore to throw doubt on the combination by which their assistance was afforded us is quite absurd.

That the tardy arrival of the Prussians rendered the victory more complete is, I feel confident, quite correct. Had the French been engaged earlier in the day with them, the last body that attacked us would not have been so committed. So far, the delay in arrival was most fortunate. Still, however, had they arrived earlier, we might have beaten the enemy sooner, and have had more daylight to take advantage of our victory.

That the position of Waterloo is by no means a strong one cannot for a moment be disputed. How far the statement that the Duke had the year before selected it is correct I will not pretend to say; but I will mention an anecdote told me by poor Sir Frederick Ponsonby after the battle, and which I heard him often repeat. He said 'he knew it to be a fact that the Duke had himself halted some regiments on the Brussels side of Genappe, meaning to have halted his army there, having that town and the small river that runs through it in his front; but that Delancy, his quarter-master-general, who had been sent to the rear, came to him and described the position of Waterloo, and that the Duke determined to retire from that on which he then was halted to take up that on which the battle was fought.'

The French made a great mistake in attacking the position of Waterloo. They should have masked Hougoumont and penetrated with all their forces between us and the Prussians by attacking our left; or else they should have attacked Hougoumont in a different manner from that in which they did attack it; not advancing against the garden and wood, but occupying in force the height above it and driving our troops out with their artillery; and then turning our right altogether, advancing, getting possession of the road to Brussels at the point of junction with that from Nivelles and that from Genappe. They might thus have bothered us dreadfully.

With respect to the meeting of Wellington and Blucher I have no doubt in my own mind that when I saw the Duke he had met Blucher.

I think his words were, on my telling him (after congratulating him on his victory) that my brigade was in perfect order, reformed after their attack, and ready to pursue, 'Our troops have had a hard day's work; the Prussians will pursue the enemy; do you bivouack your brigade.'

I am not quite certain, but I believe he said he had settled it with Blucher that the Prussians were to pursue. Certain I am that what he said conveyed the conviction to my mind that he had seen Blucher.

The morning after the battle, at, or soon after daybreak, I proceeded from the village of Hilaincourt over the field of battle to Waterloo, to see Lord Anglesey.

I called on the Duke; it must have been about, or soon after, four o'clock; he had just had his breakfast.

He asked many questions about the field which I had just crossed over, and was very much surprised indeed when I assured him of the very large number of the enemy's guns that I had seen on the field.

He told me no return he had received at all amounted to what I had described, and I am quite certain that he was not, at that time, aware of the full extent of his victory. He told me, I recollect full well, that as far as he had then heard, the prisoners sent to the rear were about 1200.

If anyone can tell you exactly about the time we advanced it will give you the time of the Prussians being generally engaged; but I should certainly say that they were before Planchenoit very soon after half-past seven, if not as early. There I saw them when, with the 18th Hussars, I got into the high road beyond La Belle Alliance. Some Prussians also had reached it, and I have no doubt some were cut down by the 18th for French; for I saw two or three who were wounded with the sabre on the road the next morning.

I do not think any large force of Prussians reached the high road short of La Belle Alliance. I am certain some came along the original position of the French, from the direction of the fire. The fact was that after the attack of the Prussians theirs might be called the general action; fighting had in a great measure ceased along our line, excepting on one front, *i.e.,* the attack of the Imperial Guard; so that the Prussian army must of course cut a conspicuous figure at the moment chosen for representation on the model.

In truth, I care not what others may say, we were greatly indebted to the Prussians, and it was their coming on the right and rear of Napoleon that gave us the battle of Waterloo. We might have held our ground, but we never could have advanced but for the Prussian movement. You are quite right in saying there is not the slightest ground for jealousy; and I must say those are most unjust to the Prussians who refuse them their full share of credit for their most effective aid at the end of the day."

In the last journal ever kept by Sir Hussey (or as he then was, Lord) Vivian, he again refers to the assistance rendered by the Prussians in these terms:

June 18th—the 27th anniversary of the battle of Waterloo. This naturally led to the events of that day becoming a subject of conversation with some of the foreigners here (Baden-Baden), and I regret exceedingly to find that there is an impression in the Prussian army that something said by the Duke of Wellington (or perhaps *not* said) has led to a feeling that his Grace has been unjust towards the Prussians, and not disposed to give them the credit they deserved for the assistance they afforded.

I have no recollection of the Duke having shown any feeling of this sort. There was something he said about the movements of the Prussian army which I remember gave offence. Be this as it may, as no one had a better opportunity of seeing the effect of the arrival of the Prussians on the field than I had, I take this opportunity of again recording the opinion I have, in my journal and also repeatedly to individuals when speaking on the subject, expressed.

The arrival of the Prussians was most opportune, and was of the greatest importance. I never was more surprised (and standing on the left of our line I had an opportunity of seeing everything that took place) than to see the very large force that Napoleon was enabled to oppose to the advancing Prussians, and most especially at the number of guns that he opened upon them; and I could not help feeling and saying at the time to those around me that had this body of troops been employed earlier in the battle to turn our left and attack the front of the position on which I was then standing, it might have made a vast difference in the state of affairs; and, moreover, I could not afterwards help thinking that the arrival of the Prussians at this moment, after our army had been so long engaged and suffered so severely, was most fortunate, as it engaged a body of the enemy which might otherwise have assisted in the last desperate attack on our centre, and, considering the enormous losses we had sustained, might have enabled Napoleon to force it.

At all events, whether such might or might not have been the consequence of the non-arrival of the Prussians, of this I am confident, that it was their arrival which enabled us to advance. We might very probably have maintained our ground; but it is not possible that, with the few men we had left in the field (Lord Uxbridge, in passing from the left to the centre, told me he did not think we had 5000 men under arms in the centre, so severe had been our loss), it is quite impossible to suppose an attack on the enemy's line, even if their attack on ours had been defeated, would have been attempted.

To the happy arrival of the Prussian corps, and the gallant attack it made on Planchenoit and on the right of the French, the British were most undoubtedly most indebted, and I cannot for a moment fancy that the Duke of Wellington has ever expressed himself otherwise.

★ ★ ★ ★ ★

Captain Siborne in pointing out that a mistake had been made as to the real position of the Prussians at the close of the day in the model he had prepared and exhibited, explains that the Prussian authorities assumed that the defeat of the Imperial Guard and the advance of the whole line happened at one and the same moment; whereas in reality there was an interval of at least twelve minutes between these two incidents.

He says:

The Prussians have not hitherto been cognisant of the fact that when the British line advanced Vivian's Light Cavalry brigade was attacking and dispersing Napoleon's last reserves of both cavalry and infantry, posted on the French left of La Belle Alliance—the very centre of the enemy's line; that Adam's infantry was attacking and defeating the rallied force of the first attacking column of the Imperial Guard upon the height situated midway between La Belle Alliance and La Haye Sainte; and that Vandeleur's Light Cavalry brigade was pushed forward in support of Vivian.

These attacks, planned with consummate judgment and electric decision, and carried into execution with perfect order and unequalled gallantry, could not, from the configuration of the ground, be observed by the Prussian army; to which circumstance may be attributed the origin of the mistake concerning the actual disposition of the Duke of Wellington's forces at the moment of the general advance of his line, which induced the Prussian authorities to confound that advance with the defeat of the attacking columns of the Imperial Guard.

Sir E. Wood, in *Cavalry at Waterloo*, remarks:

Modern cavalry soldiers who read these articles will be astonished to see how the generals displaced the commanding officers in leading charges.

Vivian went so far as to halt his second line (the 18th) till he could charge with the first line (the 10th) and return to lead the 18th. He only failed to lead the third regiment from the darkness preventing further attacks being executed.

★ ★ ★ ★ ★

At Waterloo Sir Hussey Vivian rode a milk-white troop horse of the 10th Hussars.

It is a curious fact that this great battle received different names from each of the three chief nations engaged in it. The French call it "Mont St. Jean" (the name Sir H. Vivian thought most appropriate); the Prussians call it the battle of "La Belle Alliance;" whilst the English call it "Waterloo," which, as a fact, was the name of a village some distance in rear of the position, but was where Wellington slept after the battle had been won.

The movements of the Allied forces after the battle, during which time Sir H. Vivian's brigade acted as the advance guard, are given in Sir Hussey's diary as follow:

June 19.—The army marched by Nivelles.
The Prussians by Quatre-Bras.
I moved to Houtain, near Nivelles.

* * * * *

In the course of the evening the Duke of Wellington established his headquarters at Nivelles.

* * * * *

June 20.—The army moved, leaving Binche on its left, and Mons on its right.

I went to Avesnes.

* * * * *

Vivian's Hussar brigade took the outpost duties on the Sambre. The British cavalry were cantonned in the villages of Strepy, Thieu, &c.; Vivian's brigade in those of Merbes St. Marie, Bienne, Le Hapart, and Mont.

The Duke's headquarters were at Binche.

* * * * *

June 21.—The army moved to Bavay.

I moved to Battayan.

* * * * *

The Duke's headquarters were at Malplaquet.

* * * * *

June 22.—The army to Cateau,

My brigade to St. Benin. All these marches were from morning till night.

June 23 and 24—Le Cateau.

On June 23 Wellington and Blucher gave to the great mass of their troops a halt, not merely for the sake of affording them a rest, but also for the purpose of collecting stragglers and bringing up the ammunition and the baggage.

It was from here that Sir Hussey wrote the letters from which quotations have been given. At the end of his letter to his wife he says:

> From daybreak until sunset have we been marching; now the infantry are so fatigued that it has been found absolutely necessary to rest.
>
> The reports of the cavalry are that the French are completely dispersed. If so, we shall get to Paris without a shot, and that I indeed expect, although some say he will rally at Laon. A desperate man will do anything, but such an attempt would but hasten his end.

June 25.—The army to Joncourt.
My brigade to Crissour, near St. Quentin.
June 26.—The army to Beauvais and Lanchy.
My brigade to Mattigny on the road to Nesle.

★ ★ ★ ★ ★

Vivian's brigade was again the advance guard at Mattigny, near the Somme, having its pickets on the river.

Vivian had on this day sent forward Lieut. Slayter Smith of the 10th Hussars, *en reonnaisance*, as far as Nesle, with directions to proceed, if possible, as far as Roye and gain information concerning the movements of the French army.

Lieut. Smith having reached the latter place, ascertained that French troops had left the town the night before and that a body of *gendarmerie* had marched out at one end of the town as he and his party had entered the other.

On returning from Nesles he had proceeded but a short distance when he perceived a carnage moving rapidly and coming from a cross road. He ordered the driver to halt, and found in the carriage a military looking man who acknowledged himself to be Gen. Lauriston, A.D.C. to Napoleon, and stated that he was going in the first instance to his country seat at Vaux, and then to join the King, Louis XIII. He added that he had gone to Paris to raise a party for His Majesty, and that he had not only failed in the attempt but had narrowly escaped being arrested. Having given this explanation, he entreated Lieut. Smith to allow him to continue his route, but the latter, considering it his duty to make him a prisoner, took him that night to Sir Hussey Vivian, who then desired Lieut. Smith to proceed with the General to the Duke of Wellington.

On reaching his Grace's quarters at one o'clock in the morning and intimating his errand, a curious incident occurred. There was no guard at the house, not even a sentry; and Smith had some difficulty in arousing a sleepy servant from among his fellows to announce him. The Duke was engaged in conversation with a Frenchman. On a table appeared the debris of a repast. Having explained the name and rank of the individual he had brought, the Duke said to Lieut. Smith, "Bring him in." On hearing the name of Lauriston, the Frenchman, who had been sent to the Duke by Fouché to treat for a cessation of hostilities, became greatly alarmed and begged to know how he might escape without being recognised.

The Duke remarked "There is but one door and one window; take your choice." The Frenchman preferred the door, and escaped by passing behind the Duke's back as Lauriston entered.—*See* Siborne.

The Duke subsequently sent Lauriston to the King as a prisoner instead of a volunteer.

★ ★ ★ ★ ★

June 27.—From Mattigny to Vassalin, in front of Roye.
The army about Roye.

June 28.—My brigade to Mouchy and Auteuil.
The army on the high road to Pont St. Maxence.

I was quartered at the *château* of Gen. Count Curial, whose wife had left it only three days. A most admirable house, gardens, fishponds, &c.

Madame la Comtesse Curial, horrible to relate, left an infant child in the house to the care of a wet nurse. My wife would not have done so, I am sure.

June 29.—Marched from Mouchy to Senlis.

In the evening rode to see Chantilly, the magnificent residence of the Prince de Condé. The great *château* is destroyed. Two smaller ones, together with the palace of the Duc d'Enghien, and the stables, are standing and give a good idea of the extreme magnificence of the place when in all its splendour.

★ ★ ★ ★ ★

The advanced guard (Vivian's brigade), supported by that of Arentschild, crossed the Oise at Pont St. Maxence, and reached Senlis.

★ ★ ★ ★ ★

June 30.—Marched from Senlis to Vanderlan, between Louvres and Bourget, on the road to Paris,

During the latter part of the march we have had the misfortune to follow the Prussians, who have plundered and destroyed everything, without considering that they are, by this means, not only making enemies of the French, but actually starving us, their Allies.

Our poor soldiers get nothing scarcely, in consequence of this most terrible conduct of the Prussian army; and the officers encourage it!

"*July 1.*—Halted at Vanderlan. The British army entering into position; the Prussians crossing at Argenteuil and St. German to surround Paris.

The Prussians had a severe affair of cavalry at Versailles.

At ten o'clock at night received orders to march to Le Bourget, to support the First Division, encamped there.

Arrived at one o'clock, and put up in the most wretchedly plundered house I ever saw.

July 2.—At Le Bourget.

The Prussians had a severe affair with the French near Mont Rouge, in which the French, who attacked, were repulsed with considerable loss.

The Prussians lost between 2000 and 3000.

July 3.—Le Bourget.

This day we learnt that an armistice was concluded, and that the French army was to evacuate St. Denis on the 4th, Montmartre on the 5th, and Paris on the 6th.

July 6.—At Le Bourget.

Extremely unwell with pains in my side and back; so bad as to be scarcely able to turn or move in bed.

Lord Castlereagh called in passing through.

July 7.—Received orders to march and cross the bridge of Argenteuil, and march to Puteaux and Suresnes, very delightful villages on the Seine, opposite the Bois de Boulogne.

I was quartered at the house of the Duke de Felthe, and received every mark of civility from the Duchesse—an old lady, very fat, but very agreeable.

July 8. —At Puteaux.

Some Prussians and British had entered Paris the day before yesterday.

Rode into Paris and saw the king enter. The rascally French made a great cry of '*Vive le Roi.*'

July 9.—Went into Paris to stay.

My brigade at Puteaux and Suresnes.

July 10.—Paris.

All the British and Prussian generals dined with the Duke at Verrey's,

Got leave to go to England.

July 11.

★ ★ ★ ★ ★

This date is entered in the diary, but nothing further is written; and under the circumstances that is not surprising.

For his services at Waterloo Vivian was mentioned in despatches and received the thanks of both Houses of Parliament. He also received the following decorations: the Order of Maria Theresa from the Emperor of Austria; the Order of St. Vladimir from the Emperor of Russia; and that of Hanover from the Prince Regent.

On the restoration of Louis XXIII. Sir H. Vivian's brigade, composed of the 12th Lancers and 18th Hussars, formed part of the Army of Occupation in Picardy; services less brilliant than those previously performed, yet certainly most useful and important.

When Sir Hussey returned to Truro (his native town) after the battle of Waterloo, the whole town was *en fête*. Numbers of the inhabitants went out to meet him and, taking the horses out of his carriage, dragged it in triumph through the streets. A similar enthusiasm greeted him on the occasion of a public dinner given to him at Truro on July 31.

The army returned to England in 1818, and with it Sir H. Vivian, who now found himself, for the first time in twenty-three years, unemployed. Great reductions in the military establishment of course took place, and on September 10, 1821, his favourite regiment (the 18th Hussars) was disbanded, upon which occasion Sir H. Vivian was presented by the *soldiers* of the regiment with a silver trumpet and banner, purchased by their desire with part of the prize money accruing from the horses of the enemy captured by the brigade at Waterloo. It bore the following inscription:—

> On September 10, 1821, the day on which the 18th Hussars were disbanded, this trumpet was presented to Major-General Sir Hussey Vivian, K.C.B. Having commanded them upon many glorious occasions, they offer to him this memorial of the last victory in which it was their fortune to be led by him, as an assurance that, while he gained their admiration as a soldier, he secured their lasting and unfeigned esteem as a friend, and in the hope of living in his recollection and estimation when they shall have ceased to exist as a corps.

> This trumpet, on September 10, 1880, the fifty-ninth anniversary of the disbandment of the regiment, was entrusted by my father, the second Lord Vivian, to the care of the present regiment of 18th Hussars, "believing that in this record of glorious deeds, the memory of his father, who led the regiment to victory on many occasions, will be cherished in the corps whose admiration he secured."

In 1819 Sir H.Vivian was despatched to Newcastle-on-Tyne and thence to Glasgow, for the purpose of quelling riots which had broken out at those places. This service was promptly and efficiently performed. In 1820 he was elected a member of Parliament for his native town, and he continued to represent it till 1826.

From 1825 to July 20, 1830, Sir H.Vivian held the appointment of Inspector-General of Cavalry. On January 22, 1827, he was promoted to the rank of Lieut.-General, and on the following day received the Colonelcy of the 12th, or Prince of Wales' Royal Lancers.

From 1826 (when he gave up Truro) till 1831 he represented Windsor in Parliament, but in 1832 he again returned to Truro, which he represented till 1835.

In 1828 he was created a Baronet—a coat of arms full of heraldic allusions to his distinguished career being at the same time granted to him. On July 1, 1831, he was appointed to the command of the forces in Ireland, and this, coupled with the failing health of his wife, caused him to retire from Parliament. From 1830 to 1837 he was Groom of the Bedchamber to William IV.

In 1833, whilst in Ireland (the first Lady Vivian having died), he married a second time; the lady of his choice being Letitia, daughter of the Rev. J.Webster, by whom he had one daughter.

On May 4, 1835, he succeeded General Sir George Murray as Master-General of the Ordnance, and was made a Privy Councillor. On January 29, 1837, he was transferred from the 12th Lancers to the Colonelcy of the Royal Dragoons, and on May 30, 1837, was advanced to be a Knight Grand Cross of the Bath. In this year also he was elected for East Cornwall, and continued to represent it till 1841.

In 1841, on account of his declining health, Sir Hussey was obliged to relinquish his seat in Parliament and to give up his post as Master-General of the Ordnance. On retiring from the above exalted position he was made a Peer and took his seat in the Upper House. This last earned honour he did not enjoy for long, for he died suddenly at Baden-Baden from aneurism of the heart, on August 20, 1842, at the age of sixty-seven. He was buried quietly in St. Mary's Cemetery, Truro, in the same vault as his father and mother, against the eastern wall of the enclosure.

Although he concealed the fact from his wife and relations, yet it is clear, from various entries in the last diary he kept, that Lord Vivian was well aware that his end was likely to be sudden, owing to the condition of his heart.

In closing this memoir of his life I feel that I cannot better portray my grandfathers character than he himself does in an entry made in his diary just one week before he died:

> This morning, after a short walk, the pain in my chest and arms was beyond any I have before felt, and the shortness of my breath was very troublesome. God's will be done. I hope when the time comes I shall meet my end as becomes a man and a soldier, and that God, in their distress, will support my dear wife, my children, and my family.
>
> My anxious endeavour, I trust, through life has been to do my duty towards the Almighty Creator of all things, acknowledging that from Him all blessings are derived, and sensible that I am never carrying out His will and the purpose for which I was sent into this world, better than by doing all the kindness and all the good I can towards my fellow-creatures.

ALSO FROM LEONAUR
AVAILABLE IN SOFTCOVER OR HARDCOVER WITH DUST JACKET

THE FALL OF THE MOGHUL EMPIRE OF HINDUSTAN by H. G. Keene—By the beginning of the nineteenth century, as British and Indian armies under Lake and Wellesley dominated the scene, a little over half a century of conflict brought the Moghul Empire to its knees.

LADY SALE'S AFGHANISTAN by Florentia Sale—An Indomitable Victorian Lady's Account of the Retreat from Kabul During the First Afghan War.

THE CAMPAIGN OF MAGENTA AND SOLFERINO 1859 by Harold Carmichael Wylly—The Decisive Conflict for the Unification of Italy.

FRENCH'S CAVALRY CAMPAIGN by J. G. Maydon—A Special Correspondent's View of British Army Mounted Troops During the Boer War.

CAVALRY AT WATERLOO by Sir Evelyn Wood—British Mounted Troops During the Campaign of 1815.

THE SUBALTERN by George Robert Gleig—The Experiences of an Officer of the 85th Light Infantry During the Peninsular War.

NAPOLEON AT BAY, 1814 by F. Loraine Petre—The Campaigns to the Fall of the First Empire.

NAPOLEON AND THE CAMPAIGN OF 1806 by Colonel Vachée—The Napoleonic Method of Organisation and Command to the Battles of Jena & Auerstädt.

THE COMPLETE ADVENTURES IN THE CONNAUGHT RANGERS by William Grattan—The 88th Regiment during the Napoleonic Wars by a Serving Officer.

BUGLER AND OFFICER OF THE RIFLES by William Green & Harry Smith—With the 95th (Rifles) during the Peninsular & Waterloo Campaigns of the Napoleonic Wars.

NAPOLEONIC WAR STORIES by Sir Arthur Quiller-Couch—Tales of soldiers, spies, battles & sieges from the Peninsular & Waterloo campaingns.

CAPTAIN OF THE 95TH (RIFLES) by Jonathan Leach—An officer of Wellington's sharpshooters during the Peninsular, South of France and Waterloo campaigns of the Napoleonic wars.

RIFLEMAN COSTELLO by Edward Costello—The adventures of a soldier of the 95th (Rifles) in the Peninsular & Waterloo Campaigns of the Napoleonic wars.

AVAILABLE ONLINE AT www.leonaur.com
AND FROM ALL GOOD BOOK STORES

ALSO FROM LEONAUR
AVAILABLE IN SOFTCOVER OR HARDCOVER WITH DUST JACKET

ZULU:1879 *by D.C.F. Moodie & the Leonaur Editors*—The Anglo-Zulu War of 1879 from contemporary sources: First Hand Accounts, Interviews, Dispatches, Official Documents & Newspaper Reports.

THE RED DRAGOON *by W.J. Adams*—With the 7th Dragoon Guards in the Cape of Good Hope against the Boers & the Kaffir tribes during the 'war of the axe' 1843-48'.

THE RECOLLECTIONS OF SKINNER OF SKINNER'S HORSE *by James Skinner*—James Skinner and his 'Yellow Boys' Irregular cavalry in the wars of India between the British, Mahratta, Rajput, Mogul, Sikh & Pindarree Forces.

A CAVALRY OFFICER DURING THE SEPOY REVOLT *by A. R. D. Mackenzie*—Experiences with the 3rd Bengal Light Cavalry, the Guides and Sikh Irregular Cavalry from the outbreak to Delhi and Lucknow.

A NORFOLK SOLDIER IN THE FIRST SIKH WAR *by J W Baldwin*—Experiences of a private of H.M. 9th Regiment of Foot in the battles for the Punjab, India 1845-6.

TOMMY ATKINS' WAR STORIES: 14 FIRST HAND ACCOUNTS—Fourteen first hand accounts from the ranks of the British Army during Queen Victoria's Empire.

THE WATERLOO LETTERS *by H. T. Siborne*—Accounts of the Battle by British Officers for its Foremost Historian.

NEY: GENERAL OF CAVALRY VOLUME 1—1769-1799 *by Antoine Bulos*—The Early Career of a Marshal of the First Empire.

NEY: MARSHAL OF FRANCE VOLUME 2—1799-1805 *by Antoine Bulos*—The Early Career of a Marshal of the First Empire.

AIDE-DE-CAMP TO NAPOLEON *by Philippe-Paul de Ségur*—For anyone interested in the Napoleonic Wars this book, written by one who was intimate with the strategies and machinations of the Emperor, will be essential reading.

TWILIGHT OF EMPIRE *by Sir Thomas Ussher & Sir George Cockburn*—Two accounts of Napoleon's Journeys in Exile to Elba and St. Helena: Narrative of Events by Sir Thomas Ussher & Napoleon's Last Voyage: Extract of a diary by Sir George Cockburn.

PRIVATE WHEELER *by William Wheeler*—The letters of a soldier of the 51st Light Infantry during the Peninsular War & at Waterloo.

AVAILABLE ONLINE AT www.leonaur.com
AND FROM ALL GOOD BOOK STORES

www.ingramcontent.com/pod-product-compliance
Lightning Source LLC
Chambersburg PA
CBHW031617160426
43196CB00006B/175